VÁCLAV HAVEL
THE AUTHORIZED BIOGRAPHY

VÁCLAV HAVEL THE AUTHORIZED BIOGRAPHY

EDA KRISEOVÁ

Translated by Caleb Crain

ST. MARTIN'S PRESS
NEW YORK

Published by permission of Rowolt Berlin Verlag Gmbh, Berlin

Design by Sara Stemen

Library of Congress Cataloging-in-Publication Data
ISBN 0-88687-739-3

First edition: September 1993

10 9 8 7 6 5 4 3 2 1

To Vašek

▪ Acknowledgments

For their kind assistance and collaboration during the writing of this book, I would like to thank: Olga Havel, Ivan Havel, Jan Lopatka, Andrej Stankovič, Jiří Gruša, Pavel Landovský, Anna Freimanová, Andrej Krob, Zdenek Urbánek, Jan Grossman, Miloš Forman, Sergej Machonin, Věra Jirousová, Ivan Vyskočil, Vilém Prečan, Anna Fárová, Milena Tomíšková, Jitka Vodňanská, Dana Němcová, Jiří Křižan;

and also those who are no longer with us, but who left behind them written records, memoirs, and letters: Mrs. Božena Havel, Mr. Hugo Vavrečka, and Mr. Václav Havel;

and also those who helped me put the book together: Tomáš Kosta, Arita Hucková, and Dušan Seidl.

—*Eda Kriseová*
Červená Lhota Castle, 1990

▪ Contents

The author of this book is presenting her view of my life and work. It is *her* view, and I can hardly judge to what extent it is true. I can only hope that it will bring readers closer not only to me, but, through me, to this country as well.

—Václav Havel

▪ Preface

When my book about Václav Havel was published in Czechoslovakia, I received a great many letters from people thanking me. They thanked me for writing a book in which good conquered evil. The story I wrote told that it was worthwhile to speak the truth, to not be afraid, and to stand up for oneself under any circumstances. It said that fear weakens people and that it is necessary to face fear with bravery, which in the end will prevail. And that a person who is not afraid can go into a dark forest or anywhere else and no evil can touch him. For that matter, that in the end "truth and love will win out against lies and hatred,"* but it takes work. People wrote to me that the book gave them courage and made them want to be heroes. Ordinary people—Czechs, Moravians, and Slovaks—understood my intent: amid uncertainty and confusion it is good to write and read about a hero, about someone who grew up in a family that under the old regime had no right to live.

Intellectuals, or rather literary critics, attacked me for having written a pretty story, a fairy tale. True, the hero came straight out of prison into the castle of the Czech kings and Roman emperors (the largest inhabited castle in the world, by the way). And I could go on: the most powerful rulers in the world visited him, he received honors of a sort not received by any Czech or Slovak spokesman in the past four hundred years. In him, the world saw new hope. They saw someone who could lead a confused people out of the errors of their ways. For a few months, many of us even forgot about the misery of this world. It was like when a person falls in love: he has new hope, joy, and strength.

Václav Havel was president for 935 days. People expected too much from him in too short a time. They wanted to be as rich as the Swiss

---

*An early slogan of Václav Havel and Civic Forum.

and as socialized as the Swedes. They wanted him to return to them everything the Communists had taken away; maybe they even wanted back their youth of forty years ago. And the hope that a magnificent life was awaiting them. Havel was like a good king. He would have been happy to do everything for his people, but he had bad advisors, the way it always is in fairy tales. The people projected their desires as well as their bad qualities onto the people in power. Václav Havel started to appear to citizens as too moral, too intellectual, too soft, and not strict enough. In fact, too democratic. Maybe they longed at this moment for someone who resembled them more.

When will things be all right?

They already are. But people have quickly forgotten how things were before. They are like the woman in the Chinese folktale who had two daughters. One sold umbrellas and the other sandals. When it rained, the mother wept that they would not sell any sandals, and when it was warm, she wept that they could not sell any umbrellas.

Maybe Havel was too far ahead for people to be able to identify with him. And thus it was the pragmatists who won, as they have so many times before in the history of humanity, and the philosophers who lost.

From great joy and euphoria, people and nations pass into great sadness and depression. Nations behave just like individuals. It takes a long time for them to find their balance. As they grow wiser, they will begin to resemble the king who ran so far ahead of them. Then they will start to be happy when it rains because they can sell umbrellas, and when the sun is shining, sandals.

I know for a certainty that Václav Havel's career as a politician is not over, that it is only beginning. I am glad he had left, because this has made it possible for him to return.

And I am glad that I am guilty of writing fairy tales.

VÁCLAV HAVEL
THE AUTHORIZED BIOGRAPHY

▪ Prelude

One day a gentleman visited the Havels' house, and when he left, little Václav remarked how strange it was that this gentleman did not have a hump on his back.

"How come you say that, Venoušek*?" his mother asked.

"Because with the kind of face he has he ought to have a hump." His mother took this opportunity to deliver a mild reprimand. She explained to the child what a bitter fate nature dealt to hunchbacks, and how sad a mother was if her baby was born with a hump.

At this, Václav observed, "Well, I guess so, but think how unhappy a camel mother would be if her baby was born without a hump."

1 ▪ The Search for Everything Forbidden

In 1956, in the samizdat journal *Revue K* there appeared, amid stories by Bohumil Hrabal and other poems and writings, an essay by Václav Havel, "On the prose of Bohumil Hrabal." It was an attempt to understand a writer who had already matured. Hrabal was over forty, and he had not yet published a single book in his own country. The twenty-year-old Václav wanted to know why Hrabal wrote even though he could not publish, and how, in general, a literary work is created. The essay reminds one of American-style handbooks about "How to make love/enjoy life/learn English," and the like. More than anything else, a young person longs for guidance, and this was the sort of guidance Havel wanted to find. The tone suggests a child who, as he dissects a mouse, is trying to find its soul. In this essay on Hrabal, there is still

---

*Diminutive for Václav; others commonly used are Vásek, Váša, and Véna.

a childish curiosity and none of the humility that only later—when life becomes complex and facing pressure one matures—reconciles one to the mystery of being. Havel is trying to take the measure of an individual author's work by rational analysis and to find the system in it, how the stories are arranged into parallel and sequential episodes. Analysis is brought nearly *ad absurdum*; later he learned to wield it with more skill. Nonetheless, I find in this essay a new and revealing idea.

I am afraid that Václav Havel will not want to reprint this essay in his collected works, even though the essay is remarkable chiefly for how completely its author, unwittingly gives himself away. Without meaning to, he reveals that he read the critical monthly *Kritický měsíčník* and literary magazines from the First Republic* and that he had learned much from the work of great Czech critics of the late nineteenth century and First Republic such as Václav Černý and František Šalda. His language is flowery, very much in the style of the First Republic; it is serious in an old-fashioned way; and all this gives the essay an uncommon polish. It is as if the author were attempting to bridge the gulf between the 1950s and the years of the First Republic, the era in which he was born and whose spirit presided over his childhood home—as if he were trying to fill a certain gap.

The idea I find revealing is that here Havel formulates what a writer is and what distinguishes him from other people. He is searching for who he is, where he is headed, and what he is setting about to do. He wants to know as much about this as possible, and so he studies the work of another author with great care.

> . . . *Hrabal doesn't want to be a writer; he simply wants to write better.*

---

*Reference is to the Czechoslovak nation that was founded in 1918 following the First World War and that fell in the Communist takeover of February 1948, and subsequently was derided as bourgeois and decadent; the works of the period were banned.

But why does he need to write? What drives him to it? What is
it inside him that distinguishes him from the other railway men,
metallurgists, and assistant factory workers, among whom he be-
longs? It is, I think, the intensity with which he lives his life, the
intensity with which he sees the world around him, with which
he considers his situation, with which he tries to recognize and
understand life around him. This intensity, which we can describe
as an intensity of existence, *requires him in the last instance to*
express himself through his writing, vision, and life, to translate
his recognition and understanding of the world into a written
world.

It is also important to note that, in this essay, Havel discovered a
great underground writer long before the literary critics recognized
him and his books began to be published.

At age fifteen, Václav became interested in poetry. He wrote poems,
which surprised his father, because his was a family of engineers.
Suddenly they had a poet, who read every sort of philosophical book
he could find in the family library.

With friends his own age—all born in 1936—he founded an intellectual circle or literary group, the "Thirty-sixers." They were high-
school age, but because of some blemish on their political dossiers
most of them had regular jobs and could only study at night. They
organized symposia and congresses, and even published a typewritten
magazine. Mainly—and for hours, heatedly—they debated. What
they did was dangerous, but they didn't realize it. They were fifteen
years old and they were not yet altogether responsible legally. If they
had been over eighteen, they could easily have ended up in a Stalinist
concentration camp; they could even have been sentenced to death.
In their innocence, they gravitated straight to what was being kept
from the young generation because they were supposed to be brought
up strictly with Communist ideology. They should have been grand-

children of Gottwald,* members of the Socialist Youth Movement, striking blows against prejudice among themselves, filtering out and eradicating everything they inherited that was not created by the working class and its avant-garde, the Communist Party.

Most of Havel's friends were ideological renegades. For them, the greatest adventure was the search for hidden treasures of Czech literature and history. In the Havel's library were *Free Directions* (*Volné směry*) and *Critical Monthly* (*Kritický měsíčník*). These magazines were something altogether different from what was being published then; in fact, even the language was different. Václav began to read very early, and he read everything he could. At age ten, apparently a passage in the biography of the noted Czech historian František Palacký made a great impression on him; the passage reads, ". . . already at age five he had read the whole Bible." Since he harbored great ambitions and didn't want to be someone who became famous only after his death, as his mother wrote in her diary, Václav did not begin to read the Bible, but instead the ten-year-old plunged into Alois Jirśek's thousand-page *F. L. Věk*, the epic novel of Czech history.

And, as he read, he whispered to himself, ". . . already at age ten he had read all of *F. L. Věk*."

A friend of his father's arranged for the young poet to visit the great Czech lyric poet Jaroslav Seifert. Václav brought the master his first attempts at poetry and received a letter in return. He then visited Seifert, at his apartment, together with Jiří Kuběna, one of the Thirty-sixers and a budding poet, and Miloš Forman. Forman, at that time, was studying at the film school of the Academy of Performing Arts (FAMU). He was allowed to study because his parents had died in German concentration camps. The Communists did not dare challenge him; that would have been a little too much, even for them. Vašek gravitated to film, theater, and poetry, and he was glad that Forman,

---

*Klement Gottwald, the Communist Party leader of Czechoslovakia after the takeover.

four years older, had befriended him, and that through him, at least, he could have some contact with the school, where he longed to study. At the school they screened foreign films that did not reach the cinemas. At the Café Slavia,* Forman recounted for Vašek what he had seen and what it had been like. In those days, art schools maintained a high standard, one which they probably never reached again. After 1948 the so-branded bourgeois intellectuals could not participate in civic life, publish, or perform in public. But they were able to stay safely out of the way in art schools. There, it seemed, no one would hear about them. Only much later did the Communists figure out that these teachers were the most dangerous, because they spread the infection of thinking into young minds. Later the art schools became so-called cadre schools, and particularly after 1968, they were carefully cleaned up.

Milan Kundera taught at FAMU during the 1950s. He was not one of the dangerous Communists. Students liked him, trusted him, and did not fear him. Only a few years older than they, he was already a professor, thanks, of course, to his membership in the Party. He taught well and allowed students to write things that would have put their lives in danger if written beyond the protecting roof of their *alma mater.*

It was about this time, probably at the Slavia café, that Forman and Havel decided to write a screenplay that Forman would shoot as a film for class. At that time, Kafka was a forbidden author. The conference in Liblice that cleared his name did not take place until 1963. They had learned about Kafka from a German book Vašek had. It was Max Brod's book on Kafka, and in it they read that Kafka had spent summers in Siřem-Zürau, where his sister Otla leased a cottage. There he wrote *The Castle*. The Castle is, in reality, a granary standing on a hill. If you take a copy of *The Castle* with you, you can walk around Siřem

---

*Located just across the street from the National Theater, it is noted as a gathering place for actors, writers, and artists.

and find for yourself the exact topography described in the novel. This was enough to engage the two literary adventurers, and they decided to go to Siřem.

Havel brought with him the German book by Brod and Kafka's *Castle*. In the book there was even a photograph of Siřem. Together, they walked through the whole town, asking, "Excuse me, isn't there a cottage around here where Franz Kafka's sister used to live, and where he came to visit on holidays?" But no one knew anything about it; the memory of that village had been perfectly, appallingly wiped out. No one who had lived there before the war lived there any longer. The Germans had driven out the Czechs in 1938, and the Czechs in turn had pushed the Germans out in 1945. The village had no history, not a single old-timer remained; it was as if one of Kafka's horrible visions of the end of Europe had been fulfilled. The two of them walked everywhere, asking and asking. Unfortunately, Kafka's cottage was not photographed in the book, so they had no way of recognizing it. Finally an old man advised them to go to the municipal council because there they knew everything. They went to the municipal council and Miloš Forman describes what happened:

"The chairman of the municipal council sat there. When we told him we were looking for this cottage and we needed to find out where Kafka's sister had lived, he listened to us and said:

" 'I don't know, but let's ask the party chairman.' He called out, 'Lojza, come here.'

"Lojza came and said, 'What?'

" 'Two comrades have come from Prague, see, and some Kafka guy, do you know some guy named Kafka?'

" 'No. Wait a minute. Kafka. Where's he live?'

" 'No, no, he was a writer, before the war. And he lived here at his sister's house.'

" 'I don't know, man,' Lojza said. Then he gave us a lecture about how those Germans were nasty and how the Communists are good. We were sitting there, we looked at each other, and Václav, you know him, he just kept asking questions and he was awfully polite. Even as a ten-year-old, I remember, he was the most polite and well-mannered child I've ever known.

"The party chief's conclusion was that no Kafka had ever lived there. So I took the book out and said, 'But there was a Kafka, there really was; look, Mr. Secretary, this is that Kafka fellow, here's his photograph.'

" 'Jesus, that's Siřem all right,' cried the party chairman. He was delighted that his village had made it into a book published in Germany.

" 'Who was this Kafka? What'd he do?' he asked again.

"And then Vašek told the story about Kafka and showed him Kafka's photo. It was a photo taken a few months before his death, and Kafka looked very beautiful in it. The party chairman looked at him and said, 'What a pretty boy, shit, he was pretty, and where does he live?'

"We explained that he had died of tuberculosis, and that this disease makes its victims very beautiful. The skin lightens strangely, as if it has received a kind of depth, and the face takes on an especially inspired expression. Vašek held forth enthusiastically, and they listened to how tuberculosis makes people beautiful before killing them, and suddenly the party chairman blurted out, 'Hey, that's why I'm so damned ugly, it's because I'm healthy!'

"We couldn't hold back any longer. Vašek started to laugh like a madman and we had to leave. Then we struggled with the screenplay and we didn't write anything, because it was clear the name Kafka couldn't even be pronounced without running the risk of punishment."

Miloš claims they were in Siřem in 1954, but Václav says it was not until after the conference at Liblice, when Kafka had already become fashionable. On account of this discrepancy, I thought I wouldn't be able to use the story, but then I thought it would be a shame to leave it out. It seems to me that it is not important when it happened, because Kafka's predicament—like Švejk's* and like the spirit of them both—lingers in this country.

Today, their idea for the film is quite timely, and I would not be surprised if it were actually made. In the film, a land surveyor comes to Siřem, where it has been decided that a Kafka sanctuary will be built, an artificial Kafkaesque world, to attract tourists. The land surveyor who has to put it together cannot get the project moving, because everywhere he runs into indifference and bureaucracy. During the construction of the tourist attraction, the story of Kafka's *Castle* repeats itself.

Václav adds that they did not write the screenplay because Miloš had second thoughts about it. They decided that the film required a knowledge of Kafka that could not be assumed in audiences here.

They never wrote the screenplay, but they continued to meet in the Slavia and together they visited great Czech artists, then forbidden or at least silenced. They discovered people they respected. They were pleased when these people talked to them, when a few even befriended them.

"I still remember," Miloš Forman says, "how Vašek discovered the poet Vladimir Holan for me and once even brought me to visit him. Holan lived in a little house on the Kampa below Jan Werich, the actor and playwright. I didn't really listen to what people were saying, because I was utterly fascinated by him. It was daytime, afternoon, but the room was absolutely dark, lit by one small bulb. He lived his life so that daylight never reached him. He was a wizard, a mystical creature, and I could only gawk. Vašek knew him fairly well, because otherwise we wouldn't have been admitted; he didn't accept visitors."

Another newly discovered island, in the Rilkean sense (we are, after

---

*The central character in Jaroslav Hašek's *The Good Soldier Švejk,* a hilarious four-volume satire on military bureaucracy and an indictment of war. Švejk, seemingly dimwitted but always smiling and loquatious, symbolizes the little man who beats the system. He survives by always following his orders to the letter.

all, in Prague), was Jiří Kolář, the poet and artist. These people, all outcasts, connected the young Havel with another world, noble and just. Because they demanded high moral standards in art and particularly in literature, they did not publish. People such as Kolář, Jiudřich Chalupecký, and Professor Černý stood out like long-established beacons. They had much in common with the world Havel grew up in, which had honored values that in the new world counted for nothing. Among them was Zdeněk Urbánek, the writer and translator. Our wonderful old friend Zdeněk remembers that he saw Vašek for the first time in the middle of the 1950s at a gathering on a street named either Kozí [Goat Street] or Kozácká [Cossack Street]; he no longer remembers which. Kozí [Goat Street] would have suited the street much better, because it slanted, and goats enjoy grazing on steep slopes. A handful of people had turned up there. Probably there were only two of them, but they gave the impression of at least four; or maybe there were three, who gave the impression of five.

At any rate, the young people, among them Václav, had probably read all the books Kolář had published before 1948 and some of the samizdats that came out in the fifties. Jiří Kolář belonged to a group of poets and painters* who met in the Café Slavia. They wrote and exchanged their work with one another, the way we did later in the seventies and eighties, and they published the texts as samizdats. They did this so they could maintain some continuity with themselves, with their past lives, and with the rest of the world, and so they would not go crazy.* Unconsciously, Václav somehow belonged among these outcasts, but surprisingly, so did his friends, Jiří Kuběna, Josef Topol, Věra Linhartová, Miloš Forman—all those who were not writing *engagé* or ideological literature but instead were looking for something more substantial and real. They found it at Kolář's table in the Slavia.

---

*In 1942 these people, who included theorists as well as avant-garde poets and painters, formed themselves into a group known as Group 42 (Skupina 42) for the purpose of exhibiting and publishing together. The group was active from 1942 until the Communist takeover in 1948, when they were no longer allowed to publish.

They had been sitting in the Slavia for a long time, never suspecting that at the next table sat the very people they had been longing to meet. Zdeněk Urbánek remembers that Kolář was very affectionate toward them during these visits.

Later, during Václav's first successes at the Theater on the Balustrade, Kolář said that Václav's poetics weren't clean. The expression caught on: "Hey, you, keep quiet; your poetics aren't clean."

2 • Olga

It is still 1956—in Václav Havel's life, a year more meaningful than any other. In the spring, Václav began to go out with Olga:

> Day dawns; the frogs in your fishpond
> croak wildly; silence; not a soul anywhere.
> We stand alone beside a wall set with
> glass splinters
> to make life difficult for criminals.
> Metaphors come to me, about myself—a criminal
> and about your face—a wall with splinters, so that
> my path to your soul should be more complicated.

Olga used to sit with him in the Slavia. She wanted to be an actress; she was pretty and elegant. The milieu she came from was different than his, and that greatly interested Václav. Her family were workers who lived in Žižkov. In her upbringing and her nature, Olga was Vašek's other half. Olga says of herself that she grew up in the streets and then had to take care of her sister's children. She was as cruel, she says, as the scourge of God, but they all loved her.

They were so different, but they became close to each other, and from that time they never separated. In 1956, in Revue K, Havel published a long poem about Olga. I quote from it again:

Half a day has passed since we last spoke.
You, Žižkov daughter; me, still untested
haunter of writerly cafés. Us two,
somewhere on the edge of spring.

From that time on, Olga went everywhere with him, and they did everything together. She is the first to read his manuscripts. She built his famous fence* with him. Once when Václav got lost in the forest at Hrádeček, he wandered back and forth yelling, "Olga!"

3 ▪ Kafka, Ionesco, Beckett

Franz Kafka is to this day Havel's favorite author. It astonishes me how, from the start, Havel found and chose what was genuine and right. He was faithful to his loves and his role models, sometimes adding new members to his pantheon but never throwing anyone out. He systematically discovered the best that those before him had gathered, almost unerringly.

Kafka and Havel have in common their recognition of the absurd dimension of the world, their experience of exile, of shyness, of persistent doubt in themselves and their abilities, and a sense of guilt and of their own particular obscurity. It is surprising how much they have in common—a Jewish intellectual from the beginning of the century and a scion of a bourgeois family dispossessed of its property, living in the margins of society. Many have identified with Kafka; many have imitated him. Many have felt they had a similar sense of life because they were persecuted. Usually it is a delusion, but with Havel it makes sense. Both foretold the future shape of the world in their work. Kafka's vision was unhappy, even tragic. Havel's world was in

---

*The picket fence around the garden at Hrádeček, the Havels' country cottage. Havel is proud of it, and of having built it himself.

such misery it could only get better. The more I peruse his writing, the more visionary he seems to me. At times I have to laugh at how perfectly he predicted his own future, and that makes me as anxious as the present does.

Both are interested in the loss of an individual's identity, in a person's position as the victim and target of manipulation by an impersonal power. Their points of departure are different. Kafka's nightmare came true. Havel's dream is still coming true. I would not like to analyze this any further, because it is still playing itself out.

In the second half of the 1950s, Havel was also fortified by his reading of Beckett and Ionesco. He discovered his theme and it has preoccupied him to this day. It is often said that every author has one theme that he spends all his life coming to terms with; he struggles with it, and the older, wiser, and more experienced he becomes, the closer he comes to its resolution. He never decides, however, on a definitive answer, because there isn't one; he can only come closer to it—just as in life there is no destination, only the journey. It is important to be on this journey and to move toward a destination, but it is a destination we will never reach. Human life is a person's struggle with order, or with God—the name does not matter. It is impossible to conform to order, but order is necessary to live, and the struggle with it shapes one's life.

Havel's theme is pseudorenascence. The system is deteriorating, but its leaders still believe it has the right to exist. Everyone knows the king is naked, but the king maintains he is clothed. People allow the system to be revived, because they have adapted to it, they are used to it, and so they shape the same reality again and again. But a lie only begets another lie. An ideology that people identify with and to which they yield prepares them to be the way it needs them to be. Then people would rather not think anything, and therefore they can, in the course of a few hours or even a single moment, change from one opinion to the very opposite. This is the theme of human identity and existential schizophrenia. Havel reveals this mechanism. It is not surprising that when we read his play *The Memorandum* today, it seems prescient to us. He foresees the day when the world will have evolved so far that no one cares anymore whether a person who claims to believe something is serious or not. If he were serious, he would probably even be considered a lunatic and a fool.

4 • First Publication, First Public Appearance

In 1956, another important event took place. At the time, Václav was a student in the Czechoslovak University of Technology (ČVUT). He had tried several times to get into the film school of the Academy of Performing Arts (FAMU), but he had not been accepted. There were always many candidates applying to art schools, and so a far stricter set of "cadre" rules applied than for a technical college. The socialist regime favored science and technology; it wanted to outstrip the Western imperialist states with their much-mocked wealth, and therefore they set guidelines calling for many students to be accepted into the technical schools. But it was nearly impossible to get into a college geared toward the humanities if one's parents were not members of the Communist Party of Czechoslovakia. For someone with bourgeois origins, it was simply out of the question. Because Václav was in danger of being drafted into military service, he panicked and registered at the faculty of economics of the Czechoslovak University of Technology. They accepted him into the department of public transport. He thought that later, somehow, he would enter the Academy of Performing Arts (AMU), which turned out to be altogether impossible, and finally, in 1957, he had to enlist anyway.

It was then, in 1956 when he was still a student at the Polytechnic, that he delivered his memorable address at the meeting of young writers at Dobříš, although he left the school soon after that. It was after the famous twentieth congress of the Communist Party of the Soviet Union at which Khrushchev denounced Stalin and the cult of personality. At the second congress of the Czechoslovak Writers' Union earlier that year in Prague, Seifert and the poet František Hrubín had addressed the assembly and for the first time criticized the government's politics. They had spoken about writers who had been imprisoned and whose works had been thrown out of the literary canon in the fifties. Something was beginning to move; life was again breaking through the thick crust and a slender spring was gushing up to the surface. Soon after that, *Květen* was founded as a magazine for the young literary generation.

Although its editors and writers were mostly Communists, they had tried to improve upon socialist realism; there was a kind of shift, even if it was a vague and modest one. They no longer wanted to describe the official view of the world; they wanted to write about everyday life. Havel wrote a letter to the editors in which he pointed out various insufficiencies and imperfections—chiefly, that the magazine took no interest in his friends from Group 42, that they did not write about them at all. Of course, the editors and authors of *Květen* knew nothing about Group 42. They printed the letter and called for a discussion in the pages of *Květen*. Thanks to this, Havel became known as a young author. He was invited to the conference of young authors at Dobříš and there found himself among renowned writers of the school of socialist realism.

Not long before, in that baroque, slightly haunted castle,* the writers of socialist realism would get drunk and celebrate death sentences pronounced on their colleagues during the trials of the early 1950s. In Dobříš they had their luxury suites. They formed a new nobility to replace the exiled Colloredo-Mansfelds, the former owners of the castle. Dobříš castle was and is a symbol of the immorality of writers, their pride and sense of superiority, the loyalty and flunkeyism they showed toward rulers who in return gave them perks. Surprisingly, even today Czech writers do not want to give up the castle.

---

*In the appropriated castle at Dobříš was the so-called House of Writers, a retreat for writers loyal to the Communist regime.

In 1956, Václav Havel traveled to this castle as a student in public transport, and after he delivered his address, no one could talk about anything else. Some spoke of his address as "daringly critical" and bold; others condemned him for speaking about art and creativity while in Hungary they were defending socialism with their blood. He spoke of the oppression of literature, of forbidden poets, of those they had blackballed from literature. He laid out the hypocrisy of his audience—they declared they wanted to right old wrongs, the errors of the cult of personality, but they didn't mean it seriously. Here Václav was already confronting his theme of pseudorenascence, which has played itself out so often in our lives. As far as principles, they said, there was nothing to change; they were all correct. It was only people who were not perfect, who made mistakes. Havel chewed out the writers for saying it was necessary to correct the old faults, set right the blunders, and open the windows and doors to truth, but then taking no real interest in what had happened in the past. They covered their heads with ashes, but everything remained as it was before. It was clear from their reaction to his address that they didn't even want to hear about the many things they ought to do. Havel told them everything he had against them. They looked at the blond young man, a little chubby, with clear blue eyes, who, it seemed, was bringing them a message. He looked a little like an angel, and he spoke the truth, which they were reluctant to accept. Later they had to take note of him, and of the fact that a new generation had sprung up, a generation that had nothing in common with their ideals, the ideals off of which they had lived so well. They were surprised to discover that this new generation criticized them, and that in the pages of *Tvář*, the Writers' Union's literary monthly for young writers, opponents to them had sprung up. And they started to defend themselves.

5 ▪ Seven Letters to Melin

At the close of the 1950s the new generation was coalesing in its resistance to all regulations and orders, against any violation of life. There were no longer any *svazáks*—members of the Socialist Youth Movement—who, singing *častuškas*,* judged their fellow students and expelled them from school for their political and religious convictions. This was no generation of *svazáks*, at once cruel and sentimental. In the spirit of political directives, the *svazáks* had wrecked the careers of fellow students who disagreed with them, but in the next breath they had been able to wax tender over anything simple, plain, and everyday—and particularly over themselves. For the 1950s—with their tension between the winners who asserted their power and the losers who were suppressed and locked away, or at least silenced—the bell had tolled.

Václav Havel had other teachers of philosophy than Marx and Engels. The philosophy of Havel's teachers was somewhat more rigorous and complex. Perhaps it was thanks to them that he managed to avoid the temptation of Marxism or any other kind of ideology. His teachers were the philosophers J. L. Fischer and Josef Šafařik. *Seven Letters to Melin*, which Šafařík published after the war in a small edition, was Havel's Bible in his youth. I read it much later, and it bewitched me as well. In it, an engineer escapes to philosophy, like all great men in a moment of supreme danger, and with erudition and patience he blames science and technology for causing the contemporary fall of humanity. Šafařík makes each person responsible for his own life. I would like to cite some lines that describe those who have fallen victim to ideology:

---

*A *častuška* is a Russian ditty on a timely topic.

"Moral reasoning produces morality exactly as rarely as natural science produces nature; or aesthetics, art. If you accomplish morality by threats, you have produced prudence—a nice facade, but not, in any way, morality. Either the reality and value of life lies in our nature, or there is no help for us." . . . *"What is morally negative in human nature, i.e., what is hard for the conscience to bear, is revealed in the inclination to assume the collective form, to carry out one's individual mission only to the minimum. What is despicable in a person is revealed in the tendency to clothe oneself in moral obligation, in the service of external authority and power."*

At the end of the 1950s, social structures were reviving and they began to live a life of their own. Society can never be changed by any kind of orders from above. Change must form below and wait for the opportune moment. This is also the only possible means of defense against the oppression of totalitarian power, against orders, against conformity. People usually begin to come together first on the cultural plane, and there they create political pressure in the name of demands for a need to live. At the end of the 1950s, small theaters sprouted up like mushrooms after rain. Their art was a reaction to the preceding leadership. Suddenly it was as if audiences wanted nothing but to amuse themselves, meet people, sing, and dance.

In *Seven Letters to Melin*, Josef Šafařík wrote this about art:

Art is nature and has no goal other than nature's: life itself. The artist may be led by any kind of tendencies or biases; however, if his work is supposed to be art, he may not be tendentious, i.e., the biases may not enter his work as ideas, as truths, or as precepts, but rather in the way they enter nature: as living, concrete individuals. Nature is not tendentious; it does not treat us to ideas and truths, but even so. . . . If the work is supposed to be artistic, then in the work itself we must not read or hear even a word about these biases and ideas. As much bias should be hidden in the work as is hidden in nature, i.e. as much as there is in "readers." Nothing more and nothing less may be required of the artist than that he create a living reality. But this makes as much sense as to require him to live. Either he lives, and thus creates; or he creates, and thus counterfeits and stagnates within. . . . The artist does not create out of his understanding; he creates out of his experience. Earlier we noted the essential difference these two words signify for us: the difference between "spectator" and "participant." Simply put: understanding is saved in memory and in consciousness; experiences refashion themselves into a living constitution. In the first case, you insert a new datum into a system of data; in the second, something in you dies and is born again. . . . In the first case, you act according to what you know; in the second, according to what you are, or to put it more precisely, what you are becoming.

The world of "official" literature and culture did not interest Havel; he was not a student; he was not receiving any schooling; he had to supply it all himself. He did not dally over translations of L. I. Timofeyev's Soviet theory of literature;* he did not concern himself with phony historiography; he did not have to pass exams in any of this. He was able to devote his time to his self-education, even if some years he had to work as well, or study some other things. Infallibly, what attracted him was whatever preserved continuity with the First Republic, whatever was still founded on a base of solid European culture and was not subservient to orders from above. More than anything, that was Group 42.

Havel was not alone. He had several friends who with equal zeal dug through the official snow job and searched for what remained from before. They were Miloš Forman, Věra Linhatová, Josef Topol, Jiří Kuběna, and later Jan Zábrana. For them, Group 42 was the most recent example of a living, breathing achievement in Czech poetry, in Czech art. Havel's friends organized various quasi-official perfor-

---

*Timofeyev's *Fundamentals of the Theory of Literature* was commonly assigned as a college textbook.

mances in the Artists' Club (*Umělecká beseda*), through which they also published a samizdat. They considered this other culture their natural world; official culture they avoided. They reckoned that even some of the older authors were in their camp—for example Josef Škvorecký and Hrabal, who wrote but were also not allowed to publish anything. Václav was, I suppose, much like a number of young intellectuals of the 1970s and 1980s. So far he had not done anything to get himself condemned or imprisoned, and nonetheless somehow of his own free will he drifted among the forbidden—as the authors at *Revolver Revue* and other samizdat magazines did in the 1980s. These people did not even try to be officially accepted. For them, it was not worth it to humiliate and debase themselves, to accept conditions and commands. They were free from the outset, and the price they paid was publication only by typewriter or in exile. For them, as it would be for Havel before them, it was an adventure to smuggle books from abroad, or to look at them secretly with the consent of a conspirator-librarian in the university library, to read forbidden authors and forbidden thoughts. Almost everything we in Havel's and my generation learned and studied in the fifties was against the will of the regime and in resistance to it. They were always forcing something on us, commanding us, shoving our noses into one thing, so that we would not see something else.

From Group 42, Václav received a university education in the ethics of writing, something he couldn't have gotten at the time in a philosophy department. He had someone to turn to, someone to debate with, someone to learn from. He had, therefore, everything, and he was satisfied. The symbol of all this was Kolář's table at the Slavia.

6 • Military Service

"It's very important that Vašek did time in the service," says his friend, actor Pavel Landovský, "because his whole life he mixed in circles of prominent fools, who got out of the service in the "aussies,"* or who had "blue booklets."† Just city kids from Prague. There's something entirely Old Testament about it, that the service in the course of two years makes a teenager into a man. In the service, a guy has to keep company with people he wouldn't hang out with on the outside, where he would have avoided them. After these two years he learns how to bear his fate in this world. Vašek can handle so many things today because he had a background in coercion. As a civilian he was coerced many times, but it started in the service, with the engineers. He could have come up with flat feet or something else, but he never shirked anything. I've always had the feeling that a fellow should stick his nose into everything, and if it doesn't get cut off, keep going. Nothing human was alien to Vašek. . . ."

Within days of their father's sixtieth birthday, both sons were conscripted. By extending his studies Václav had delayed enlisting so his service would coincide with Ivan's.

On September 12, 1957, Havel's mother arranged a family party at the Barrandov Terraces.

In the late 1920s, Havel's father had bought a hill outside Prague called Barrandov. He planned to build a fashionable district there, modeled after the English garden cities. In five months he set up a dining and entertainment establishment called the Barrandov Ter-

---

*From the abbreviation A.U.S., for *Armádní umělecký soubor*, the Forces Arts Ensemble.

†Issued by the government, "blue booklets" resembled passports in size and shape and certified the bearer's *zdravotní nezpůsobilost vykonávat vojenskou službu*—"inability to perform military service for health reasons."

races. It was the most outstanding summer establishment in Prague. The ground work, construction, garden layout, and outfitting with furniture and restaurant equipment took just five months and nine days! During the opening, on St. Václav's Day, 1929, fifty thousand people visited.

In 1957, Barrandov Terraces had long since ceased to belong to the family, but all the family celebrations traditionally took place either at Barrandov or at the Lucerna Palace, which the family had also built and owned. On this occasion, they were celebrating the father's sixtieth birthday and the sons' departure for military service.

All four realized that their family life together was coming to an end. The parents stayed behind with their own worries. They sent letters and packages to Václav in České Budějovice and to Ivan in Hummený.

In Prague, on the train platform, Václav met Andrej Krob, who later became a good friend. Andrej also remembers an attractive blond standing there in a rayon raincoat. Olga. Understandably, Andrej wanted to know who the pretty woman was with. And then he noticed the chubby short fellow beside her, and said to himself: Damn. Later he noticed that this little fellow was, absurdly dressed according to regulations, just like in the manuals under the title, "Military Bearing and Dress," the section that outlines how a cap should and should not be shaped, how many buttons should be where, how pants should be tucked into drill boots, how many centimeters of what should show. Andrej often ran into this model soldier with the sharply pointed cap on his head. He went around with a box full of papers for the political-education office. He struck Andrej as an eccentric, and so for a long time they did not become close.

Vašek at that time was friends with Karel Brynda, later the head of drama at the theater in Ostrava. They founded a troop theater company—culture, particularly if it was ideological and educational, was well supported in the military service then—and for their first production, they performed *September Nights* by Pavel Kohout. Havel played the villain Lieutenant Škrovánek so well that the troop commander began to suspect that Havel was showing his true face. The commander felt he had better relieve Havel of his duties as a panzer, which the commander considered an honor. This saved Václav from the responsibility of dragging a bazooka with him on marching exercises along with everything else, and from cleaning it every week.

Once, when Andrej was in the sick bay with Havel and Brynda he discovered they were writing theatrical pieces because they gave themselves away by constantly guffawing. They were writing a serious drama, concerned with military problems, a socialist-realist and "boldly critical" play, as the times demanded. They had great fun with it, and they figured the trips to drama competitions would shorten their time in the service. At first it worked, and the play was successful in the lower levels of competition. When, however, they were supposed to go before the all-army review in Mariánské Lázně (Marienbad), it occurred to the *politruk** to investigate the authors' class background and political credentials. The play, it seemed, was threatening to win the top prize. They discovered that both authors had the kind of background that made it impossible to believe they took their play seriously. The investigators were right. To Mariánské Lázně, nonetheless, our heroes went; they performed outside of the competition, and only so they could be exposed and the play condemned as anti-army. The theater company had to return all the flowers, wreathes, and medals they had won, and the matter was hushed up.

In the army, then, Havel first wrote a play in which he himself performed; thus, he founded "author's theater," which later became his destiny.

---

*"Political commissars," from the first syllables of the Russian words *politicheskij rukovoditel.*

7 ▪ *Spiritual Legacy*

While Václav was in the service, clouds were gathering over Havlov. Havlov was the summer family seat that Václav's paternal grandfather had built near Tišnov in Moravia. For fifty years the family had gone there. Václav and Ivan spent a good part of their childhood here, attending school in nearby Žd'árec. Friends of their parents and grandparents had visited there. But now for the Havels one loss followed another. The Works Council of the Revolutionary Trade-Union Movement in Kuřim decided that they could set up a young pioneers'* camp at Havlov. The Havels offered Havlov to a school in Žd'árec with the condition that they set aside several rooms where the Havels could keep their furniture and stay in the summer. But the District National Committee in Tišnov made an executive decision to award all of Havlov to the Works Council of the Revolutionary Trade-Union Movement of the Machine-Tools Factory in Kuřim. The property passed into the Works Council's possession for 70,000 crowns, its estimated value, which, however, the Havels never received.

In October 1958, the family had to leave Havlov. At the same time, they lost the rest of the furniture and things from the suburban home of Václav's maternal grandparents, the Vavrečkas, in Zlín, from their Prague apartment, and from Havlov itself. Havel's mother sold some things on the spot for peanuts; another portion the Works Council of the Revolutionary Trade-Union Movement simply took.

The loss of Havlov was offset in the 1960s by the acquisition of Hrádeček.† Ivan traveled there with his family; Václav's father was

---

*A sort of Communist Boy Scouts.
†The Havel's country cottage situated in Northern Bohemia near the Polish border. Even under the Communist system and nationalization, it was still sometimes possible to manage, to obtain certain things, as was the case with Hradeček.

there almost constantly after the death of his wife; and friends came to visit.

In his memoirs, Vaclav's father ends the history of Havlov with this laconic conclusion: ". . . when you returned from military service [Vašek and Ivan], there was no longer any Havlov. Although I was very fond of Havlov, I was reconciled to what happened, for I saw that after socialism I would not be able to hold on to it."

Gradually, the Havel home in Prague and the plots at Barrandov were nationalized. Václav's mother gave up her share in her parents' suburban home in Zlín because she would have had to repair it, and she could not afford to. But what most annoyed her was the nationalization of the family art collection, which she had donated to the Museum of Decorative Arts and the National Gallery.

And so, by the beginning of the 1960s, the property of the Havel family had been liquidated. At that same time, Václav was entering the Theater on the Balustrade, so that during the 1960s, when his plays began to be performed at home and abroad, he would become, relatively speaking, "upwardly mobile," as his father said in his writings.

Václav's father worked until 1963, when he was sixty-five years old. His net income was 1,200 crowns a month. As a former capitalist and exploiter, he was never allowed to hold any position of authority. They calculated his pension to be 600 crowns. As a pensioner, he depended on his wife's support. She was employed from 1960 on by the Prague Information Services. She acted as a tour guide for foreigners, took care of the Bethlehem Chapel, and for the longest stretch worked in the Old Town Hall. There she was a guide, an information officer, and sold tickets and souvenirs. She figured that in 1973, at sixty years old, she would be able to retire. Sadly, she did not live to see it.

I remember once when a foreigner and I were visiting the Museum of National Literature, I started talking to a little old lady. She looked like someone's fairy godmother; she had white hair divided in the center at a pink part, and because the library was cold, she wore a scarf on her head. I remember her big, dark, lively eyes, an eighteen-year-old's eyes in a pinkish wrinkled face. Out of the face of the old woman shone the face of a girl—some women age into youth and into girlish shyness, and blushing. We were talking about something or other and I don't know how we came to the subject of Havel. "Do you know him?" beamed the old woman. "How lovely. I used to know his mother; we were together in the Bethlehem Chapel. His mother was very nice; I remember her warmly. She was a lady," whispered the woman. "And Václav turned out well for her. We follow what he writes through the foreign radio broadcasts, and we pray for him. When you see him, please tell him one of his mother's co-workers from the Bethlehem Chapel sends him greetings." I was happy to deliver the message.

In the case of grandfather Vavrečka, Václav's maternal grandfather, I sense a great affinity not only with Václav, the writer and politician, but also with Ivan, the roboticist, mathematician, and philosopher. His daughter Božena persuaded her father to write out his memoirs for his grandchildren, for Ivan and Václav. He wrote a bit for them, but was reluctant to write more. Grandfather Vavrečka teased his daughter a little about her maternal love—the way she worshiped her children as could be seen in her diaries and in the albums she decorated with her sketches. He remembered that sometimes she also got angry, for example when Ivan did not eat or Vašek pouted. In a large note-book, he addressed Božena with love and for her sake wrote down his meditations, which read like something the author of *Seven Letters to Melin* could have written, or like some of Václav's later letters from prison:

> *I have, as you know, a strong inclination to the natural sciences, and I read chemistry, physics, or biology with the same interest and relish as a good novel. I know, however, that the scientific method ends where the fateful fall of human life begins, and where the history of nations and humanity is woven. We will never be able to direct our fate or the history of our nation on the basis of*

scientific knowledge. It is impossible to refute the supreme natural law governing the whole world, the rule of cause and effect which rules all objects and phenomena. However, we also may not forget that no one can know all the causal conditions and links in the world—there are considerably more of them than there are cells and atomic combinations in a human brain. Even in pure mathematics, it is impossible to solve certain equations with total precision. As soon as there are three bodies in space, the simplicity and clarity of mechanics ends. Without question, there are many things that can be managed purposefully, systematically, and rationally—we dedicate the larger part of our life's work to these goaloriented activities; every day, however, we find evidence that the most important events, actions, and turns, in private as in social life, spring in the end from creative inventiveness, from lucky or unlucky inspirations, rather than from the teleological use of our consciousness and experience.

The world's kaleidoscope is formed above all from countless individual personalities and numerous national characters, whose actions and interactions are incalculable. There have been instances when Saint Bernards, trained to save lost travelers, have clawed a child to pieces when playing. Among people are wolves, tigers, hyenas, vipers, sheep, bulls, and pigs, as if nature first drew a sketchbook of diverse characters, then mixed them into one hodgepodge of a human being. How can science manage the world when we do not know what is hidden in people? My highest praise goes to those whose instincts tell them what the score is.

8 • *Grandfather Vavrečka*

Hugo Vavrečka knew Tomáš Bat'a, founder of a huge and prosperous shoe manufacturing enterprise, from his youth. Bat'a wanted Vavrečka when he was a student of electrical engineering, to explain to him the principle of electricity. Bat'a more or less understood direct current, but alternating current was not clear to him. Later, whenever he introduced a new technology into his factory, he would consult the student. Sometimes it bothered him that he was not paying for the ideas, so he would start the conversation far afield, as if he were interested in discussing something else, but in a few moments he would give himself away. He couldn't keep it up, because he was in a hurry; his time was expensive. Sometimes he was quite generous and would run in and shove an envelope with a few banknotes at the poor student. Maybe Bat'a wanted to do a good deed while something was working out for him, Hugo Vavrečka suggested with his dry humor.

Vavrečka understood not only technology but also politics. Later, when Vavrečka became ambassador in Vienna, Tomáš Bat'a accompanied him as an adviser on economics, business, investments, and trade. While he was the director of the ministry of foreign affairs and an active diplomat, Hugo Vavrečka could not participate in Bat'a's business, but he had a good business sense and he enjoyed following the rapid development and rise of this purely Czech enterprise. For instance, he criticized Bat'a for the dowdy display windows and bad service in his shops, particularly in Prague. Bat'a listened to him and re-did his shop windows. He applied Vavrečka's ideas in production, in retail, in technology, and in organization. Bat'a offered Vavrečka a position in his business, but Vavrečka had a dream for Central Europe he wanted to realize. Instead, he accepted the position of consul in Hamburg, then served as ambassador to Budapest, and then to Vienna.

This grandfather appears to me to be genetically the closest to Václav. He was a politician, a diplomat, and he had an original plan for Central Europe. He wrote wittily, and he was a homegrown philosopher. In his memoirs, grandfather Vavrečka wrote:

> On Christmas Day, 1919, Dr. Edvard Beneš, the minister of foreign affairs, called me to the Castle and offered me a position in the foreign service: either as a delegate in Budapest or as consul in Hamburg. I accepted Hamburg, filling the post in February 1920. Meanwhile I called on President Masaryk,* who followed my actions with interest and did not conceal that he counted me as one of his "pupils,"—i.e., as an adherent of his opinions and methods. He relied on my judgment, and when we parted, he remarked, "When you finish your task in Hamburg, you ought to take economic matters in central Europe in hand. Our whole future will turn on how we manage to lead and form central Europe—Austria, Hungary, and the Balkans." He pointed a finger upward and said:
>
> "That's the most important question."
>
> When I reached the door, he turned around once more and said:
>
> "That, of course, and Russia."
>
> Years later, Karel Čapek shared with me that in his Conversations,† Masaryk mentioned me and my articles several times. Once he said:
>
> "Vavrečka is one of those who turned out well for me."

After consultation with foreign minister Dr. Edvard Beneš, Hugo Vavrečka, as ambassador in Budapest and later in Vienna, attempted to link Hungary, Austria, and Czechoslovakia in close cooperation.

As the first official ambassador to Hungary, Hugo Vavrečka had much to deal with. Every day there were border clashes, espionage affairs, insults to Czechs, haughtiness to Slovaks, and attacks in the

---

*Tomáš Garrigue Masaryk. The first president of the Czechoslovak Republic.
†Karel Čapek's book of conversations with Masaryk, published in three volumes from 1928 to 1935.

newspapers. Our ambassador however took the view that "quiet patience and tenacity can accomplish more in Hungary than in any other of our neighbor nations." In Budapest society, he earned the moniker "the Czech optimist." "Particularly because," he wrote, "I looked for ways to bypass Hungarian affectation with humor, and I was not afraid to go out among the people. From the first I went to the cafés like any other resident (not like the diplomats of the great powers, who showed themselves only in horse-drawn carriages, automobiles, and theater boxes) and people knew that I was not afraid to walk down the street, even during nationalist demonstrations. Nothing ever happened to me, and the politicians soon began to seek me out for discussions."

As ambassador in Vienna, Hugo Vavrečka continued to pursue lines of cooperation with Hungary and Austria. An autonomous central European orientation in these countries, without domination by any great power, was his goal. Unfortunately, it did not turn out that way, although his concept gained many adherents among politicians, high officials, and businessmen in all these countries.

In the 1930s the line of development was interrupted by a great world crisis; Europe plunged into a new war.

In his memoirs, Hugo Vavrečka writes with no small visionary talent and political prudence:

> *I realized that my conceptions and plans for the realization of closer politico-economic cooperation between Czechoslovakia, Austria, and Hungary were premature. My belief that someday this cooperation of the nations living together in the Danube region must come about was never shaken. In 1932, however, I recognized that it is a process that will take many generations before it matures into a more stable sociological formation, and that above all it must somehow survive the "Greater Germany" complex, that natural propensity of ethnic Germans to join together into a single unified state, . . . and for our nation, the fateful question is whether or not our nation will be able to exist.*

To contravene the rise of such a German complex, Vavrečka was constructing in central Europe a higher supranational form. In 1932, when he discovered that everything in Austria was moving toward *Anschluss*, and his life's work was collapsing, Hugo Vavrečka left the diplomatic service. In July of the same year, he signed a contract with Tomáš Bat'a, who twelve days later died in an airplane accident.

Grandfather Vavrečka, whom Václav and Ivan loved greatly, left behind many stories, some written in his native dialect—Lechish, which is quite unintelligible to Czechs. He also wrote a science-fiction novel and one play, all between the years 1905 and 1911, before he married and raised a family. (An adaptation of one of his stories came out as the film *Lelíček in the Service of Sherlock Holmes*.) He held patents for several inventions in physics and electronics and he wrote a philosophical essay, "On the Beginning and Ending of the World."

9 ▪ His First Plays

At the close of the 1950s, a process was running its course—Václav Havel calls this the process of social self-awareness and self-liberation—and gradually it led to political changes at the end of the 1960s.

Theater of the sixties was once more nonideological; it did not moralize or give a prescribed "official" picture of the world, as had the "Stone theaters"* of the 1950s. It was no accident that the process of social self-awareness began in small theaters. Theater is a collective experience. Suddenly, groups of people heard what for a long time no one had been allowed to say, even in secret. They heard it in a darkened theater, and they reacted anonymously, but every one of these performances was a kind of holiday. The spectators were seized and bound. They began to free themselves from fear, to formulate their feelings, to laugh. Society woke slowly from its lethargy, fear, and

---

*The large official theaters, the only ones that existed in the 1950s.

indifference. Until this time, theater had taken itself too seriously; it was supposed to "mirror contemporary of burning reality acts," be *engagé*, show what was good and what bad, distinguish the ideologically positive characters from the villains. Now, finally, it stopped aspiring to moral and political judgment. On the small stages, there were no psychological dramas to be found. In this comparatively happy period, Havel began to write plays.

"What exactly is absurd theatre? How would you define it?" asks Karel Hvížd'ala in *Disturbing the Peace* (a book-length interview with Havel whose Czech title translates as *Long-Distance Interrogation*).* Václav defines it thus:

> Personally, I think it's the most significant theatrical phenomenon of the twentieth century, because it demonstrates modern humanity in a "state of crisis," as it were. That is, it shows man having lost his fundamental metaphysical certainty, the experience of the absolute, his relationship to eternity, the sensation of meaning— in other words, having lost the ground under his feet. This is a man for whom everything is coming apart, whose world is collapsing, who senses that he has irrevocably lost something but is unable to admit this to himself and therefore hides from it. . . . They [absurdist plays] cannot be taken literally; they illustrate nothing. They merely point to the final horizon of our common general theme. They are not overblown, highly impassioned, or didactic. They tend, rather, to be decadently joking in tone. They know the phenomenon of endless embarrassment. Often the characters are silent; often they run off at the mouth in stupid ways. They can be seen as outright comedies. The plays are not—and this is important—nihilistic. They are merely a warning. In a very shocking way, they throw us into the question of meaning by manifesting its absence. Absurd theatre does not offer us consolation or hope. It merely reminds us of how we are living: without hope. And that

---

*Václav Havel, *Disturbing the Peace: A Conversation with Karel Hvížd'ala*, trans. Paul Wilson (New York: Alfred A, Knopf, 1990).

is the essence of its warning. Absurd theater, in its particular (and easily describable) way, makes the fundamental questions of the modern human dimension of Being its themes. [Disturbing the Peace, pp. 53–54]

Havel's first absurdist play was *An Evening with the Family*, a one-act play influenced by Ionesco. Then he wrote the first version of *The Memorandum* and began to contribute theoretical articles to the magazine *Divadlo (Theater)*. At the time he worked as a stagehand at the ABC Theater in Prague, where he was accepted because his father interceded for him with Jan Werich, the theater's artistic director. The ABC Theater was somewhat like Kolář's table at the Slavia, because it too linked the First Republic to the present day. It was one of the last slender threads linking what came before with its weak reflection in the present. It was like when, during a drought, a forest begins to burn, and then the flame mysteriously burns down but still smoulders in the roots, so that it might still flare up again, unexpected. The fire no longer has its original wolfish strength; it is old and sputtering, but there is still something in it of the fierce, young flame of long ago.

During each performance, the ABC's employees waited for Werich's dialogue with fellow actor Miroslav Horníček in front of the curtain during intermissions and the spectators looked forward to it as they had once looked forward in the interwar period to the *Liberated Theater* of Jiři Voskovec and Werich. The audience understood every signal, every gesture. Werich and Horníček could draw the link between the stage and the audience masterfully, even though there was practically nothing they were allowed to talk about. Mysteriously, without words, a conspiracy between actors and public was created every time. A sort of peculiar magnetic field arose. Even when the main performance was a little stale, these dialogues held their own. In fact, Werich later had to leave the theater. In the ABC Theater, there was humor, clowning, practical jokes, improvisation, poetic symbols—everything that was missing in the stone theaters or had been explicitly prohibited. Havel spent one season at the ABC and remembers it fondly.

In a 1976 essay with his proverbial methodicalness and rage for order, Havel numbers and presents the essential phenomena that he regards as "a fortunate interplay of several quite accidental circumstances" in his life.* Until their dying day, many people of his generation will offer the excuse that having a bourgeois origin made it impossible for them to attend school, and so they remained without an education. Many will complain until the end of their lives about the unfavorable circumstances that prevented them from developing as they might have under more favorable conditions. How many frustrated hopes and jilted lives! But if a person truly wants and is destined to be somebody, he will be somebody. The social Darwinism of the 1950s was harsh. Because of it, though, we have survived everything. Those of us who have survived.

Havel considers his circumstances to have been positive from the beginning. He writes:

> Thanks to the apparent disadvantage of coming from a bourgeois background and growing up in a Communist state, I had the opportunity, right from the start, of seeing the world "from below," that is, as it really is. This helped me to escape certain eventual illusions and mystifications. [Open Letters, p. 4]

He praises the circumstances that defined him: He could not have fallen for the ideology of communism even if he had wanted to. His ancestry and his family's experiences prevented that. He thereby avoided a great deal of trouble that others fell into. Some of those who did fall for communism in the beginning still cannot come to terms with this burden today. A sense of delusion ruins their memories of youth, because everything they believed and did was denounced and turned out to be false. Later, the unpleasant experience they suffered,

---

*"Second Wind," in Václav Havel, *Open Letters*, trans. Paul Wilson (New York: Alfred A. Knopf, 1991), p. 4.

when they, too, were excluded from the banquet of life, helped to open their eyes, but it is difficult for them to get over this trauma. For some, life has split in two halves: the period when they were fools, and the period when they saw clearly. They are unable to identify with the first part, and their life is not whole.

The amount of purging an individual for his acts seems to depend directly on the amount of suffering. As long as a person wants to return to the truth, he can achieve it, albeit with great effort. Havel from the beginning loved exclusion and condemnation. He would not have become a capitalist, even if he had lived in a free state, and he would not have been a prominent Communist, even if there had been no trouble with his political background. He would always be, as he himself thinks, a writer, but I am not sure what kind of writer. The absurdity he experienced from early childhood on perhaps determined that he would write absurdist plays, perhaps determined his absorption in the problems of the world. In *Disturbing the Peace* he says:

> *I'm a writer, and I've always understood my mission to be to speak the truth about the world I live in, to bear witness to its terrors and its miseries—in other words, to warn rather than hand out prescriptions for change. Suggesting something better and putting it into practice is a politician's job, and I've never been a politician and never wanted to be. Even as a playwright, I've always believed that each member of the audience must sort the play out himself, because this is the only way his experience of it can be authentic; my job is not to offer him something ready-made.*
> [*Disturbing the Peace, p. 8*]

But in this country it is difficult to be a writer and avoid politics. When the regime lies about the weather, when one is constantly swimming in official half-truths and dialectico-metaphysical statements that claim to constitute reality while denying it, anything that points to truth, any true statement becomes political. Truth is somewhere between what truth is and isn't. In the end, every authentic act is political, because it takes a stand against the other politics. The criticism of politics is also politics. At a certain juncture, life is so deadened and fettered by ideology and by the regime's desire to hold on to power that any free act in the defense of life and in the name of life manifests itself as political. Havel was always more and more implicated in politics, because whoever says A, must inevitably also say B.* As soon as a person protests against something, he calls up a reaction, to which he must in turn react.

10 · Background: Bourgeois

It is time to consider who this man who has appeared in public life is, to consider the purposefulness and logic of his behavior. In all his actions there is a peculiar tenacity that always commands him to pick up the pieces from his last encounter and go on to the next. Why doesn't he leave well enough alone and adapt to the circumstances? Why is he different?

The Communists could only come to terms with him by single-mindedly assigning him the label "bourgeois." That is something no one can do anything about. You can never get rid of it.

Václav, in truth, is never going to get rid of his impressive, powerful family. They are Czech bourgeois, who long ago under the Hapsburg monarchy laid the foundations for the prewar prosperity of the First Republic and influenced the education and culture of their fellow citizens. The rise and fall of the Havel family, like that of the Vavrečka family on Václav's mother's side, seems to typify the fate of this country and sheds light not only on our past but also on our present and future. What happened can never be undone, but today a new Czech national bourgeoisie is rising and forming, like during the nineteenth

---

*See *Disturbing the Peace*, p. 89, for Havel's discussion about his political involvement.

century. Will it be as educated and cultured as the last one, a liquidated class whose remains still survive, here and there, in old age and poverty?

Vácslav Havel, Václav's grandfather, built Prague's Lucerna Palace, an arts and entertainment center that was on a par with that of any great European city. It was his life's work. He loved Prague and wanted to do something that would promote Prague from an Austro-Hungarian provincial town to a great city.

In 1907, he bought Bělský Palace in Vodičková Street, off Wenceslas Square, and figured that gradually he would buy all the plots up through Štěpánská Street. As a ten-year-old boy, his son, also named Václav, watched his father sketch out his plans. Grandfather Vácslav smoked a Virginia or a Trabucco cigar while he worked, and from time to time he consulted his wife, Emilie. In his memoirs, Václav's father writes:

> When his project was finished, he showed my mother his suggestion for the façade on Vodičková Street. As soon as she saw it, she exclaimed that it was like a great big lucerna, or lantern. My father jumped at her remark, saying:
> "That's a good name for the whole building. Lucerna. It is a Czech word that even a foreigner could pronounce well."

During the first stage of development, from 1907 to 1908, they built the building on Vodičková Street and its courtyard wing. Grandfather Havel built Lucerna in three stages at his own expense with the help of bonds and mortgages. He and his wife, Emilie, guaranteed the repayment of the loans with all their property as colateral. For the Jubilee Exhibition of the Prague Chamber of Commerce, they opened the coffee and tea house Yokohama. The manager was the great Czech traveler Joe Hloucha, who wrote one of the best travelogues about Japan.

The Japanese teahouse in Lucerna had parchment tables, Japanese lanterns, bamboo furniture, *japonerie*, all originals brought by Hloucha from Japan. Girls waited tables in kimonos. The Yokohama was very popular in Prague; everything Japanese was very much in vogue during the Art Nouveau period. The Hloucha family ran the business until 1928, when the Havels installed the Winter Garden in its place, where students who needed to earn money for school waited tables. Václav's father, who was studying engineering, was one of the leaders of a student club in the 1920s. The club collected money and managed to build a student dormitory in two years—Kolonka na Letné (the Students' Hostel at Letná Park), which then served for fifty years instead of the originally planned five to ten.

During the first stage, Havel's grandfather also built Bio Lucerna (Lucerna Cinema), which he enlarged to its present form five years later when he bought another plot of land. It had a modern décor and turbine ventilation with hot-air heating—all cutting-edge technology for its day. The films were mostly German, with Czech subtitles projected from slides. In other Prague cinemas only one pianist accompanied silent films, but at the Lucerna an eight-to twelve-piece orchestra would play. The conductor saw the film first, selected music for it, rehearsed it with his orchestra, and played it for each film. Bio Lucerna was also the first in Czechoslovakia to launch sound films, thanks to Miloš Havel, Václav's uncle. On August 13, 1929, Lucerna presented the Czech premiere of the American film *Showboat*, with many black folk songs, the most popular of which was "Old Man River." Miloš Havel was then chairman and majority shareholder of the A-B Corporation and the prime mover behind the construction of film studios at Barrandov. Before World War II, he organized production of Czech films under the aegis of the A-B Corporation.

The Lucerna Cabaret was a great cultural boon to the small-town life of pre-World War I Prague. Václav Havel and his friends Jaroslav Kvapil, Karel Hašler, and Ignát Herrmann put together a world-quality cabaret not only in its decor and ambience but also in its artistic program. The decor, late Art Nouveau, was designed by Josef Wenig, painter and set designer for the National Theater. Here, Hašler's old

Prague songs became famous, as did Hašler and Rudolf Friml's tramping songs. Until then, Prague had only had small, smoke-filled night clubs.

After World War I, grandfather Havel remodeled the cabaret into the Comedy Theater. In the center he built a fashionable folly—a curved, retractable stage that could be lowered to floor level and double as a dance floor. Jiří Voskovec and Jan Werich performed with dancer Milča Majerová for the opening show. Was there anything more wonderful in Prague? Hard to say. But surely cabaret never again matched these high standards.

The ambitious concept of a single enterprise for entertainment, haute cuisine, and culture was crowned by the construction and inauguration of the Great Hall in 1920. The hall was submerged three stories below ground; above it stood a seven-story building. It was the largest underground concert hall in Prague. For the construction of the hall, Vácslav Havel innovated the use of steel-reinforced concrete for the pillars and ceilings, designed and engineered by Stanislav Bechyně, later a member of the Czechoslovak Academy of Sciences. The construction was a worldwide rarity. It survived a fire in 1927 without damage. The only thing the Havels did not finish was the ventilation and air conditioning for the hall. The equipment was only manufactured in the United States, and while they were waiting for it to come to Europe, war broke out. And then after the war, the Communists nationalized the Lucerna Palace.

During the time of the First Republic, famous concerts were held in the Great Hall. Artists such as Jan Kubelík, Ema Destinová, Pablo Casals, Richard Strauss, Josephine Baker, and Maurice Chevalier performed. Meetings, demonstrations, country dances, Graeco-Roman wrestling, Ping-Pong tournaments, ballet and artistic productions were held there. Since its founding, the Communist Party of Czechoslovakia had held its congresses there.

11 • Mother and Father

In 1904, Grandfather Václav Havel built house number 2000* in Prague on what was originally called Palacký embankment, later Rašín, after the war Vltava, then Engels, and today Rašín again. That's the way it is with almost every street in Prague. He built two houses there at the same time, in the Art Nouveau style. Both have globes made out of wire on the roof. The Havel family moved into house number 2000 in 1905.

To the same house, to the very apartment where Václav Havel lives today, his father brought his young bride, Božena Havel, née Vavrečka, to live. When she was born in Brno on February 15, 1913, her father, Hugo Vavrečka, was an editor at *Lidové noviny*. In 1914, when war broke out, Vavrečka had to enlist as a naval officer at Trieste. After the war, he went to Paris as a member of the Czechoslovak peace delegation. Božena lived in Brno, and then the whole family moved to Hamburg when her father was sent there as consul. Later Vavrečka was named ambassador in Budapest and then Vienna, as mentioned earlier. His daughter was a sensitive and cultivated girl, fluent in several languages, whom everyone in society loved. She returned to Prague from Vienna and lived with her younger brother, Ivan, whom she cared for, in her father's official quarters on Havlíček square, later Gorky, today Senovážné.

Božena attended university where she studied painting and French. She often saw Václav's father in Prague society. She invited him to

---

*Every building in Prague displays two numbers: the first, in blue, refers to its location on a street, as in America; the second, in red, is a number assigned by district authorities when the building is registered. The lower the red number, the older the building. Thus, in theory anyway, Václav Havel built the two-thousandth house in the fashionable and central Nové Město district.

tea, and he invited her on a date. It was for November 24, Emilie Havlová's name day, which the family always celebrated. Havel's father chose that day because he was particular about that date, and later he confessed that the invitation was in fact an offer of marriage. The autumn of 1934 was a very happy time for both of them. They went to the movies and the theater together. During the wedding scene in *The Beggar's Opera*, a fork flew out of an actor's hand, punctured Božena's stocking, and injured her foot. She considered it a lucky sign. It was like something out of a girl's romance novel: a happy ending with a marriage. Mayor Baxa officiated on June 14, 1935, at the Old Town Hall. It would never have occurred to anyone that thirty years later, Mrs. Havel would be at the Old Town Hall again, selling postcards and giving guided tours. For their honeymoon, they traveled to Switzerland.

In October 1936, they brought their firstborn son back from the maternity hospital to the newly furnished apartment at number 2000 on the embankment. There was no question he would have the same name as his father, grandfather, great-grandfather, and great-great-grandfather. Two years later, Ivan was born. It was already after Munich, and hard times had set in. For the Havel couple, the hard times would never really end. They had a difficult life, in which they gradually lost everything they had, but they bore it bravely and together.

On the anniversary of their first date, Václav's father took his wife to the hospital. It was exactly thirty-five years later. She never returned from the hospital.

12 ▪ *On the Balustrade*

In 1960, the magazine *Kultura 60* invited Václav Havel to write about Prague's small theaters. At the time, these were the Theater on the Balustrade, the Rococo Theater, the Semaphor Theater, and the Reduta. Havel's article spurred discussion, and the magazine invited representatives of the small theaters to their editorial offices. One who come was Ivan Vyskočil, co-founder of the Theater on the Balustrade. He met Václav there.*

At the Theater on the Balustrade in the 1960s, Havel got a rare opportunity to write for a theater he knew, and to participate and cooperate in the creation of performances. Zdeněk Urbánek describes that time: "It was the ultimate in direct contact between playwright and stage. I hope—and I think Václav will confirm this—that it felt like that to him. The way he collaborated on the performances, I compare without any qualms to Shakespeare, whose plays I translate and who fascinates me. Shakespeare wrote some of his greatest roles with specific actors in mind."

The Czech public were beginning to question the logic of the utopia in whose name they were being oppressed. They wanted to know what it was all about, and Havel's actors were able to reveal this with increasing precision and skill. The theater had political significance; it shaped the intellectual climate. As Havel writes in an essay in 1976:

. . . the more we were able to do, the more we did, and the more we did, the more we were able to do. It was a state of accelerated metabolism between art and its time, and it is always inspiring and productive for phenomena as social as theater."
["Second Wind," Open Letters, p. 6]

At the Theater on the Balustrade, where he spent eight of the happiest years of his life, Václav made good on what had been invested in him during his childhood and early youth.

When Havel arrived, the troupe was in crisis. Jaromír Vomáčka, a musician and one of the most optimistic and inspired people the theater had, was leaving. Vyskočil had discovered him when Vomáčka was still a nightclub pianist at the Olympia. What a musician! He bet Vyskočil he could write a knock-out tune that in half a year would be

---

*Vyskočil subsequently offered Havel a job at his theater, and so he left the ABC Theater.

playing on every merry-go-round in the country. He wrote "Blow out the Chinese lanterns, lanterns" and "The little Black Kitty." Vomačka performed in *Faust* at the Theater on the Balustrade and did a remarkable job of smoothing out the various rifts and clashes that arose in the theater every now and then. Zuzana Stivínová, another great stage personality, was also leaving. Václav Havel impressed the older Vyskočil as a clever, keen fellow. Václav confided in him that he also wrote plays. Vyskočil needed an author, an actor, and a factotum, although everyone at the Balustrade was happy to help with errands and small tasks. At the time, Vyskočil was producing *Sad Christmas*, and he was planning text-appeals* after the performances. Because they were largely improvised there was an amazing amount of interest in the text-appeals, which lasted from eleven until four in the morning. Most of the people in the audience were students.

Immediately, Václav set to work not only settling feuds but also arranging physical things in their proper places with his proverbial methodicalness, which can sometimes seem pedantic. Ivan Vyskočil says: "What got me more than anything else was how great it was to talk to him. I needed to make a lot of things clear and I could accomplish that just by talking. But he unnerved me with how he had everything in order. When I visited his house, it was like being in an office. The whole kit and caboodle: letterhead, files—he even had a paginating stamp. I said to him, 'When you finish something, *do you take it to your own mail room? And then stamp it?*' I think he did it to build character. His organization made me even more of a slob; I was always losing something; I could never find anything. He looked like a koala bear, and that always made me laugh. He was especially astounding when he got a little plastered and waxed lyrical. That's why I was so fond of him. It was a big contrast to his "bureaucratic

---

*Events featuring jazz, prose, and poetry, with authors reading their works, usually written especially for the performance. They were modeled on gatherings held in the 1950s in New York and San Francisco in "bohemian" circles.

self," his meticulousness, to the Havel who took every task seriously, was always diligent, and never quarreled about anything.

"We did *Sad Christmas* first, in 1960. He worked on it as a 'techie' and helped build the set. That was another contrast. When he picked up a hammer, you thought: workers' compensation payments are just over the horizon—but what a surprise when he made some pretty little thing."

The young Havel wrote plays and articles and took night classes at the Academy of Performing Arts (AMU), where he was finally accepted once it no longer really interested him. At night he made props with his future wife, Olga, who was an usher at the Balustrade. Havel remembers Ivan Vyskočil as a great innovator, provocateur, and obsessive, who no doubt had a lot of ingenious ideas, but who could not handle the practical management of a theater. On the one hand, Vyskočil impressed Havel as a real expert on theater, but on the other hand he annoyed Havel with his sloppiness and inability to organize things, an inability he would not recognize, and so refused to abandon the organization to someone else.

"The premiere of *Sad Christmas* was a scandal. Sergej Machonin, the theater critic, wrote the review for *Literární noviny,** talking about ideological diversion and how I had stained the theatrical escutcheon of the Theater on the Balustrade. The unions stood up for me, but the management drew up a formal complaint."

Václav did not sign the indictment, even though the rest of the theater did. On The contrary, he stood up for Ivan Vyskočil.

Sad Christmas had no script; not even a manuscript exists, because Ivan Vyskočil was so disorganized. The play was about antimortaline, a pill that prevents death—makes people immortal. It is manufactured in crematoria and funeral parlors distribute it. Since no one is dying, the raw material from which the antimortaline is made begins to run

---

*The official cultural and literary magazine of the Writers' Union, published weekly.

out and it seems that by New Year's Day, everyone will be mortal again. The trick is to find more raw material. Everyone starts to murder everyone else, and in the end only the strongest survive: grandfather Hobi, founder of the antimortaline company, and his secretary. The company slogan was "Live to see worlds yet unseen/with Hobi antimortaline!" Ivan Vyskočil gave the text of the play in its final version to the director Nikolský. He staged it in Moscow, held a premiere, and got into even more trouble. His theater ceased to exist; the Balustrade at least managed to survive.

"They had to suppress us," remembers Ivan Vyskočil, "because the Balustrade was the first absurdist theater, a model in our country. People were not used to it, and it particularly incensed the officials. No one had started to use the word 'Absurd' pejoratively yet, but they found other epithets such as modern, existential, antisocialist, and likely to offend 'the sensibility of our people.' *Sad Christmas* collided head-on with the militancy of those who claimed a monopoly on truth."

Then Vyskočil began to write *Hitchhiking* with Havel—five scenes, two of which are Havel's: *Ela, Hela, and Stop* and *Motormorphosis.* Havel wrote *Motormorphosis* for a larger cast than the Balustrade had at its disposal, and the actors were not up to performing it. It also would have been difficult to stage. In the end Vyskočil and Havel agreed they would not produce it.

The premiere of *Hitchhiking* stirred up even more tension within the theater. The tension was not merely political.

"Vašek was remarkable, particularly when we were on tour," says Ivan Vyskočil. "These trips were where we earned our keep. Once we were booked to perform for a ridiculous Miners' Day in Horní Suchá. We performed in an open-air amphitheater and slept in barracks. The amphitheater also had a merry-go-round and swings. The only one of us the miners would pay any attention to was Ljuba Hermanová. During the performance, these drunk miners and bureaucrats kept coming on stage. We didn't know what to do with them, so we thought up a quiz show. We made two teams of three local drunks. Vašek was a wonderful moderator, and when the quiz was over, the drunks were ready and willing to leave the stage. After intermission they begged to do it again, so we had to run a quiz show in the second act as well. Then *Rudé Právo** published a letter to the editor saying that on Miners' Day in Ostrava, actors from the Theater on the Balustrade had performed while intoxicated. I had to go to Ostrava, where I discovered it was one of our 'co-performers' who had written the letter. I forced him to write a retraction, but *Rudé Právo* never printed it.

"Vašek was great on tour not only because he supervised everything carefully, but also because he knew how to have a good time. He liked to meet people; he was happy when they welcomed him into their group at the pub, he brought beer, for everyone, he beamed, and he sang. He can't sing too well, but he likes to sing. It's the *verbuňk*† in his background. . . . "

"When we sat in the lobby of the theater," Vyskočil continues, "the tenants would complain about us now and then, especially the ones from the building next door, which belonged to the Union of Catholic Journeymen. The building caretaker, I think her name was Mrs. Šrajerová, she wasn't on our side at first, but then we won her over. And to have the caretaker on your side in the Old Town district is like winning the lottery. Míla Kučera used to drive us all home when it was too late for city transportation. He drove a streetsweeper; today he drives a taxi in New York."

In *Motormorphosis* the character of the "inaugurator" first appears. This is the seed for the "inaugurator" and "liquidator" in *The Garden Party*, and for the principle of eristic dialectics. Eristic theater tries to show that every situation is authentic; dialectics is clash and play. Havel was already interested in researching what the concepts meant: the inaugurator, the liquidator, how they pervade each other, how one changes into the other through dialogue. Meanings shift and change.

---

*The official newspaper of the Communist Party of Czechoslovakia.
†A Moravian Slovak men's dance that speeds up as it progresses. Originally, it was danced during conscription levies, and a song about military service was sung as it started.

Eristic dialectics originated with Schopenhauer. Havel is methodical; he sticks to the formula; he keeps everything trapped in boxes until he shuffles everything around.

13 ▪ *Enter Jan Grossman*

Under Vyskočil, Václav probably put up with a lot. It had been a period of confusion and constant change. But a new era began with the entrance of Jan Grossman, who became head of drama. Vyskočil founded the dramatic company of the Theater on the Balustrade and set its course; Grossman developed it. Jan Grossman used to say, according to Václav Havel, "Theater should be done well, but it must not take itself too seriously." Without making much ado about it, from 1962 to 1968, Grossman, with Havel whom he chose to be his playwright and closest collaborator, turned one of Prague's least impressive theaters into a focal point for the art. It's paradoxical. The National Theater was never able to pull it off, because they always took themselves too seriously. They had to moralize, and be highly artistic, official, and representative. Anyone who takes himself too seriously runs the risk of becoming ridiculous; that's the comedian's first rule. Anyone who can laugh at himself is free. The person who knows he is awkward, foolish, and unseemly, who has some perspective on himself, is safe. But he must not hide anything or be afraid for himself. He must stick his neck out, again and again. Like Grossman and Havel.

The Theater on the Balustrade, when its golden era began, looked very different than it does today. The headquarters were in a corridor where the restroom is today. Mr. Vodička, the producer, sat there at an ancient desk circled by tattered curtains which could be drawn if the producer was not "in." Jiří Vyskočil was the manager; old Mr. Zborník handled the books; Mr. Beneš was in charge of the technical crew; and Eva Überhüberová was the secretary. Vodička kept a pipe and a telephone on his desk. When there was a phone call, the others could hear everything; there were no secrets.

"What impressed me about Venoušek," remembers Mrs. Tomíšková, a secretary for the theater, "was what a decent, modest person he was. Just to avoid taking a bow, he would hide in the attic, in the bathroom, or run from the building altogether. With Venoušek and with Mr. Grossman—they were my favorites—there was no difference between the crew and the actors. They ran things differently there than in other theaters. The secretary's office was something like a confessional, and I don't remember anyone being jealous or saying things behind each other's backs. That sort of thing happened later, in the 1970s. The atmosphere changed completely. I can't even describe the kind of muck there was then. But in the 1960s everyone stuck together. Like the time Sloup got drunk before the afternoon performance of *The Garden Party*. The performance still took place; the understudy substituted; everyone was willing to help him. Nobody told on him; everyone always made excuses for each other. I remember when the great Soviet mime Leonid Georgeyevich Yengibarov came from Moscow while the pantomime troupe that shared our theater was on tour. Vašek came to me suggesting we give the stage to Leonid after the evening performance. Leonid arrived in the morning, in the afternoon we called a few newspapers, and that evening the theater was bursting at the seams with people."

Jan Grossman wrote the following in the preface to Václav Havel's *Protocols,** a book published by Mladá Fronta in 1966:

> *In fact, great theater does not only reveal itself and its own story. It also reveals the audience's story, and through that, the audience's urgent need to compare their own experience—their own "subject matter"—with the subject matter offered them on stage.*
>
> *This kind of theater does not end with a performance, but on the*

---

*Protocols contained his plays *The Garden Party* and *The Memorandam*, two essays and a collection of typographical poetry.

contrary, the end of a performance is where it begins. I believe that Václav Havel has shown evidence in his plays of a genuine dramatic talent that very few in contemporary Czech theater possess.

After Charter 77—the first joint declaration by the Czech opposition—when the regime was striking back at dissidents, particularly in the media, they interviewed a few people from the Balustrade on television, asking them who Václav Havel was. The Balustrade staff answered skeptically, "Was there somebody with that name here? Oh yes, I think he was a stagehand who also wrote plays."

Grossman came to the theater as director while Vyskočil's and Havel's *Hitchhiking* was still running. It had been playing for two years, and the people working in the theater were quitting. That doesn't mean *Hitchhiking* was a bad play; it was actually excellent as a text-appeal, but nonetheless something had to happen with the theater. It was dying of consumption, although beautifully. Grossman, Vyskočil, Miloš Macourek, and Havel dreamed up *Mrs. Hermanová's Best Years*.

Ljuba Hermanová as an aging star! The collaborators were at a loss as to how to handle the subject, until finally Grossman's idea won out: if they didn't know what to do, they ought to admit that in the script. The play featured *Ljuba* Hermanová, her husband, a scriptwriter, and a dramaturge. Macourek was a well-known cynic (once, when they were in despair over the script, he came in and said, "Gentlemen, what if we were to kill Ljuba?"). But they put together a performance that was successful. They toured all over with it.

No sooner did they have firm financial ground under their feet than they began to prepare *The Garden Party*. Text-appeal theater couldn't sustain itself forever even if it had been important to the early cultural revival; it was an ephemeral thing. They were looking for drama. Otomar Krejča directed Klaus Hubalek's *In Thebes There is Burial No More* at the Balustrade; it was a modern version of *Antigone*. The author recast the story in the present day. It had great significance for that time, because once again the world seemed to be full of cowards and traitors. Krejča's grasp of the material was inspired, and the actors put on a stupendous performance. This new *Antigone* stands out today as one of the Balustrade's best productions, when it was at the height of its fame. Other performances of that caliber include Jarry's *Ubu Roi*, Beckett's *Waiting for Godot*, the classic one-acts of Ionesco, a dramatization of Kafka's *The Trial*, and Havel's *The Garden Party, The Memorandum*, and *The Increased Difficulty of Concentration*.

Libor Fára worked at the Balustrade as the artistic director at the time. He designed all the sets and programs. He used few materials, but his creations were inspiring and varied. Anna Fárová, his wife, remembers that the Balustrade was their daily haunt. Libor spoke ironically and skeptically about Havel: "Once Vašek entered the theater, there wasn't room for another author to get in." He meant it, though, as a compliment.

Anna's father, a former diplomat, read Václav's political writing in 1968 and noted presciently: "He has the makings of a great politician."

There were other noteworthy theaters in addition to the Balustrade; each of them played its own distinctive and original role. The Semaphor Theater was constantly full; it may have expressed the living spirit of our generation the most meaningfully and accurately, just as the Beatles represented that spirit for the world. We identified with the hippies and with the antiwar movement in the West; the Beatles are still a symbol of our youth. It is a shame we were never able to see them ourselves or hear them with our own ears. We frequented the Semaphor Theater; the poetry wine cellar *Viola*; the Rococo Theater, which Darek Vostřel directed; and the Paravan, J. R. Pick's literary cabaret, at the Reduta. Suddenly there were places to go and not enough time to get to them all. Later, with great delight, we went to Krejča's Theater Beyond the Gate and to The Dramatic Club, directed by Jaroslav Vostrý. We went to the cinema, because there were even some movies worth watching. It was the period of directors who wrote their own screenplays and whose films went on to impress the world as the Czechoslovak "New Wave." It's enough to mention their names: Jan Němec, Ivan Passer, Jiří Menzel, Ester Krumbachová, Věra Chytilová, Evald Schorm, Miloš Forman, and Pavel Juráček. They were close friends of Václav Havel's. In music there was the Czech "big beat" and we had "happenings." There were even things to read, because the works of writers such as Škvorecký, Hrabal, Vladimir Páral, and Věra Linhartová began to appear.

It reminds me of recent events here, and I wonder why it is at times when everything is forbidden, even history, that the situation always suddenly explodes; the ice cracks, and people's silent thoughts, creations, and defiance suddenly fly out like a cork from a bottle. Society develops in shocks; for a long time nothing happens, and then everything happens. We are always ahead of the times or behind the times, but we rarely manage to be with them.

14 ▪ *The Garden Party*

At one of the remarkable get-togethers during which Ivan Vyskočil used to tell about what he had seen, felt, and experienced but which regrettably he never recorded, Ivan told a story that Václav later used as the subject matter for his play *The Garden Party*. It was a brief story: a person has lost his sense of identity for so long that one day he goes to look for himself in his own apartment. At that time, Havel already knew Grossman. They had met sometime in 1956, right in front of the Theater on the Balustrade. The young poet and essayist Havel had brought Grossman, his senior and the editor of Československý spisovatel,* his essay on literary philosophy.

Václav's father, who worked for the Czechoslovak Association of Physical Training, arranged a three-week retreat in the Krkonoše Mountains for his son and Grossman. The location was so secret—so that they would not be bothered—that to this day neither of them can remember where it was exactly. It seems it was in Harrachov, ac-

---

*A publishing house.

cording to the actor Pavel Landovský's recollection. Landovský describes it a heroic act on his part to have broken through the conspiracy, found them, and convinced them to let him join the group. Jan Grossman tells the story:

"I don't know where we were, because we never even crawled outside. We sat in the hotel day and night; we each had our own room, very posh. Vašek worked and gave me what he wrote; we almost never spoke to each other. He would more or less shove the pages under my door, the way they shoved food through that hole for Charles IV when he was praying in the chapel at Karlštejn. His writing went back and forth between us. I had to fight off the attacks of charming waitresses; Vašek told them he couldn't go anywhere because he had a very strict boss. Vašek loaned one little chambermaid a copy of Kafka's *The Trial* we had with us because I had just made a dramatization of it. When she returned it to him, poor woman, she said he had written it very nicely.

"I'm fond of *The Garden Party* not only because I was most involved in its creation but also because even today the play bears traces of the author's search for a personal poetic. I say that with admiration and love for Vašek. Like when you read Chekhov's *The Seagull*, then *Three Sisters*, and what he wrote later. *The Seagull* is fragmentary, but it has oomph; in its scope and in a few places it's enormous; at the same time it's as clumsy as a puppy. After *The Garden Party*, Havel suddenly caught his breath; it was as though he had shaken the puppy awake; he delivered the play and it was ready to perform. But I'm even fonder of *The Memorandum*, because there we tried out the principles I returned to when I produced *Largo Desolato* at the Balustrade. A geometric style, symmetry, repetition, echo, purity, the theme of a continuous merry-go-round. Vašek compared it to musical composition."

In the preface to Havel's *Protocols*, which includes *The Garden Party* and *The Memorandum*, Jan Grossman noted:

In The Garden Party *and* The Memorandum, *the main character in the plays is a mechanism for controlling people. In the first play, that mechanism is the cliché. It is conceived as a variation on the observation that a man never makes his clothes, but rather the clothes make the man: that is, a person does not use clichés; instead, the cliché uses him. The cliché is the hero of the piece: unprompted, it plots and complicates the conflict, determines human actions, moves the story along, and, drawing further and further from reality, produces its own new reality. In* The Memorandum, *too, the mechanism comes from the realm of language: this time, man is governed by an artificial, synthetic language that is supposed to perfect communication and make it precise, but in fact it leads to a further interference in human relations and to a more persistent alienation. . . . It is possible to say that the theme of the mechanism is psychologized in* The Memorandum. *. . . "Psychologization" means here only Havel's more developed ability to interpret the material in many situations and spheres. The theme of the abstract linguistic mechanism is naturally reflected in other mechanisms: of cowardice, of power, and of indifference. Each of these mechanisms by itself and in conjunction with the others thus forms a more stratified and—compared to* The Garden Party—*more complex picture of human depersonalization.*

Grossman collaborated on *The Garden Party* with the author. Since Grossman did not want to give the impression he was making theater only for himself, and since he felt somewhat unsure of himself, he asked Otomar Krejča to direct it. At the time, Krejča was rehearsing *Romeo and Juliet* in the National Theater, and he took on *The Garden Party* in addition. He brought with him from the National Theater the stage designer Josef Svoboda, who conceived the set. Zdeněk Urbánek remembers:

"The height of theatrical fashion then was the one-way mirror. Svoboda suggested it; I don't know what it was supposed to be good for. It had no function in that play, unless maybe during the party festivities some fools might stick their heads out of it and then disappear. Grossman and Václav attended the rehearsals and the monstrous thing bothered them. Since they had to share the theater with Ladislav

Fialka's pantomime troupe, they rehearsed in a large hall in the Břev-nov district and the mirror had to be moved there. Every night, the last person to leave the hall had to take the key with him and arrive first the next morning. They didn't dare tell Krejča or Svoboda, 'Please get rid of it; it's in the way.' Also, the mirror cost a lot of money, about as much as five productions at the Balustrade. One night, someone slipped into the hall—I don't know if this is still an actionable crime or if the statute of limitations has run out—and smashed the mirror to pieces. It was investigated, but nothing was discovered, so Svoboda made a new set. It reminded one a little of the Atomium at the Brussels World's Fair of 1958. Spheres connected with little sticks circled the whole stage. Strange symbolism; maybe it was supposed to be people in the atomic age disintegrating and losing their identity, but it didn't really fit. Krejča was directing with a heavy hand, and the actors were carrying on as if it was a heavy, serious drama. Grossman and Václav got up the courage to say he should let it go a little, let the actors speak in a normal tone of voice. Krejča came around, and in the end, suprisingly, it turned out well."

Jan Grossman directed *The Memorandum*. Havel's third play, *The Increased Difficulty of Concentration*, was also produced at the Balustrade in the 1960s, directed by Václav Hudeček.

Grossman and Havel made quite a team, and not just as creators of plays. The actress Marie Málková remembers the celebration for her graduation in 1962. The group was sitting in the restaurant, waiting, but Havel and her future husband Grossman still had not come. She went to see where they were, but the Balustrade was dark. She knocked for a long time before they came. They did not want to turn on the lights or let her in; they whispered through the door that they were lying in wait for a thief. Every day, of late, something had been discovered to be missing from the theater, from valuable items to utterly ridiculous ones. For instance, Grossman's old pants, which he wore during rehearsals, or a bottle of Becher. Havel and Grossman didn't wait out the thief that night; they finally gave up and went to the restaurant. Later it was revealed that the guilty party was a kleptomaniac who lived one floor up. When the police took possession of his apartment, they displayed the stolen goods. Grossman's pants and Becher were there.

In those days, Pavel Landovský was watching the Balustrade through the keyhole. He had a crazy longing to join the theater; he befriended Vašek, but Vašek had no influence over personnel decisions.

"I decided to make it happen, and so I hounded them. They're intellectuals, I said to myself; they won't hold out. They'll have to face what a person like me can do when he gets it into his head. And there were awful scenes. Vašek was more or less on my side, but Grossman, he'd whizz away from me, he'd turn green. I'm an unbelievable detective; I cornered them at their hideout in the mountains where they were writing *The Garden Party*.

"I got a clue from Viola Zinková, who told me they'd gone, and Olina* or Havel's mother tipped me off that they'd gone by bus. From the bus schedule and the time they left, I figured out where they'd gone, and then I checked by phone. I was working like a detective; it was great fun. I got there by hitchhiking. Grossman, when he saw me, went to sleep, and Vašek and I played chess. That's when I discovered that he plays chess well; he's got a stubbornness in him that won't give up on mastering those sixty-four little squares. He didn't guess; he deduced. In prison, chess was our salvation.

"I always taught Vašek about life," Pavel remembers. "We were the same age, but I was always a half year ahead of him in life. I showed him what I'd discovered. He was a kid from Prague, and kids from Prague until a certain age don't see how the world works. Kids from small towns and villages have the whole picture: the local poor, the local idiot, the madman, the criminal, the parish priest, the landlord, the peasants, the cottagers. Equipped with this experience, I had a peculiar audacity. My parents were immigrants, Russian Czechs; at home we talked about it a lot; I was a thoroughgoing anti-Communist.

---

*Olga.

That brought Vašek and me together, because we were both upstarts. We weren't allowed to study. They threw us out of everywhere. He was going to be a chemist and I was going to be a toolmaker. When Stalin died, I got into the firm's trade school. I tried to get into acting school many times, until Vlasta Fabianová, an actress at the National Theater, told me: 'You'll never get into school, don't even try. Sneak off somewhere, better if nobody from Prague sees too much of you, and act.' So I snuck off to Šumperk and then to Klatovy.

"I brought Vašek to Klatovy on a motorcycle, and he saw ham-acting for the first time there. The Theater on the Balustrade was a modern theater, and they were all slick dudes from school. I don't think much of actors who rattle off somebody else's text and aren't story-tellers themselves. Vašek saw ham-acting for the first time, and he lit up. He heard actors say lines like, 'Careful, boss, let's not overrehearse this.' He discovered Schlagwort* theater—i.e., when an actor delivers his lines, he quietly indicates to the other guy that he's done and the other can start talking, because the other guy usually isn't paying attention. Vašek sat in the dressing room like Alice in Wonderland; he watched how the old folks did their make-up. He saw a performance where twenty-five-year-old me dressed up as an old man and played the father of a sizeable family. It brought him to life, because he suddenly realized that theater is foolishness and at the same time an unbelievably demonic foolishness. The theater was packed; people wanted to see this ghastly thing.

"He was happy to be friends with me, because I knew how to have a good time. He used to say: 'I'm Landovský's barnacle; I stick to him and I can slip into any bar.'

"I dragged him along with me, and they would always say, 'There's a gate† here, Mr. Landovský.' 'What gate?' I'd say, and I'd shove him into the bar, past the grill, behind bars, into a world regular mortals

---

*German for "slogan" or "catchphrase."
†The seedier bars in Prague have an iron grill at the entrance that looks like the gate of a prison cell. The grill is locked, and the porter expects either reassurance or a bribe before he will admit someone who isn't a regular.

never see. Once—this was a little later—this guy started discussing something with him at a bar. I came up and asked, 'Where do you know him from?' And this guy says: 'I was in jail for two years, and I had a special chore. I spent two years scissoring him out of books of Czech literary history.' "

In the 1960s, Havel worked both at the Balustrade and as an assistant director for several of Alfred Radok's productions in the Prague Municipal Theaters, including the stagings of *Swedish Matches* and *The London Pickpockets*.

In 1986, Havel wrote the following about Radok the director on the tenth anniversary of his death:

> *Radok's radiation, uncommonly strong, remained in the invisible rather than the visible range of the spectrum.*
>
> *When I consider what all of Radok's varied stagings and artistic performances had in common, it occurs to me that it was a certain magic, an element of the irrational, the presence of mystery and the sense for mystery, the courage to let himself be carried away by the strange, inexplicable impulses and ideas of the subconscious and fantasy, by diverse archetypal images (sometimes, too, Freudian symbols: remember the ingots that danced with ballerinas in the first Laterna Magika production). Obsession, passion, irony, absurdity, paradox, grimacing, despair—all of it was revealed, whether in one size and shape or another, always anew in what Radok did. . . . He was not, of course, a magician who wanted to bewitch the audience and the world. On the contrary, he was a shaman, continually awe-struck by the mystery of the world, humbly bowed before it and humbly offering it an entrance. He was a sort of medium for something higher, something he did not try to claim he understood. . . . When his magical imagination charged him, everything had to stand aside—including his own methods (on whose rational exterior he took such pride).*

In 1963, the Fáras introduced Havel to Arthur Miller. Anna was a friend of Arthur's wife, Inge Morath, the renowned photographer and portraitist. The historic meeting of the two playwrights took place in the Fáras' studio, and Inge Morath photographed the encounter. Václav worried the whole time about his car, which he had to go pick up from the service station. It bothered him to tell Miller why he had to go—after all, could an American understand what a stroke of luck it was to be first in line at a service station and have your car repaired? On top of that, Václav needed the car that evening, so throughout the entire meeting, he worried about whether he should tell this to the great writer, and if so, how. Finally the desire for his car won out. For a long time it bothered him how he had behaved.

On December 3, 1963, for the first time, a full-length play by Václav Havel was performed on its own at the Theater on the Balustrade— *The Garden Party*.

In July 1964, Olga Šplíchalová and Václav Havel sent out wedding announcements, declaring they had married. The only people at the ceremony were the two of them and the witnesses: Libor Fára and Jan Grossman. Two years later, Václav attended the wedding of Marie Málková and Jan Grossman. They had three witnesses: Havel, Zdeněk Urbánek, and Dr. Vodičaka, the manager of the Theater on the Balustrade. From Mr. Grossman I thus learned the important fact that you can have as many witnesses as you want at a wedding.

15 ▪ *Tvářists* and *Tvář*

In the 1960s, Václav Havel was not only the successful playwright and dramaturge of the Theater on the Balustrade. In 1965, he also became a member of the editorial board of the Writers' Union's literary monthly, *Tvář*. He learned a great deal there in political struggles with those who tenaciously refused to give others a chance to express their ideas; they refused only because those ideas differed from theirs.

Havel talks about it in *Disturbing the Peace*:

> *It was a step that turned out to be far more important in my life than it first appeared to be. It was the beginning of the period, which lasted for several years, during which* Tvář *struggled for its existence; it was also the beginning of my "rebellious" involvement with the Writers' Union, also lasting several years; at the same time, it was the beginning of something deeper—my involvement in cultural and civic politics—and it ultimately led to my becoming a "dissident." I began as a kind of working stiff at the Theatre on the Balustrade, someone who lived only for his work in the theater, and was no more than a curious observer of anything beyond that. Thanks to* Tvář, *I stepped outside this circle, without really knowing where the inner logic of the step would take me. . . . When I joined the editorial board of* Tvář, *my involvement in the struggle for the magazine's survival began. It was a period of endless debates, meetings, and arguments; it was my private school of politics. [Disturbing the Peace, p. 77]*

Tvář was founded in 1963 as a magazine for young people at the third congress of the Writers' Union at the request of Jiří Gruša. From time to time, the Writers' Union tried to renew and rejuvenate itself. Every such attempt was, of course, inspired by a movement within the central committee of the Communist Party. The movement might remain hidden to those on the outside, but the Writers' Union would find out about it. They wanted to win over young people and toward that end give them something that would show the world they were treating young people well. Throughout the forty years of Communist rule, the announcement of a magazine for young people was a reliable signal that conditions were loosening, and the banning of one meant the opposite.

The regime was not too ingenious—it attempted cosmetic change and partial renascence (or pseudorenascence) with a kind of regularity. Sanctions and bans always followed. In essence, nothing ever changed; not only did the central committee of the Communist Party carefully guard against this, but so also did the leadership of the Writers' Union. Nonetheless, these feuds and scandals wore the regime out and had the unintended result of revealing its true nature. In the feud over *Tvář*, we saw the true face of the representatives of the Writers' Union and the ideological writers—that is, those who had been active *svazáks** in the 1950s. Later, some of them became reform Communists[†] and after the 1968 Soviet occupation, many of them drifted to the samizdats, joining the people they had fought earlier. In 1963, the poet and novelist Jiří Gruša delivered a speech at the third congress of the Writers' Union. It was a kind of manifesto, which he had written in collaboration with Ivan Wernisch, Petr Kabeš, Jiří Pištora, Karel Tomášek (under the alias "Lidin"), and Milan Uhde. They did not suspect it would be the declaration of a generation. Or that the magazine these writers would get, *Tvář*, would from the beginning have to fight fiercely for its existence against Communists and reform Communists—i.e., everyone who had power at the time—would draw the profile of that generation. Or that the magazine would in the end be permanently banned, but the generation definitively established.

This generation differed from its predecessors chiefly in its lack of ideology. Its members had inherited the regime in its final form; they could not change anything about it. No one asked them if they liked it or not. In other eras, the generation gap was twenty years wide, but here ten was enough. They had missed the active experience of the 1950s, the possibility of choice, the period when society strictly divided those who had power from the oppressed, those who owned literature from those excommunicated from it, friends from enemies. The people who had lost their positions were jailed or sentenced to death only for having had a different political opinion. It is a great burden the Communists drag with them, even if by now they have exposed their own illusions and mistakes.

---

*See page 16.
[†]Havel calls them "antidogmatics." They still considered themselves Marxists but favored a more liberal interpretation of Marxism in practice.

The new generation was unusual and different. Politically, it had a low profile. It was not yet clear who was who. For these reasons, right from the start, the older generation did not entirely trust it. After all, they were accustomed to seeing enemies everywhere; as the saying goes, "He that is not with me is against me." They were not accustomed to being tolerant, to allowing different opinions. In addition, they did not understand the "*Tvář*ists" too well, and they were suspicious, as are all people who think ideologically. Many of them, at the time, criticized the Party and its past and believed they were already "living in truth." The trouble they got into validated them and gave them credentials to show off. To be in trouble was fashionable. But they were not much interested in people who had known the score for years and had suffered for their truth. The critics within the Party had the impression that it was enough if they themselves started to address the issues with great uproar and fanfare.

The fight over *Tvář* was a fight between a nonideological generation and people who were not used to criticism from below or from peers. They were only used to criticism from above, which, unfortunately, was usually accompanied by a purge. From the first issues of *Tvář*, they had the feeling they were being purged and that they had hired their own purgers. Literature was supposed to be an institution authors were installed in and then expelled from. Still, it was they who published *Tvář*, and they were the Writers' Union. What was printed in *Tvář* and later in *Sešity pro mladou literaturu* (Note books for Young Literature) expressed an entirely different perspective, a different style, a different take on life. This kind of clash between generations is common in normal societies; it surprises no one, even when it is extremely sharp. But this was not a normal society, because it was ruled by an omnipotent state police, tied to those in power. It is not surprising that when Gruša* left Prague after one of the scandals, it

---

*Gruša, deprived of citizenship and exiled in 1981, is now the Czech ambassador to Germany.

was said that he had been sentenced to ten years in prison. Those in power could do anything, and everyone knew it.

Tvář wanted to create a bridge between the past and the present, to arch over the ideological abyss and link what was best in the First Republic, in the postwar period, and also in the underground after the Communists seized power. Its second task was literary criticism of what was published. This bridge was disturbing for ideological reasons more than anything else, and the literary criticism did not please the writers it failed to praise. Jan Lopatka says about it: "They [the Writers' Union] exercised what they felt to be their natural right, the right of the majority over a minority. Ipso facto, they said, 'Why do we have to support someone who writes that we are idiots?' Thus, the fate of *Tvář* was sealed, and from January to October 1965 the Writers' Union tried to quash the magazine. *Tvář* was then printing 5,000 copies of each issue, all of which sold out."

In 1965, Václav Havel became a member of *Tvář*'s editorial board. It was Jan Lopatka who invited him to join. Jiří Němec also played a significant role at *Tvář*. No member of the editorial board was a member of the Writers' Union, not even Havel. Membership on the board was offered to Havel with the condition that he join the Writers' Union, because *Tvář* needed to have someone in the enemy camp. From *Tvář*'s point of view at the time, Havel was an author the regime approved of. Similarly, when, as *Tvář* took off, they asked for formal registration as a magazine, the Writers' Union set the condition that the editor-in-chief had to be in the Party. None of them were in the Party, and they searched in despair until they found František Vinant. In the same way, many unpublished writers took Gruša to be an establishment author since he had delivered a speech at the third congress of the Writers' Union.

Havel was not good friends with any of the *Tvář*ists. Much separated them, little united them. Havel's contemporaries at *Tvář* struck him as more or less establishment writers. While he had moved in the underground in the 1950s, had not been able to get into school, had worked as a lab technician, and had published in samizdat, they had studied at gymnasia and then at the philosophy department at Charles University. They worked as editors at magazines and publishing houses, their first fruits were printed early on, and they lounged around writers' clubs. But in this country, the powers-that-be managed on several occasions to achieve the impossible: They brought together people who never would have suspected they had anything in common. In the 1960s, it was not yet as striking a phenomenon as it would be in the 1970s, when Charter 77 united people who were enemies in the 1960s—for instance, Zdeněk Mlynář, who later permanently outlawed *Tvář* and the *Tvář*ists. At the time, no one, not even in his wildest dreams, could have imagined that one day oppression would drive them and Mlynář into a single fold and unite them in a common goal.

Václav accepted the job in 1965. *Tvář* was, after all, closer to his heart than any other literary movement or group of the day, because it published everything it considered good, without regard to how it might be pigeonholed. It was a sort of island of freedom in an ocean of bondage. In the very first issue there was an epigram that said a great deal about the magazine: "It is only by what we do not say that we can recognize ourselves."

At a meeting in 1965 of the Czechoslovak Writers' Union that commemorated the twentieth anniversary of the republic's liberation at the end of World War II, Havel delivered an incendiary speech, in which *Tvář* firmly went on the attack. The speech begins with an analysis of what he calls "evasive thinking" and of what is at the root of the ritualization of language, false contextualization, and a certain dematerialized way of thinking that he calls "dialectical metaphysics." Evasive thinking invariably diverts attention in one way or another from the matter at hand. Our era is marked by the conflict between "thinking evasively and thinking to the point." Thinking to the point calls things by their right names and does not tangle things up with a ritual series of *but*s, *to a certain extent*s, and *on the other hand*s. Havel went on to subject the Writers' Union to thorough criticism:

The main speech at this conference was entitled "The Tasks of Literature and the Work of the Czechoslovak Writers' Union," which may leave us with the impression that the job of the Union is to assign tasks to literature. In reality, it should be the other way around: literature should set the tasks for the Writers' Union. The point is that every good writer is the best judge of what his job is. The Writers' Union should merely provide the necessary backing so that writers and magazines can best fulfill the tasks they set for themselves. . . . This doesn't mean laying out a program so vague it can accommodate everyone, but helping each writer to be himself to a maximum degree—unique, well defined, and clear on how to go about fulfilling his own program. . . . In its own way, literature always was, is, and must be intolerant. ["On Evasive Thinking," Open Letters, trans. Paul Wilson, p. 19]

There are people in the leadership of the Union who are not tolerant of Tvář. As writers, they need not be tolerant, but as members of the Union's leadership, they must be. They have behaved intolerantly not only toward Tvář but also toward their older colleagues who were banned in the 1950s. Professor Černý, Jindřich Chalupecký, Jiří Kolář, Richard Weiner, Ladislav Klíma, Jakub Deml are still waiting patiently for the publication of their writings, although what they wrote is among the best of Czech literature. . . . [Not included in the abridged version of the essay in Open Letters; translated by Caleb Crain.]

I think that the Writers' Union makes sense only if it ceases to act as a broker between politics and literature, and starts defending the right of literature to be literature. . . . Only in this way can literature be as well, and in the best sense of the word, a political entity. ["On Evasive Thinking," Open Letters, p. 24]

Havel's speech was a great success, even though it attacked everyone who applauded it. Pavel Auersperg, secretary of the central committee of the Communist Party, is said to have gotten angry and to have told

Jan Procházka, "This guy is going to be dangerous to us." It was the second writers' conference Havel had broken up.

Once again it was clear that the best defense is a good offense. *Tvář* was left alone for a while, but in September, the attack began again. Jiří Šotola attacked it in the September 4, 1965, issue of *Literární noviny*, protesting its literary criticism. Famous authors and members of the Union could not stand the criticism Bohumil Doležal and Jan Lopatka wrote in *Tvář*. The Union declared that *Tvář* was not what it was supposed to be, and had been founded to be. It should have been a magazine by and for young people. *Tvář*'s enemies hoped to lay their hands on young writers who would claim that they did not feel *Tvář* represented them. This was one of the regime's usual techniques. "Who does *Tvář* serve," they would then ask, "if it does not speak for the young generation?" But they couldn't find any young writers who would take a stand against *Tvář*. Even the most loyal thought a public denouncement of the magazine would be embarrassing. So *Tvář* held on into the fall; it was a real battle from one issue to the next.

On October 14, the Union decided the magazine would stay just as it was, except they would change the editor-in-chief, the editorial board, and the magazine's objectives. The editors organized a signature campaign, and 270 people signed the protest against the quashing of *Tvář*, which in those days was a gigantic success. It was a blow to the members of the Union's leadership, for it showed that they were not as progressive as they had pretended to be.

And another blow soon followed. The *Tvář*ists read through the by-laws of the Writers' Union and came across a rule that said it was possible to call an emergency session if they collected signatures from a third of the membership. It had probably never occurred to the men who wrote the by-laws that anyone would take them at their word. The federal constitution and the laws were full of these leftover demo-cratic clauses that no one took into account and whose only purpose was to give the appearance of a democratic society. The *Tvář*ists had stumbled across the possibility of fighting the authorities on the basis of laws the authorities themselves had decreed and formally recognized. The same legal principle underpinned Charter 77 twenty years later—i.e., that the government had signed the Helsinki Accords. Already in 1965, Havel and the *Tvář*ists realized it was a good idea to take the regime at its word. When they had started to collect signatures and it seemed likely they would get a third, it was a horrible predicament for the Party. What was to be done? Call a congress on account of a pair of unsatisfied individuals who had got the notion into their heads to force the issue, or disgracefully overturn the by-laws? They brought the writers before the central committee in small groups and tried to persuade them not to sign the petition—in exchange they would publish all their books, etc. The above-mentioned Pavel Auersperg met with Havel. He promised that if Havel were to end the signature campaign, he would receive his own magazine, admittedly without the *Tvář*ists on the editorial board, but they could still publish in it.

On the other hand, the head of the cultural section of the central committee of the Communist Party threatened Dr. Vodička, the manager of the Theater of the Balustrade, saying he would close the theater because Havel was dramaturge there. Dr. Vodička told Václav not to travel around the republic promoting *Tvář*; they were going to close the theater because of it, and anyway his head was already this big from the whole thing. Havel answered, *"I wasn't there; I just turned up there."* Dr. Vodička was always astonished by the incredible facility with which this young man, who came to the theater when he was twenty-three and left it when he was thirty, could lead people—himself, especially—into madness. Havel could not have stopped anything, even if he had wanted to.

In the end, they did not get hold of a third of the membership, which was understandable under the circumstances. The *Tvář*ists founded the Young Authors' Caucus soon after. The Union declared it illegal, and the censor's office sent Colonel Hubený to attend the Caucus meetings. He was charged with watching to see we did not take any votes at our illegal meetings. If there had been voting, the meetings would have become actionable. The *Tvář*ists therefore decided everything without voting, and the colonel's superiors fired him for incompetence.

At the same time, the Commission for Young Literature sprang up under the aegis of the Writers' Union. Václav Havel, Jan Beneš, and Jan Lopatka were appointed to it. The Commission was supposed to untangle and resolve questions regarding the publication of young authors according to the regime's wishes. At the end of November, the central committee of the Writers' Union met in Bratislava and decided that *Tvář* would be a house magazine—i.e., a sort of propaganda press.

Thus, the existence of *Tvář* came to an end. The Writers' Union explained then, as it had explained many times before and would many times in the future, that it made no sense to defend small things when big things were involved. The antidogmatic politicians still did not understand that freedom is indivisible, and therefore their time would come in the end. They made a tactical retreat, and so they lost. They also did not know, because it did not figure in their system of morality, that someone who wants something good may not do something evil to attain it, that there is no such thing as a smaller or bigger evil, and that a small lie can eclipse a great truth. That evil things cannot serve good ends, and that it is not possible to win through compromises. In the end, their compromises swept them away. In 1967, at the fourth congress of the Writers' Union, a letter from Solzhenitsyn was supposed to have been read. Eduard Goldstüker protested that it was none of our business, it was a private affair of our Soviet comrades, and we shouldn't meddle. The story of *Tvář* all over again.

In 1968, *Tvář* was revived and moved once again toward fulfilling its two original goals: to be a bridge and to create literary criticism. The chairman of the editorial board was Václav Havel. Two issues of that volume were printed. In 1969, there were another six issues. In June of that year, the magazine was permanently discontinued.

In *Disturbing the Peace*, Václav Havel assesses the period of the struggle over *Tvář* as follows:

> *Still, I think our efforts had a great importance, one that has not been recognized, even today. We introduced a new model of behavior: don't get involved in diffuse general ideological polemics with the center, to whom numerous concrete causes are always being sacrificed; fight "only" for those concrete causes, and be prepared to fight for them unswervingly, to the end. In other words, don't get mixed up in backroom wheeling and dealing, but play an open game. I think in this sense we taught our antidogmatic colleagues a rather important lesson.* [Disturbing the Peace, p. 83]

As later became clear, he was right. The Writers' Union was afraid that the *Tvář*ists would break up the 1967 congress. The secretary of the Union promised Havel that the magazine would be revived if they would behave and the congress turned out well. In the end, it was the antidogmatics who broke up the congress, the reform Communists from the *Literární noviny* circle.* In *Disturbing the Peace*, Havel claims it was *Tvář* that radicalized the antidogmatics, and if so, then *Tvář* had an essential role in paving the way for the Prague Spring of 1968. The antidogmatics were thrown out of the Party in the fall of 1967, and *Literární noviny* was shut down. This foreshadowed what would happen in January. The Party had to reform itself, to distance itself from Novotný's† bureaucracy. The reform Communists took up that challenge. They thought up the term "socialism with a human face," and they tried to humanize their ancient creation.

It was only in November 1989 that I realized once and for all that 1968 was not the most vital adventure of our lives.

---

*They opened up the congress to be a forum to speak the truth, to speak frankly about the political situation in the country and the need for reform.
†Antonía Novotný, the Communist Party leader who had succeeded Klement Gottwald as president of the republic in 1957.

16 ▪ *The Academy of King George*

What has made this agile, not very tall man, who runs more often than he walks and moves with a gentle clumsiness, what he is today? He has light, curly hair, blue eyes full of innocence, and a boyish smile. Everything interests and astonishes him as if he had just seen it for the first time. He has so much energy that he exhausts everyone around him. Sometimes he manages to stay up all night, spend an hour in the morning in the bathroom, and then set off for work. He is always thrifty. He is happy to sit in a fourth-class pub drinking beer with his friends. A sweater and jeans are his favorite clothes. But then he can put on a tuxedo, appear in a dance hall, and dance a six-step, left-hand waltz. With a white silk scarf around his neck he looks like young Swann. He is so polite people think they can take the upper hand with him. This impression arises because he is impersonal; he is always concerned with the matter at hand, never with himself. This sometimes confuses people, if they are not also capable of this kind of impartiality, if they do not know how to be like that—to open themselves up to every risk.

I do not know whether these qualities are inborn or a result of upbringing. But I do know that it is difficult to devise a strategy for a campaign, insist on one's principles, and at the same time honor the mystery and surprise that life reveals to us constantly and embrace it.

Havel graduated from the district grammar school in 1947, and his mother decided he should leave home to experience life on his own at a boarding school. At the castle in Poděbrady, there was a boys' prep school modeled on the English boarding schools at Eton and Harrow. It was called the Academy of King George of Poděbrady. Orphans who had lost their parents in the war, such as Miloš Forman, studied there. For this good deed, the school received funds from the government, and so the headmaster, Mr. Jahoda, could choose the best instructors. Thanks to the instructors and the financial resources, it was a good, modern school with fine facilities. There were cabinet-making, locksmith's, blacksmith's, and bookbinder's workshops. Children from Poděbrady also attended; when classes ended, they went home, while boarding school life started up for the others.

An incredibly incongruous group of children were brought together there: orphans and the children of distinguished bourgeois and Communist families. The Communists began to send their children there when they won the elections. At the end of the war, some of the orphans had been living like wolves. This was not the case with Miloš Forman, who was, as he himself says, well protected and cared for by his uncle and other relatives. But the children who ran wild up to the end of the war would ask for chewing gum, "and if you didn't give it to them, they'd stick you with a jack-knife and that was that."

The school administration handled the problematic and peculiar social situation with a policy of strict discipline. It was something like the army, but on a higher level. Mrs. Havel sent her oldest son here. Ten years old, he was assigned to a bedroom for younger students. Every bedroom for younger students had one older student who acted as an adviser, and in Vašek's bedroom, this adviser was the fourteen-year-old Miloš Forman.

"I was terribly annoyed," Forman recalls, "because I would rather have been with boys my own age. Fourteen-year-olds have more interesting conversations than ten-year-olds, so I didn't like the job. I took it because there were certain advantages. Everything there was on a strict points system. Anyone who had an average better than one point seven didn't have a required study period, didn't have to sit somewhere in a classroom, and after school he was a free man, like the kids from Poděbrady. The job of adviser, a clean closet, and a neatly made bed went into figuring your number. Either you were the best behaved, and then you were a free man, or you were the worst."

"Do you remember anything that he was famous for, or that distinguished him from this crowd of boys who got on your nerves?"

"Two incidents are fixed in my memory. He simply hasn't changed since. When he played soccer, he couldn't shake the idea that a good soccer player is always near the ball. So he was always chasing the ball, and the upshot of it was that after ten minutes he had to go lie down, because he was worn to a frazzle."

"But he can run a long distance, and he's a good tactician," I protested.

"He was always running after that pigskin," concluded Miloš. "And I remember another incident, the time we got a bicycle and learned how to ride it. The director of the workshop brought us to the front gate and helped us mount the bicycle. You rode away from the gate, you turned around the statue of George of Poděbrady, and back to the gate again. Everybody did it that way, until Vašek. They sat him on the bicycle, pushed him off—Vašek rides forward, we're waiting and suddenly we see he isn't turning around the statue of King George, instead he's riding straight ahead, toward Nymburk. We stared like idiots while he disappeared, and then we started yelling, 'Professor, Professor, Havel is escaping!'

"This magnificent professor came out, a stickler for detail, and he said, 'Oh yes, I see he is escaping; I shall go after him on my motorbike.' But that didn't happen right away. The teacher had to slip into his leggings, tie on his leather helmet, put on his gloves, don his motorcycle goggles, equip himself with everything just as it should be, before he would ride off. He caught Havel somewhere near Nymburk. He discovered that Havel had not been escaping, but he'd been scared to turn and didn't know how to stop. Since he was relatively small, his legs couldn't reach the ground to brake himself. He didn't know what to do so he kept on going. If the teacher hadn't gone after him, he might have gone straight to the Soviet Union."

In all, Václav Havel spent three school years in Poděbrady. Ivan Havel came to Poděbrady two years later. He was even younger and Forman was not the least bit interested in him. Furthermore, he only stayed there briefly during the 1949–1950 school year.

In February 1948 the memorable year of the Communist takeover, the students went on a field trip in the mountains. They had just returned and were waiting in the train station at Mladá Boleslav for the arrival of the Prague train. And then they heard Klement Gottwald, the Communist leader, over the train station's loudspeakers. Miloš noticed a curious thing: in their class—i.e., those born in 1932 and later—90 percent were convinced it was a hoax. The older students, starting with those born in 1931, began at once to chant slogans and volunteer for youth organizations. Forman maintains that the generation of 1931 and the generation of 1932 are divided as sharply as if by a knife.

17 ▪ *The Fateful Year of 1968**

I remember a meeting some students held with a writer who was well known at the time. The writer, a ruddy, fat man, arrived with a sense of humor. He told us gossip about the Novotný bureaucracy and the central comittee of the Communist Party, and he was honestly enjoying himself. The tension in the hall grew. People got embarrassed, until everyone was sweating except him. He continued to tell his revealing jokes. When he was finished, he wanted to discuss what he

---

*At the beginning of 1968, progressive Communists in the leadership decided that political reform was needed to keep the whole system from toppling. Alexander Dubček, a Slovak, was elected to replace Novotny as first secretary of the Communist party, and began a wide-ranging program ("socialism with a human face") to democratize the Communist Party and assert more independence from Moscow. A period of openers and cultural freedom ("The Prague Spring") followed as the nation gave Dubček its support. Despite Dubček's assurances that Czechoslovakia would not abandon communism and leave the Soviet bloc, the Soviet Union was uneasy. When their demands for a halt to liberalization went unheeded, on Aug. 21, 1968, Soviet tanks invaded and occupied the country. An immediate negative international reaction forced the Soviet leaders to retain Dubček and his associates in office, but by April 1969 Dubček lost his office, and was replaced by Gustáv Husák.

had told us. And one of us told him he was in fact a traitor and reminded him of his past—when he had been the central committee's enfant terrible. All at once, the writer burst like a bubble. In my whole life, I've never seen someone so dejected. He seemed actually to have forgotten who he was; he simply had not identified himself with his past. This was typical of the reform Communists at the time. Some people simply are not bothered by their internal contradictions.

I also remember the enormous misgivings I had about the Party leadership's ability to make a decision, about their sessions, postponements, and eternal promises to resolve the essential issues. The Soviet Union, which I had once visited, seemed to me to be a frightening, irrational colossus, capable of anything. I was terrified on the one hand by its sentimentality, and on the other by its cruelty. Later experience taught me that the two complement each other, that cruelty can be a product of weakness and uncertainty.

In short, I was disappointed in 1968. In the end, it exploded—but strangely and incompletely. During the Prague Spring of 1968, the forgotten national myths—that, the Czechs were always the good guys and the chosen people, and would invariably stand up with strong spirit against numerical superiority and violence; that we were always first in everything, even liberalism—resurfaced, and everyone was buoyed by them. Everyone felt like a mythological hero. The leaders acted as if they had already won, but behind them stood the gigantic colossus, and nobody knew what it would do. It was like the fairy tale of Little Red Riding Hood, when the wolf is lying in the bed instead of the grandmother. It was terrifying. And the worst of it was that nothing could be done about it, because the leaders would not take advice from anyone. They wanted to be popular and celebrated—just like that writer—and they did not think about what they did not want to think about. They were witnesses; they could guarantee us nothing.

In April 1968, Václav Havel wrote an article for *Literární listy* entitled "On the Theme of an Opposition." It was perhaps the only published article to suggest political pluralism—that is, the end of single-party rule. At the time this idea was considered to be extremely bold and daring. Havel now says that he no longer believes all of what he wrote in the article, but this does not diminish its significance at that time. Later the text was used as evidence to prove the counterrevolutionary nature of the press. In essence, Havel expressed an opinion then common among our intellectuals: If the Communists wanted to retain a leading role in government, they would have to earn it. It was not enough for them merely to voice what everyone else had recognized long ago.

He wrote that Communist power had destroyed, stifled, harmed, and forced into exile people who had held the opinions that the Communists were now enunciating as truth they had discovered. A party that had once made such a grievous error could not continue to have a monopoly on power, even if in some cases it now agreed with an opposition, whether it be party members who temporarily dissented from the party line or of members of the public. How could the public control the party, if the public did not have media access, ideology, machinery, propaganda, and a program for all society? How long would the party listen to the opposition, if until now it hadn't listened to the opposition at all? The contest of ideas could not replace the contest for power, and the public had the right to choose, from time to time, who would govern it. The control of power could not be left to special-interest or social organizations founded on principles other than political conviction. What could they do if those in high places refused to allow an opposition of non-Communist political parties, on the pretext that this could lead to "a return to the superseded and regressive structures of bourgeois democracy"? In his article, Havel suggested the creation of at least two parties of comparable strength— which, as we know today, would also have been undemocratic.

18 ▪ *The Tanks Rolled In*

During that week in August 1968 when Soviet tanks rolled in to crush the "Prague Spring," Havel was staying with his wife and the actor Jan Tříska at the home of some friends who were architects in Liberec. They participated in the local resistance there. Havel wrote daily commentaries, which Tříska read for the local radio station. They appeared on a television program from the studio in Ještěd; Václav wrote a speech for the chairman of the District National Committee and prepared public statements for the District Committee of the Communist Party, the District National Committee, the District Committee of the National Front, and the Municipal National Committee, which were broadcast by loudspeakers. They experienced in Liberec that swelling of harmony, brotherhood, and camaraderie—moments that are rare in the life of nations and that were repeated in our country in November 1989. In such moments, it seems that the harmony will last forever, that people will be better, *that this basic experience has changed them.* But it is not so. After the euphoria, the equilibrium returns once again to the banal and uninteresting middle ground. After the enthusiasm, the pendulum swings back to the other side, to depression.

When Alexander Dubček returned from Moscow* and wept on the radio, we knew our cause was lost. But we could not have imagined the extent of the catastrophe. On all sides I heard, "And what could he have done? We are a small country; everyone has abandoned us;

---

*On Aug. 23, Dubček and his aides were transported to Moscow to take part in negotiations, and an agreement on "normalization of the situation" was reached. Dubček returned to Prague on Aug. 27. Inevitably, after the euphoria of 1989 and early 1990, the pendulum swang back again, but not to depression, but rather, to a time of being realistic. When in 1968 it had meant silence and indifference or accomodation with the regime for those who wanted to make careers, the conditions are now human and people are able to do what they want without outside pressure.

we have to bow to pressure and lie. We've bowed to pressure several times before, and we always straighten our spine again once it's over, once the resistance to us is no longer so great."

It was above all our parents who thought this way. For them, the Germans were still much worse than the Russians.

We started down a difficult path, full of lies, compromises, and half-truths. The road to hell had no end. The unbelievable became fact, and people abased themselves. During the occupation and after it I was in Israel and was not able to share that week's experience of community and patriotism with my fellow citizens. I only had that experience twenty-two years later. If we had known it would last so long, would we have led our lives differently? But it could still have lasted till our deaths.

In the Czech Lands*, we are constantly ending something, condemning it, and then starting it all over again. Incessant beginnings and endings. How are we to catch up with countries whose development is continuous and who add to their material and spiritual wealth without interruption?

Egotism, careerism, cowardly accommodation—on these principles the rehashed political leadership founded its authority. The former malaise deepened further, because the centralized direction of society was renewed and reaffirmed. Those who had previously proved themselves incompetent returned to their jobs as a reward for their praise of the invasion. And so traitors to the nation found their way to positions of leadership. Censorship was reinstituted and the media began to lie again. All social organizations had to be loyal, otherwise they were quashed. The workers' opinions interested no one, but those in power once again declared themselves to be the spokespeople for the working class. People who worked for reform or merely let their opinions be known publicly, were condemned and vilified, with no means to defend themselves.

---

*As of Jan. 1, 1993, Czechoslovakia split into two parts—the Czech Republic and Slovakia. The Czech Lands refers to the what is now the Czech Republic.

Václav Havel analyzed this situation in a letter to Alexander Dubček in 1969. He asked Dubček to tell the truth and leave the political arena honorably, without trying to save himself.

> *Your act, therefore, will have no positive effect on the immediate situation; on the contrary, it will probably be exploited to justify further repression. But that is all negligible when set beside the immeasurable moral significance of your act for the social and political destiny of our two nations. People would realize that it is always possible to preserve one's ideals and backbone; that one can stand up to lies; that there are values worth struggling for; that there are still trustworthy leaders; and that no political defeat justifies complete historical skepticism as long as the victims manage to bear their defeat with dignity.* ["Letter to Alexander Dubček," Open Letters, *trans. A. G. Brain, p. 43]*

Alexander Dubček did not follow this advice, but he did not make the public repentance Havel's letter warned against, either. He slipped away, lived in forced isolation, and became a legendary symbol of the Prague Spring. An ambiguous symbol. Compare his retreat to the act of Jan Palach.* Twenty years later, Palach set in motion thousands of young people who felt that if they forgot about him, they would betray his act, his memory, and themselves—they felt their own lives were at stake. Palach's act endured, even though it was surrounded by either deathly silence or bullying propaganda. It plunged into the communal memory, emerged at the right moment, and brought forth the moral purification of thousands of people. Professor Jan Patočka achieved the same effect, in giving his life.[†] Dubček returned to public life twenty years later more or less as he was when he had left it, only a little older. He had preserved his face and his smile. For young people, unfortunately, he was more a symbol of losing than a symbol of the desire for truth that death does not annihilate, but exalts.

---

*In January 1969, Jan Palach, a student, set himself on fire and burned to death to protest the Soviet invasion.

[†]See p. 130 for a description of Patočka's funeral.

In 1968, people were still holding back; they were still taking into account what the Soviet Union might say, what the Communists might say, whether it would upset them too much. People were still calculating the risks. People experienced a moment of truth, but it was too late when they came face to face with the tanks. According to Havel, 1968 was a schizophrenic year, because the truth was not pronounced.

19 ▪ And Then Came Normalization

Andy Warhol wrote:

> In the 60s everybody got interested in everybody.
> In the 70s everybody started dropping everybody.
> The 1960s were Clutter.
> The 1970s are very empty.*

John Lennon said the 1970s weren't worth a damn.

And neither of them even knew too much about what was happening in Czechoslovakia.

The screw that Dr. Husák† set in place began to turn; people professed their loyalty during screening sessions and then retreated to their homes and gardens. Provocatively, they turned their backs on what was happening; those in power did as they pleased. Those who wanted to emigrate and could still make it, left. Since the Communist putsch of 1948 there had not been so many emigrants. The nation's spirit never sustained a worse blow than during the following twenty years; we never stood in a wider or drier moral desert than we did during the twenty years after normalization.

---

*The Philosophy of Andy Warhol: From A to B and Back Again (New York: Harcourt Brace Jovanovich, 1975), p. 26.
†Gustáv Husák, who replaced Dubček as first secretary of the Communist Party after the Soviet invasion.

In July and August 1969, Václav took part in conversations that led to the release of the Ten Points petition, addressed to the federal government, the federal assembly, the government of the Czech Socialist Republic, the Czech national council, and the central committee of the Communist Party. It came out on August 21, 1969; ten people signed it. In it, they repudiated the politics of normalization. That fall, they were accused of the crime of subversion of the republic. One year later, the criminal proceedings against them were indefinitely postponed.

At the end of 1969, Československý Spisovatel was still able to publish *Similes 2*, an anthology of eighteen authors edited by Havel. Soon after that, all the authors were banned, including Havel. In August 1970, Havel was publicly vilified on television, in *Rudé Právo*, and on the radio, as part of a campaign against Professor Václav Černý. In 1971–72, his name was included on a secret list of authors whose books were to be discarded from libraries. Prisoners cut him out of anthologies.

In our country he was slandered and banned, but elsewhere he was celebrated. He won Obies for the resounding successes of *The Memorandum* and *The Increased Difficulty of Concentration* at off-Broadway theaters in New York.

There were fewer and fewer friends Havel could turn to. Some emigrated, such as Věra Linhartová and Jan Tříska. Jan recognized that he could not perform in the theater and have money, a house, and a car without losing his true friends. In the end, he resolved the dilemma with a dramatic escape. Some acquaintances were so afraid that if they ran into Václav, they would cross to the other sidewalk. Dr. Vodička, the manager of the Balustrade, forbade him to enter the theater. Given his consideration of others, Václav was unhappy to cause people embarrassment, so he went out less frequently. Anyway, there was nothing to see in the theaters. Anyone who associated with him ran into some kind of trouble, large or small, with State Security. He and Olga went to Hrádeček and lived there most of the year. Václav went to work at a brewery in Trutnov. It was not because of money;

he could have lived off the royalties from his plays, which were meeting with great success abroad, but because he needed to be among people and he needed to have official employment, since he was not recognized as a writer. In a few months, he knew more about barrels and beer than people who had worked there for decades. He knew almost everything about them.

The number of people who visited Hrádeček dwindled. The regular visitors were Pavel Landovský, sometimes only for a night; Pavel Kohout, who was also something of a refugee; and their faithful friend Zdeněk Urbánek. Zdeněk had his own room at the top of the stairs, and as far as I remember, it was the only place besides his house in Střešoviče in Prague where he could write. In the mornings, he wrote; and in the afternoons, he hiked in the mountains. He saw Václav in the evening, because Václav essentially worked at night. Even today he is a night person. Night people, I once read somewhere, were keepers of the fire in their previous lives. They were the most responsible people, for they guarded over the future well-being of the community. While they stood vigil over the fire alone, they would think of many things and philosophize.

Olga often told Zdeněk to take Vašek with him to the mountains or on a walk, and Zdeněk tried to persuade him to come, but in the end they only went to the mountains together when there was a meeting with Polish dissidents.

"To get him to go now," Zdeněk says, chuckling, "we'd have to arrange a march of presidents through the Chřibský Mountains."

During the first years of normalization, many people lived a life Václav already knew well. A downward slide with no end in sight. All losses and no gains. The gains might come later, in another form. Havel's whole family had lived through this since 1948.

As Miloš Forman says,* there was a generation gap between people born in 1931 and those born in 1932. Forman remembers a quiet, calm boy who sat next to him in school—Zbyněk Janota. One day the

---

*See page 71.

students of the Academy of King George of Poděbrady learned, again via the loudspeakers of the local radio, that their fellow students, the criminal Mašín brothers, had crossed the border to West Germany and escaped. They were children from Poděbrady; the Germans had executed their father for attempting to blow up the Berlin train station. The next day Zbyněk Janota did not come to school. The day after that, his fellow students learned, again via the loudspeakers, that a group of traitors to the nation had been uncovered. They had been condemned to death and immediately executed. Zbyněk Janota was among them.

"They executed the boy who sat next to me," Miloš remembers. "They knew what they were doing when they attacked us, and not those one year older. They knew about that division."

In the middle of the third form, Václav, as the son of an exploiter, had to return to Prague. To continue in a regular course of study at a gymnasium was out of the question. Children from families of businessmen, manufacturers, intellectuals, and tradesmen had to take jobs in manual labor as soon as they had completed the minimum education required by law, to bring them closer to the working class. At first Václav was assigned to be an apprentice at Tesko, a construction company, but his mother visited the training institution and was horrified to discover that her son was supposed to work on scaffolding. She knew Vašek had vertigo. She did her utmost to save him and found him a position as an apprentice chemical laboratory technician. Two years later she found a position for Ivan as an apprentice in precision mechanics at the Signal company. She took their education into her own hands. When she died, she told her husband she could die in peace, because she had fulfilled her maternal duty. Václav was already a famous playwright; and Ivan, a successful mathematician on a research grant at the University of California at Berkeley. That was 1970. The poor mother no longer had enough strength to see her older son through the ups and downs that were to follow in his dramatic career.

She had lived through enough. After the nationalization of Havel Bros.—Prague, Inc., Lucernafilm, and the A-B Corporation studios (including the cinemas), her husband became an employee of the Restaurant Companies of the Lucerna and Barrandov. The national committee of Zlín took the suburban home of grandfather and grandmother Vavrečka, so the grandparents moved in with the Havels in Prague. Václav's mother rented out three rooms on the third floor, did the housekeeping herself, economized wherever she could, and sold off jewels and other valuable items.

Late in the evening of March 31, 1949, three young men surrounded Václav's father outside house number 2000. One of them identified himself as a member of State Security. They interrogated him later at their headquarters on Bartholomew Street about "an offer of illegal border-crossing for his father-in-law, ex-minister Vavrečka." Later that night he was brought in a green patrol wagon to Pankrác prison, where he stayed six weeks in a cell in the State Security section and another six weeks in regular detention before charges were finally filed against him. He was accused of "knowing and not informing," according to the law for the defense of the republic.

The attempt to convict Havel's father and thereby deprive him of his remaining property failed. The court acquitted him of the charges and he was released. Mrs. Havel helped the cause of justice along with the aid of some friends. But it had been nonetheless a time of worry for her. No one had known what was happening to her husband until he managed to smuggle a letter out of Pankrác prison. The old man's description of the situation in prison reminds one of his son's letters to Olga, written thirty years later. It attests to his bravery and refinement, and also reveals what good company was to be had in Czech prisons at the time:

> *I sat uncomfortably in prison for three months, ordered around by guards, in a one-person cell where there were always five or six of us. In the beginning, Colonel Lukas was among us, the one who fought at Tobruk* and was then a military attaché in Washington. During one interrogation, he was so badly beaten that he died*

---

*Modern-day Tubruq, in Libya.

*within three days. We deeply lamented his death. He was a re-
markable person and a friend while I was in jail. That sort of
thing happened more often in those days. Not everyone had it as
easy, relatively speaking, as I did. . . .*

*Happily, everything turned out well in the end, except for the
car; the salary and the job at the Lucerna (as a planner) were left
to me. I was richer for the experience. Poor Mama breathed a sigh
of relief—but not for long, as I describe further on.*

The downward slide, once begun, never stopped. Grandfather Vavrečka was tried without being detained and then acquitted, but it
worried him and the whole family. Miloš Havel was imprisoned for
attempting to cross the border illegally. He managed to reach Austria,
but he found himself in the Soviet zone. The Soviets delivered him to
the Czechoslovak authorities. He was sentenced to two years in prison
and the loss of his property. The prison was in Plzeň-Bory. Božena
Havel visited him there with her twelve-year-old son, Ivan. It was and
would be Ivan's destiny to go on many prison visits. When, in 1950,
he saw his wretched uncle behind bars, he broke out in tears.

Shortly thereafter, an *agent provocateur* tried to entrap Václav's father
at the Lucerna. The agent pointed a revolver at him and demanded
500 crowns so his brother Miloš could cross the border again. Mr.
Havel gave him the money, but immediately reported the incident to
the police.

A woman also came to Mrs. Havel and introduced herself as the
cleaning woman for an American journalist who lived in the Havels'
building. She talked about her connections with the underground
anti-Communist movement. Mrs. Havel immediately reported her,
and of course nothing happened to the "cleaning woman."

The methods of State Security at the beginning of the 1950s may
seem rather primitive, but that made them all the more dangerous.
People disappeared without a trace; people were sentenced without
any wrongdoing having been proved. Innocent people received the
death penalty. Porters decided whether the children in a building

would study or do manual labor. The waves rolled out from below, and the flow of anger, hatred, and revenge they carried was unending. During the years of rule by the Communist regime, which was based on class hatred, a negative basis, so many injustices, lies, and crimes were committed that it is only possible to start anew and not think about them. If a settling of accounts were to begin, if people began to take revenge on one another, the wrongs would never end. When I peruse the family archives and see everything that has happened to the Havels and how they have reconciled themselves to it, they have my absolute admiration. It is not by chance that a man from this family rose to the forefront of a nation so morally wretched.

In the 1950s the Communists called forth a fear that my generation inherited, although we weren't of an age to make decisions. Our parents' fear entered our subconscious minds, and we will never get rid of it. Our children no longer have this fear, because fear is not passed on by genes—it has to be taught.

The signatories of Charter 77 were the first citizens to try to rid themselves of this basic, existential fear by overcoming it. They reckoned they would be jailed and persecuted, but they realized that times had changed since the 1950s and it was necessary to take risks and confront those in power. They realized that a free act by individuals opens up realms that they cannot imagine.

The secrecy and silence of the 1950s was appalling. Everyone was afraid of his neighbor; no one trusted anyone. In their mind-set, people returned to the time of the Protectorate, except there was no longer any hope that the Germans would lose the war and everything would turn out well again. People were afraid to talk about anything in front of anyone they did not know well. They were waiting for things to fall apart, but the waiting was a kind of fairy tale. People felt that a return to the good days of the First Republic was impossible in their world. They had no way out, and their way of life began to erode. It took until almost the end of the 1960s for people to begin to pull themselves together. After a shock, society comes to its senses slowly, one person at a time.

According to Václav's father's memoirs, 1952 was the family's most difficult year. Mr. Havel had to leave the Lucerna. It had not belonged to him for three years, but they had allowed him to work there. He worked well and his employers liked him. The final parting was hard for him, because he was attached to the business by countless emotional ties, by his family tradition, by his whole life. During the construction of the second and third stages, his parents had initiated him into all the technical and restaurant details. After graduation from *Realschule* (technical secondary school), he worked as an assistant with the concrete work. He received a small business permit in the restaurant field and in addition his degree as a construction engineer.

After his departure from the Lucerna, Václav's father joined the Sokol association Vzlet,* a physical fitness organization, as manager of the transportation section. Again, he did not complain, but no sooner was the family assured that the breadwinner had a job and had calmed down than he was called before the National Committee of Prague District 1 on Vodičková Street. There they notified him that he would have to give up his five-room Prague apartment at house number 2000 to other, more needy citizens and move to Albrechtice near Liberec—that is, in Sudetenland, from which the Germans had been expelled and which was virtually a wasteland in the early 1950s.

This new setback was part of "Action B," the relocation of reactionaries, capitalists, and politically unsuitable people away from Prague. Friends tried to help. It was not only that the family would lose their Prague apartment, but they would also lose their connections in the community, Mr. Havel would lose his job, and the children would lose their chance to study. They sent a petition to President Zápotocký, the ministry of the interior, and the people's party, to which Václav's father belonged. They attempted to exchange the exile to Albrechtice for an exile to Havlov and to preserve at least a small space for stays

---

*Sokol associations are clubs dedicated to physical fitness. The first Sokol clubs were founded in the nineteenth century, when Bohemia and Moravia belonged to the Hapsburg crown, and were an early source of Czech national pride.

in Prague. That year, Mrs. Havel spent the summer at Havlov with Ivan and Václav.

When grandfather Hugo Vavrečka learned about Action B, he became so upset that he suffered a stroke. Within several days, in August 1952, he died. A month later, foreign radio announced that Miloš Havel had crossed the border into West German. Everyone was no doubt happy for him, but it meant further reprisals against the family. A hopeful hearing of the family's case vis-à-vis Action B was immediately brought to a halt, and the reprieve the family had gotten was canceled. Thus, they lost the apartment Václav and Miloš had grown up in—the apartment where Václav and Ivan were born and also brought up. The family retreated to the fifth floor, where there was still one apartment, though small and partly rented out. Václav was given a room that overlooked the courtyard, which from that time forward became his "den." His mother had a lot of work with the move. She sent a portion of their things to Havlov. The books, archives, antiques, and china were packed into boxes, which she numbered and stored in the basement. The Habaner ware* and other valuable china, amounting to perhaps three hundred pieces, she placed in the depository of the Museum of Industrial Arts. The paintings and sculpture, including a self-portrait of the Baroque painter Kupecký and portraits of the Havel ancestors, were given to the National Gallery in the belief that it was the best place to store them, and that way the family would not lose them. Later they lost all these items without any compensation. They were nationalized according to the same regulations as all the real estate.

A new, crushing surprise awaited the family at Havlov. The main building had been sealed up the day before their arrival by State Security, on the pretext that it was the collective property of Václav and Miloš Havel. They had to store all their possessions in the garage, and they had nowhere to go. Havel is father traveled to Brno, where

---

*Decorative china manufactured in the late sixteenth century by an Anabaptist sect in Moravia and Slovakia.

he proved that Havlov was registered solely as his property, and about six weeks later, State Security unsealed Havlov. For a short while, it was saved. In the small apartment in Prague, the family trembled whenever anyone rang the doorbell, afraid they would finally be evicted. Luckily, no one informed on them, and so they remained in Prague until Action B was called off. Shortly thereafter, grandmother Vavrečka died in the Prague apartment. Although Mrs. Havel's parents had once been well off, they left behind them no more than a few pieces of clothing and the beautiful memories of those who loved them.

Václav moved into his grandmother's old room on the fifth floor. He worked in the chemistry laboratory and took night classes at a gymnasium. Ivan was learning precision mechanics and also started night classes. In 1953 came the currency reform. It affected anyone with a savings account or a pension. The Havel family still had a few pieces of unmortgaged real estate, and owed no taxes. What made matters worse is that they could not sell anything to raise money, because no one could afford to buy.

The family's concerns always centered on the education of their sons (their mother wanted them to go to college as soon as they finished the gymnasium night school, no matter what the cost) and the more practical problem of the father's employment, the provisional living arrangements, and holding on to Havlov. The income from the sale of plots of land in Barrandov stopped, but both sons were working while they studied and so they began to help out.

Uncle Miloš Havel lived abroad like a disinherited son. Several times he tried to make it as a businessman, but his luck had run out. His life became a series of misfortunes and disappointments. His old friends Jan Werich, Jiří Trnka, Jiří Krejčík, and Zdeněk Štěpánek visited him abroad. Later his nephew Václav brought him joy; he was proud of him. He followed Václav's successes abroad and traveled around Europe to the premieres of his plays. They met again for the first time in West Berlin in 1965, at *The Garden Party*, which the Theater on the

Balustrade was performing there in Czech. They also saw each other in Munich and in Vienna at the premiere of *The Memorandum*.

Miloš Havel died on February 23, 1968. Václav, Olga, and Václav's father went to the funeral in Munich. They inherited 171 deutsch-marks and 5 pfennigs from the deceased. In his memoirs, Václav's father wrote this about his brother:

> *From conversations with Miloš's friends in Munich, I formed the impression that at the end of his life, Miloš had become for Munich something like what the famous Dr. Uher became for the Battalion.* Apparently he liked to sit in bars, entertain the staff, and tell them his rich life story. Wherever they knew him, they loved him. In his final photograph, although well dressed, he appears to have aged a great deal. He remembered his parents fondly. He was always especially fond of his mother.*

The name of Miloš Havel was erased from the history of Czech film.

20 • A *Letter to Dr. Husák*

Something had to happen. The trials at the beginning of the 1970s took place without publicity. It seemed that society was paralyzed and would condone anything. People who lost their jobs—either because the magazines or institutions where they worked were liquidated after the occupation by the normalizers, or because during screening sessions they were fired for failing to support the Soviet invasion—had to find manual labor. The normalizers manipulated society, which seemed unable to come to its senses after the shock.

In April 1975, Havel wrote a letter to Dr. Husák, an action which

---

*The Battalion was a notorious Prague night club and Dr. Uher was a lawyer who ended as a drinker and a practical joker.

at first struck many of his friends as sheer suicide. It was a daring gesture. People who had been only a little frightened now became more frightened, because there was no way to anticipate how Husák would behave. Until then, he had never debated with anyone in public, and he had published nothing. Protests and petitions disappeared hopelessly into the trapdoor of time; no one reacted to them; Husák carried out normalization with repulsive cunning. He kept all problems under cover; he minimized publicity; he stifled all information. In no way could Václav reckon how Husák might act. He wrote the letter and he waited to see what would happen. Pavel Landovský secretly made Xerox copies of the letter at the Academy of Sciences and took the parcel he had prepared to Slovakia. There he distributed the copies in theaters. Many actors and theater staff apparently said it was a mistake and a foolishness to write to that strumpet.

Perhaps because he was afraid, although he did not show it, Havel began his letter with an analysis of the fear that Husák's government had instilled in society. Fear as the awareness of a lasting and ubiquitous threat. A slow acclimation to fear as a tangible part of the world. It was a system of existential pressure that never left a single citizen, because even a factory hand could be demoted to a worse job, and this existential pressure was put into effect by a ubiquitous and omnipotent state police. The state police could reach into any life at any moment; it was impossible to defend oneself against them.

During a deep moral and economic crisis, this system gave power to egotistic and careerist types, unprincipled people who could accustom themselves to any kind of humiliation and who would be willing to sacrifice their friends and family if it pleased those in power. Every citizen was forced to become a hypocrite. People grew indifferent, and this was the intention of the policies the government leaders advanced. It seemed to make no sense to fight for anything; it did not seem to be worth it. People fell into apathy and grew disinterested in any suprapersonal values. They went through political rituals in order to be left in peace. The government encouraged people to care only about their private lives and to pay no attention to the spiritual, political, and moral violence around them. In Communist ideology, the individual and his humanity come first, before all other interests and concerns. Those in power always paid lip service to this principle, but in reality they wanted a satisfied, socialist Babbitt, whose private life was reduced to a quest for consumer goods. He would become an obedient member of the consumer herd, and since the economy did not work too well, he would always be kept busy ferreting out one consumer good after another. The government took care of politics and did not let anyone else meddle in it.

There was order and peace, but the price was the spiritual and moral deadening of society. The essential instrument of social self-awareness is culture, and this was totally destroyed, superficialized to the point of banality, mediocrity, and genial, Babbittish philosophizing. The question was, to what future depths of spiritual and moral impotence would the castration of the nation's culture lead? Somewhere at the root of this power which had set its course for entropy was a death wish. Those in power brought us order without life, so that even history vanished. Society regressed to a kind of prehistoric era; history was replaced by pseudohistory. We lived from anniversary to anniversary, from celebration to celebration, from congress to congress. But as those in power deadened life, they also deadened themselves. Somewhere deep below the icy crust, life continued to flow quietly and inconspicuously like a little stream. And eventually something would happen, something not planned for in the official calendar. History would announce itself. Consider what Václav predicted in 1975:

> *The more rational the construction of the official calendar of nonevents over the years, the more irrational the effect of a sudden irruption of genuine history. All its long-suppressed elements of unrepeatability, uniqueness, and incalculability, all its long-denied mysteries, come rushing through the breach. Where for years we had been denied the slightest, most ordinary surprise, life is now one huge surprise—and it is well worth it. The whole disorderliness of history, concealed under artificial order for years,*

suddenly spurts out. . . . Nothing remains forgotten. All the fear one has endured, the dissimulation one has been forced into, all the painful and degrading buffoonery, and worst of all, perhaps, the feeling of having displayed one's cowardice—all this settles and accumulates somewhere in the bottom of our social consciousness, quietly fermenting. . . . I fear the price we are all bound to pay for the drastic suppression of history. . . . ["Dear Dr. Husák," Open Letters, *trans, anonymous, pp. 77–81]*

This is a summary of the letter to Dr. Husák; with this letter, a new era in Czechoslovak history began. Admittedly, everything seemed to continue much as before, because Dr. Husák did not react. However, copies of the letter circulated; people read it and realized what perhaps everyone already knew, but in small bits. Here someone had put the pieces together for them. It was exactly what the regime most feared. So long as each person had his own concerns, all slightly different, it would not occur to anyone that there was a common denominator and single culprit, that someone had deliberately organized the system that entrapped them.

21 • The *Beggar's Opera in Počernice*

Václav Havel wrote political essays and articles, but he preferred above all to write plays.

In 1972 he wrote *The Beggar's Opera*, based on the play by John Gay, then wrote *The Mountain Hotel* and *Private View*. Zdena Salivarová had these plays, along with *The Conspirators*, published at Sixty-eight Publishers in Toronto in 1977.* Jiří (George) Voskovec, the actor, wrote a beautiful preface to the book; I quote from the high praise he gives to Václav:

---

*Audience was also included.

... *History imitates—or, if you will, fulfills—the visions of only a handful of geniuses, such as Jules Verne, and at deeper levels, H. G. Wells, Jonathan Swift, Franz Kafka, and Dostoevski. My friend, you are a member of this exclusive club. I take a deep bow before you.*

*Allow me only a few words more. It impresses me that in your most recent plays (*The Mountain Hotel, Private View, Audience*), you have adapted your own situation in Czechoslovakia's post-Dubček era into a theatrical effect which I personally refer to as the "Havel spiral." It is a movement; a vortex of nonsense; an unordered, accelerating gallop of emptiness and despair in words and deeds which, in one variation or another, concludes the three above-mentioned plays. In this incomprehensible maelstrom, whose motion is reflected in the repetition and dissolution of sentences, you and all your fellow citizens—including the leaders—circle. Only you, though you cannot resist the rotation of this tremendous tornado, maintain your perspective and manage to reconstruct the tornado in theater, as if you stood outside it.*

Above this—and this is no joke—is the whirlwind of the Great Communal Nonsense; on this tiny planet, it attacks us all, regardless of political or other affiliation. ...

In 1975, Václav wrote the one-act play *Audience*. That year Andrej Krob, his neighbor at Hrádeček, who later directed the premiere of *Audience*, staged the first performance of *The Beggar's Opera*. He talks about Václav and that first performance:

"What an ability to adapt to new surroundings! He had been in the brewery only a few weeks and he was sold on it. Basically, he didn't have to go there, but it was like a trip into another universe for him. For a few months he rolled barrels in the basement, but he soon wanted to learn how the barrels were manufactured, who made the iron hoops, what was put into the barrels, and suddenly he was giving us long lectures on the world of beer brewing. He was a world-class expert. He has an ability to understand things quickly, to perfectly analyze a situation he finds himself in out of the blue, something he has minimal information on. I've always butchered him in chess. I think he had a chance either to become president or a world chess mastermind. He'd be good if he devoted himself to it, the way he does to writing, philosophy, and politics. With him, not a single thing remains unfinished; not a single word is said in vain. Every second, every hour has a purpose, he knows what for. Even in jail he could organize his life. He's a person who's always at home. I'm one of the few people who knows it for sure. It's not only an ability to get along with everyone; it's an ability to bring other people, with their faulty, limited thinking, around to the most useful path.

"I read *The Beggar's Opera*, and I got it into my head I might stir up my slightly drab life a little. It was originally written for The Dramatic Club, but it could not be performed there. So I simply decided I would do it. We rehearsed with amateur actors for a year and a half; nobody really believed we'd manage to pull it off. Havel saw it twice: once we went to Hrádeček, we had been rehearsing it in various apartments; then Grossman and Vašek came to see the dress rehearsal. After a year and half we had reached the stage where the dialogue was in good shape and the blocking was perfect. It had a rhythm, and we needed to start performing, only the times we were in made that impossible. So we negotiated with a pub in Dolní Počernice, a district on the outskirts of Prague, and sold a limited number of tickets. Vašek considered it his premiere. It may not have been a finished performance, but in any case it was an unrepeatable one. Everything connected up with everything else. In the next room, drunks were roaring; we had muffled the doors with mattresses. In the audience were sitting three hundred wonderful, splendid, talented people whom the Communists had demoted to the nation's boiler rooms. They sat on creaky chairs. On stage, people who installed insulation in windows, stage hands, workers, repairmen, and drivers performed the play, and suddenly the action shifted from the stage to the audience. It was an enormous 'happening' with *The Beggar's Opera* as the theme. Something happened there that I've never been able to understand. For me it was a mess of fuck-ups—curtains opened poorly, slips of the tongue, sweating faces. But with the passage of time, I realize it wasn't a matter of a theatrical performance at all, but of something that managed to happen under absolutely incredible circumstances."

I reminded Andrej that he had also shot a video of Havel's play *Temptation* with amateurs. I watched it once at Hrádeček for three hours, and I could not believe my eyes. I truly believed in the amateurs in the play. Andrej also believed in them, more than he would have in someone from the National Theater.

"I'm not responsible for that success; that success is due to their intelligence, their understanding, their grasp of the text, because they knew what they were performing.

"After *The Beggar's Opera*, we went to get drunk. We reserved a room right around the corner from the police station on Bartholomew Street, the rear room at U medvídků (At the Sign of the Little Bears). We had a good time, it ended in the early morning, and we parted with the feeling that everything had gone well. For a few days things were quiet. Before the anniversary of the October Revolution,* they picked me up and started to interrogate me. I figured out that they were totally confused and didn't know what was going on. The cops probably hadn't been in Počernice at all. For one thing, we had kept it a secret, and for another, they hadn't been expecting an attack from that side at all: from workers and stagehands. I was sitting through interrogations and in Počernice people were gathering for a repeat performance, which, of course, never took place. I'd only told the head waiter that we'd do it again."

The performance in Počernice caused a big fuss. All kinds of institutions got involved. People said that it was Havel's fault, why doesn't he finally give it up? that conditions in Czech theater would set worse, that it would cease to be possible to do what had still seemed possible

---

*The Russian Revolution, which actually occurred in November according to the Western calendar.

up to that point. Since the beginning of the 1970s, this has been every opportunist's line of reasoning. If I don't do it, some swine much worse than I am will come along and do something far worse. A lesser wrong is better than a greater, and therefore we'll do wrong without qualms, with a clean conscience. They constantly retreated, but they defended themselves by saying they held on to their position.

Václav was very happy to see one of his plays on stage for the first time in years. As he himself says, it made him happier than the performances of his plays in New York or Vienna. Remember that he had been a playwright who wrote his plays for a specific theater and specific actors. And then one day he lost everything. Plays are not meant to be read, but performed. A play does not truly become a play until a theater produces it, until a director stamps his vision on it, until the actors rehearse it, until the actors and, finally, the audience members complete it. Only in a theater is it possible to create that unrepeatable, explosive atmosphere between stage and audience. Vašek had to think about it and imagine it. He imagined he was writing his plays for contemporary audiences, but the audiences were both here and on the other side of the iron curtain, where the atmosphere of society was quite different. In his article "Far from the Theater" in 1986, he wrote the following about the dilemma:

"Just as the only defense of a prisoner may be to blunt his pain by settling into an organized pseudolife, my laxness toward the theatrical life of my plays may be the only defense against the absurdity of my situation."

The performance in Počernice confirmed for him that he wrote plays that could be performed and that entertained the public.

Writing the letter to Dr. Husák had freed him, and the combination of the letter and the production of The *Beggar's Opera* in Dolní Počernice brought him a rush of energy. In an atmosphere without drama and without narrative, something was starting to happen. People once again showed signs of life. The communal experience in the theater gave strength to many people who were soon to become signatories and spokespeople for Charter 77. That free act brought liberation to

everyone who participated and whose participation created and fulfilled it.

Václav reacted against the attacks on those who produced *The Beggar's Opera* by writing a letter to Zdeněk Zuska, mayor of Prague. The
German magazine *Spiegl* published an article about it, which Radio
Free Europe broadcast. From that, State Security discovered that the
performance in Počernice was not an imperialist plot and suddenly
realized that to make a political scandal out of it was ridiculous.

"In the end, I was the only one to get in trouble," says Andrej,
"since they threw me out of the theater and I had to install insulation
in windows. I did that for thirteen years, and now I miss it. I met
thousands of people—there were so many bedrooms, living rooms,
kitchens. I saw Vašek mostly in the summer, at Hrádeček. Our cottage
was a reading room. We had dissident literature there, and people
would stay around for weeks at a time reading the books and magazines. Today, these are romantic, lovely memories of a gloomy time."

The two houses faced each other. When Havel sat in his backyard,
he could see Andrej leaving his cottage to go to the toilet. On his way,
the cherry tree would catch his eye, and he would decide to pick some
cherries. He would go to fetch a ladder. In the shed, he would see he
needed to chop some wood, so he would decide that he had better
chop wood first, and meanwhile he would discover he had already
shit his pants.

Havel was always systematic; his life was in order. Andrej is Havel's
opposite; maybe that is why they get along so well. Havel was a part
of every important moment of Andrej's life, and a photograph of
Andrej with a raised index finger is on the ceiling over Václav's bed.

In 1972, the Samizdat Press, Padlock Press (Edice Petlice), had been
founded. Ludvík Vaculík and several of his friends had conceived it.
In March 1975, Havel and Jan Lopatka met again after an interval of
five and half years, in the wine cellar U piaristů in Panská Street. They
discussed the letter to Dr. Husák, which was then sent on April 8, and
the idea of founding Expedition Edition (Edice Expedice). It would

also have to be a typewritten, samizdat press, which would parallel *Padlock* and complement it.

Padlock published original texts by authors who had suffered the same fate over the last thirty years. Expedition had a slightly different plan. Havel wanted first to borrow a few select titles from Padlock, but soon after the press was underway they began to fill out the list with their own authors. They were chiefly younger, underground writers. They too published books of essays, anthologies, and memoirs. A special feature of Expedition was that the author did not sign the book, as in Padlock, but the publisher did. Thus: "In the year such and such, Václav Havel made copies for himself and his friends." Václav took everything on himself, as always (just as, later, he told all the signatories to Charter 77 that he himself would bring the text for them to sign). Expedition books were bound plainly, in black cloth, and in the lower left-hand corner they had the gold initials "EE."

Havel did not ask the authors whether or not he could publish the books. Here too he took on all the decisions and the risk; he printed what he wanted to. Expedition Edition was a wild, "pirate" press. In the first period it published authors such as Václav Černý, Jiří Dienstbier, Jiří Gruša, Ladislav Fikar, Havel, Bohumil Hrabal, Jindřich Chalupecký, Pavel Juráček, Eva Kantůrková, Pavel Kohout, Eda Kriseová, Pavel Landovský, Osip Mandlestam, George Orwell, Jan Patočka, Jaroslav Seifert, Karol Sidon, Topol, Jan Vladislav, Jiří Voskovec, a collection of Czechoslovak feuilletons, and the anthology *The Hour of Hope*. In the second group they issued underground books: Egon Bondy (a pseudonym for Zbyněk Fišer) *Film Studies Today*, Jaroslav Hutka, Ivan Martin Jirous (also known as "Magor"), Věra Jirousová, underground anthologies, and Vlastimil Třešňák. Expedition Press published books that had been planned for serialization in *Tvář* and that were supposed to appear in the never-realized Tangent imprint at *Československý Spisovatel*. Some of these were Dietrich Bonhoeffer, Salvador Dali, Martin Heidegger, Ladislav Klíma, Jiří Kolář, Jan Lopatka, Charles Péguy, and the anthology *Glances 1*. Expedition also published essayists who wrote on the natural sciences and on the interdisciplinary relations so characteristic of scientific thought in the last few decades. This line of books was also an invaluable contribution, because it introduced people to what was then in print elsewhere in the world, though forbidden in our country. It was not possible to borrow these books from the library. Either the libraries did not have them, or it was impossible to check them out. St. Augustine, Vytautas Landsberg, Konrad Lorenz, Zdeněk Neubauer, Radim Palouš, Julius Tomin. They also published the best of the banned translators, such as Zdeněk Urbánek's Shakespeare, Jan Vladislav's Henri Michaux and Eugenio Montale, Petr Kopta's Pierre de Ronsard.

When Václav Havel was imprisoned for the first time briefly in 1977 and then for a longer period in 1979, his wife, Olga, continued with the publishing. During those periods, the volumes were signed: "In the year. . . , Olga Havel made copies for herself and her friends."

Between 1975 and 1981, 122 volumes came out under the "EE" trademark. The last book in the so-called Black Series bears the number 152. From 1975 to 1978, Daňa Horáková took care of the samizdat's logistics and editing; from 1979 to 1989, Ivan Havel and Jan Lopatka. In 1983 began the so-called Light Series. In all, about 300 titles were issued, of which thirty were seized by the police at a stage in production that made it impossible to complete the print run.

At the beginning of the 1970s, writers would meet at Hrádeček from time to time for a kind of mini congress. Two groups met there, which later united into one. There were the ex-Communists or, as they were called, the antidogmatics, who were paying for their attempt at reform socialism: Vaculík, Klímla, Kohout. And then there were those who had already been dissidents in the 1950s, whose work had come out in samizdat even then: Urbánek, Vladislav, Hiršal, Kopta. Sometimes Kliment, Gruša, Uhde, Kabeš, and Sidon came as well. The groups mixed together well, because they were all in a similar enough predicament. Some of them survived on royalties from abroad; others held manual-labor jobs, which did not leave them much time to write. The tradition founded then continues to this day. Later we traveled to Moravia and Slovakia, to various secret locations. We visited friends and offered our own homes for their visits. The meetings took place regularly four times a year. We exchanged our writing; we read works out loud. Wherever we were, the date and location of the next meeting was always written on a piece of paper. Sometimes the date and location fell into the wrong hands and we were not able to meet.

In early 1976, Havel met Ivan Martin Jirous, whose pseudonym is Magor. Magor was the manager of the rock group The Plastic People of the Universe; he was the founder and king of the Czech musical underground, a title he still holds today. Magor combined music with the visual arts, because he was an art historian at the Knights' School.* He also wrote poems and manifestos. The underground, as Egon Bondy says, was culture acting in self-defense during a period of despair; from it arose, among other things, Czech postmodern art.

The Plastic People of the Universe developed out of The Primitives Group, which had played in the late 1960s. They were markedly nonconformist, and the Communist Babbitts were soon shocked not only by the style of their music, but also by their performance, since they had long hair, used obscenities, and so forth. They revoked their license to perform in Prague and in the end forbade them to play in public anywhere. The Plastics then played at weddings, baptisms, and birthday parties. They held so-called black concerts in villages. Before the concerts the police monitored the train stations and bus stops, rounded up young people in the forests and on the highways, and directed cars to turn back. The Plastics' concerts resembled the medieval mountaintop festivals where Protestants met to hold their religious services in secret. The police broke up several concerts, beat the participants brutally, and took them away in patrol wagons. There was nothing at stake but music that didn't please the lords of power. Those in power could not believe that so many people would defy such explicit instructions merely on account of music.

The Communist regime was beginning to come into conflict with a new generation, with young people. These people did not have any

---

*The Knights' School of Pure Humor, no kidding. A private circle of artists and muscians.

blemishes on their records from 1968, because they had not been old enough to be guilty of anything. But those in power made enemies of them by refusing to let them live the way they wanted and needed to. In their arrogance, the powerful assumed they could decide how people ought to be, what ought to attract them, what should please them. Something similar happened to the powerful in 1988 and 1989. As Jan Patočka wrote in his article "Heroes of Our Time":

> *Nietzsche said that great changes come in on little pigeon feet. They are played out in secret; that is the essential thing. If they had a speculative streak, the Herods of this world would be able to nip change in the bud. It is only because they do not see what is really happening—that it is not* things *that are changing, but the* world*—that the world is protected from the greedy hands of manipulators. Where, then, do changes in the world and in history take place? "Inside," or better put, within the life of the individual.* [The Jan Patočka Reader: First Sketch for a Portrait; samzidat, 1977]

22 ▪ The Trial of the Plastics

One evening in early 1976, Havel got together with Magor. All night, Magor played Havel songs by the Plastics, DG 307, and other groups. He gave Havel his *Report on the Third Czech Musical Revival*. Vašek understood that what was happening here was an expression of something essential, that it was the authentic and existential voice of young people, and not merely noise and obscenities, as it was described by the officials. He discerned that Jirous's underground could be his allies; the regime had thrown them in the ghetto because they refused to conform. There was poetry in their music, a desire for salvation and justice, for freedom. After this, everything took place as if under some higher direction.

The regime stuck its own head into the noose. In March, they arrested the Plastics. They locked up nineteen musicians and followers of the group, and criminal charges were filed against them. They thought they were condemning a few long-haired rowdies, drug addicts, slackers, and alcoholics—people nobody knew and nobody cared about. They thought they were getting rid of the infection of rock music that gravely threatened the young generation.

At the beginning, Věra Jirousová, Magor's wife, and Jiří Němec* did not know whether or not they should ally themselves with Havel and ask him for advice and help. The friends of the Plastics were trying to figure out whether it would hurt the musicians to have Havel on their side. After all, they were only musicians, not dissidents. They hoped it was all a mistake, and that those in power would admit of their own accord that they were barking up the wrong tree. Who had ever heard of musicians being sent to prison for playing the music they liked? If Havel and his cohort were involved, State Security would not be able to back out gracefully. The case would become an affair of prestige for the regime; they would have closed off the regime's only path of retreat.

Magor dodged the police for another week, hiding in secret apartments, and in the end he decided to go all the way. Vašek came from Hrádeček and they formulated their tactics. When they emprisoned Magor soon after that, Němec and Jirousovà went to Václav, and they decided to publicize the case. Vašek arranged interviews with Reuters and with the news bureau of Radio Free Europe. They sent protests to all the embassies, and *voilá*: the world was outraged. People saw that it was not a case of political opponents settling accounts, or winners punishing losers, that it was not a fight for power, but a fight for life. That a degenerate and life-threatening power could imprison anyone for breathing, singing, or walking down the street.

---

*Němec, a political writer and psychologist, was closely involved in Jirous's underground.

Husák's government saw that it had overshot the mark, and by May the government seemed to be giving in. It was decided that the matter would be redefined and prosecuted as a disturbance of the peace. But a certain Lieutenant Koudelka in State Security's West Prague office overturned this decision; it appears that Lieutenant Koudelka had decided the Plastics' was the case that would make his career. He simply couldn't stop. He pushed the case to trial in September. Many people believed that at this point the secret police had slipped out of Dr. Husák's control and begun to do as it pleased; perhaps not even the central committee of the Communist Party of Czechoslovakia was enough to brake it. From that time on, the persecuted took advantage of the persecutors' mistakes. Even in a tennis match, the one who wins is the one who exploits his opponent's errors. It was clear that the wait-and-see game no longer made sense.

In this trial, the human desire to lead one's life freely was in the dock. It was trial in the name of sameness, indifference, bureaucratization, total obedience, and conformity. Anything that deviated from the norm in any way had to be liquidated. A new era was setting in of its own accord. We too had had such an experience. Those who had trouble getting a higher education in the 1950s and early 1960s then had quite a good start in the middle of the 1960s, and those who studied relatively easily in the 1960s found themselves in a very bad position in the 1970s. It came and went like the tides, according to fundamental laws that nobody understood. But in every case it was clear that the opposite phase was coming, and it was necessary to take advantage of it. In 1976, it seemed that society was beginning to restructure itself and resistance was strengthening. Those in power were not too clever. Gradually, they angered everyone, while offering to collaborate with no one. In their conceit, they failed to realize they were driving into a single camp people who previously did not have, and did not even want to have, anything in common. Every power eventually pardons those who have offended it, but Husák's power showed mercy to none. It nursed its grudges, and this decided its fate.

Havel's chief collaborator on the Plastics campaign was Jiří Němec, his former co-worker from *Tvář* whom he had not spoken to since he left *Tvář*'s editorial board years ago. Havel knew that Němec could handle the organization of the long-haired crowd in the underground. He understood that it did not make sense to always work with the same people signing the same set of petitions. He saw that a mass of wronged people was growing, people who wanted to join forces. The rockers had excellent training. As a group, they communicated quickly; they could have understood each other with tom-tom drums. Havel recognized this when he organized the signature campaign for the Plastics. Vašek, as was and is his wont, planned out the campaign. He always planned all of his political actions with flow charts. Much as he might sketch out the plot of one of his plays, he sketched the events he had in mind. Here I should note though that Havel's first consideration has always been to real life; he willingly and gladly changes his organizational charts and sketches new ones when events turn out differently than he has planned.

The people the message was aimed at slowly began to understand that freedom is indivisible and that a threat to the freedom of one person is a threat to the freedom of all. It might have been assumed that the people would not stand up for a few young long-hairs, whom official propaganda had described in the worst light, but the people were tired of censorship and inaction. It was clear something would have to drive events, and the Plastics were a good inciting force. Havel and Němec wrote an open letter to Heinrich Böll. The first to sign the protest were older writers to whom nothing much could happen. A big petition followed, which seventy people signed. Even lawyers and ex-Communists made themselves heard—which must have been an unpleasant surprise for the current regime.

In September, in the district court for the Prague-West region on Karmelitská Street, the trial took place. Havel wrote an article about it. He observed the court as if it were absurdist theater, as if it were something thought out and planned altogether differently that changed its shape before the audience's gaze. He wrote:

Soon, however, this façade of judicial thoroughness and objectiv-ity began to appear as a mere smokescreen to hide what the trial really was: an impassioned debate about the meaning of human existence, an urgent questioning of what one should expect from life, whether one should silently accept the world as it is presented to one and slip obediently into one's pre-arranged place in it, or whether one has the strength to exercise free choice in the matter; whether one should be "reasonable" and take one's place in the world, or whether one has the right to resist in the name of one's own human convictions. . . .

[T]he whole case was depressing simply because it had slipped out of joint. How could it have been otherwise, when this contro-versy over the meaning of life took place here, in the district court for the Prague-West region, and when no one present could do the one thing that was appropriate in this situation: stand up and shout: "Enough of this comedy! Case dismissed!"? . . . .

But none of this does justice to the experience. At a deeper level it was, oddly enough, not depressing at all. There was even something elevating about it. This was perhaps because of the very awareness that we were participants in a unique illumination of the world. But chiefly, I suppose, it was the exciting realization that there are still people among us who assume the existential responsibility for their own truth and are willing to pay a high price for it. (Whereas those who judge them can only depend on the collective backing of a colossal social power and would rather send someone to prison for no reason at all than risk even a minor blemish on their record.). . . .

Suddenly, I felt disgusted with a whole world, in which—as I realized then—I still have one foot: the world of emergency exits.
["The Trial," Open Letters, trans. Paul Wilson, pp. 105–107]

After the trial, the long-haired youths and the former Communist Party functionaries stood next to each other in the corridor and they shared a shock—the awareness that we were all threatened. There were intellectuals there, both those who had held power, deciding who could publish and who could exhibit, and those who had not, whose fates had been in their power. Everyone understood that the feuds of the past, the differences of opinion and differences in age were no longer important. As Havel described it,

> The people who gathered outside the courtroom were a prefigu-
> ration of Charter 77. The same atmosphere that dominated then,
> of equality, solidarity, conviviality, togetherness, and willingness
> to help each other, an atmosphere evoked by a common cause and
> a common threat, was also the atmosphere around Charter 77
> during its first few months. Jiří Němec and I both felt that some-
> thing had happened here, something that should not be allowed
> simply to evaporate. . . . [Disturbing the Peace, p. 132]

In the fall there were several meetings, where various types of people, including Zdeněk Mlynář, Pavel Kohout, Ludvík Vaculík, Petr Uhl, Jiří Hájek, and František Kriegel,* expressed opinions that were almost entirely in agreement. They were preparing the text of the Charter.† Philosopher Ladislav Hejdánek brought some very important information. In the digest of law, an announcement had been published of the adoption of the Helsinki Accord. For its legal authority, the Charter could rely on a human rights agreement the Czech government had in fact signed.

A model situation was created in our society, and Václav Havel

---

*Mlynář was a former member of Dubček's central committee, Kohout a playwright, Vaculík a writer and publisher of Padlock Press, Uhl a journalist, Hájek a politician and diplomat who had been a government minister in the 1960s, and Kriegel a politician who had been a member of the Dubček government.

†As Havel describes in Disturbing the Peace, these meetings were a result of probes by himself and Němec following the trial toward creating a statement demanding human rights in Czechoslovakia. Although Havel stresses that the Charter belongs to all the Chartists, it was at these meetings, after the participants had consulted with their own circles, that the Charter was written.

made an essential contribution to its creation. Later, when foreign journalists came, they were amazed at the existence of an integrated social structure that contained within it everyone from Marxists to Trotskyites, to intellectuals, to Christians, to the rock and roll underground.

23 ▪ *Kidnapping* Children

Anna Fárová recalls that on October 2, 1977, while her family was visiting the Havels at Hrádeček, two children from the household were kidnapped—Betina Landovská (age fifteen) and Gabriela Fárová (age fourteen). They had gone to the forest to pick mushrooms, and when they came to the highway, near a roadside cross, a yellow police Volga stopped beside them. The policeman wanted their citizens' identity cards. Betina's was at the Havel's cottage, and Gábina* did not have one yet. On the pretext that it was cold, the officers forced the girls into the car. Then they slammed the doors, locked them, and the car drove off quickly. The girls protested that the car was going away from Hrádeček, and asked where they were headed. They did not receive an answer. The policemen took them to Trutnov to the district police department. There they let them wait a quarter of an hour and then interrogated them separately. They asked where they had been, at whose house they had been, and what they had done there. They made Gábina Fárová breathe into a balloon that turned green twice, although she had not drunk any alcohol. Here is a segment of the transcript of the interrogation, which Gábina refused to sign:

> POLICE: How many people were at the Havels'?
> GÁBINA: About fifteen.

---

*A diminuitive for Gabriela.

P: Did you recognize anyone?

G: No.

P: What did you do all evening?

G: I chatted with a group of young people at Andrej Krob's house.

P: That was the first time you had met them?

G: Yes.

P: Do you know any of their names?

G: No.

P: How did you like the music they were playing there?

G: Well, it was very nice. Why?

P: Was it a group?

G: No, records.

P: "The Plastic People," does that mean anything to you?

G: That's English for people made out of plastic, right?

P: Well, yeah, that too, but the group, do you know them?

G: The group? No.

P: And did you hear any commotion last night?

G: Yes.

P: Starting when?

G: Maybe around six, I don't know.

P: And you were at this Havel's house after midnight?

G: We weren't at Havel's house.

P: You're babbling again, because you just said you were at Havel's.

G: That's not true. I . . .

P: Listen, how long were you at Havel's and who was there with you?

G: I have a question. Do you think you can answer it?

P: Go ahead, please.

G: Am I required to answer you? By what right am I here and according to what law are you interrogating me?

P: Look, I know more about that kind of thing than you do. Are you going to be stubborn?

G: And even if you wrote that deposition a thousand times,
I wouldn't sign it for you.

P: You can't write?

G: I can . . . but I have my reasons.

P: May I know what those reasons are?

G: I'm in the right. I was arrested because I didn't have
my citizens' identity card, which I haven't been issued.
You can give me a fine for trespassing in a field, but
you have no right to interrogate me about what I did last
night. . . .

This is only an abridged extract from the interrogation; Betina Landovská endured a similar one. Meanwhile their parents—Pavel Landovský and [Anna and Libor]—were standing outside on the
sidewalk. When the children did not return for lunch at one o'clock,
the parents had gotten frightened and begun to search for them. Some
people told them that the police had abducted them, so they went to
Trutnov. There they were told that the police had the right to hold
their children for up to twenty-four hours without giving them any
report. The parents filed a complaint against the action of the police
department: the police's step was illegal; the police had violated a
whole range of binding regulations. The whole police action had been
directed toward obtaining by illegal means further information about
the private lives of the children's parents and their friends. In their
complaint, the Faras wrote:

> *Our child has been seriously traumatized by this event. Since
> Monday, October 3, she has been bed-ridden, nauseous, and sub-
> ject to extreme mood swings, when not sleeping listlessly. As the
> doctor we called states on the patient referral form, ''It is necessary
> to consider this state as a reaction to a depressive situation.''
> Considering that our daughter was sick and unfit for normal life
> for seven days due to the illegal steps taken by these officers, the
> behavior of the police must be described as criminal acts injuring
> the health of others (according to Paragraph 221 of the criminal*

code) and abuses of the authority entrusted to a public officer (according to Paragraph 158 of the criminal code).

The parents enclosed the doctor's testimony, and of course nothing happened.

24 ▪ How the Charter Was Prepared

A team wrote the text of the Charter. A manifesto protesting the suppression of human rights in Czechoslovakia, the document announced the creation of Charter 77, an association of dissidents "bound together by the will to devote themselves, individually and collectively, to the respecting of civil and human rights in our country and the world . . ."

At first glance, the formulations of Professor [Jan] Patočka and Václav Havel predominate in the wording. The Charter, however, has no single author. Everyone who signed it is considered as having an equal share in its authorship. In 1935, Jan Patočka wrote: "Philosophy reaches a point where it no longer suffices to pose questions and answer them, both with extreme energy; where the philosopher will progress no further unless he manages to make a decision."

Patočka was my professor; I attended his lectures in phenomenology. His later lectures were on ancient philosophy. For him, Plato and Aristotle were not theoreticians in the modern sense—i.e., scholars who had collected a lot of knowledge and ideas—but people who, so to speak, had their hands around the throat of the basic, vital necessity of coming to terms with life's demand that *we do not know how to act, and we must act,* that no one will relieve us of this responsibility, and that we may not try to lighten this burden for ourselves. Patočka's own concept of existence is formulated as "living in truth." The professor spoke about the soul, and in all our university courses, no one had spoken about that before—about the soul, which surpasses itself, expends itself, and exposes itself. He even spoke about the need for a new spirituality, for a *spiritual* conversion, because otherwise we would not be able to solve the problems of this world. Not only students attended, but also professors from the philosophy department. These lectures were events or, better put, "happenings." The professor arrived and stood before us. He never sat during his lectures; he always paced and gesticulated. He digressed slowly, as if he were collecting a river from many streams, and sometimes while I followed the thrilling flow of his thought it seemed to me he might lose his way, but he never did. He always returned straight to the heart of the matter. It was as if he was searching for and finding something already said somewhere else, something he merely translated out of its meta-language, where it lay deposited in human memory forever. Once, I remember, a lecture of his did not work out. He started over several times from the beginning, then waved his hand, apologized, and left.

When they threw him out of the philosophy department*—it was like throwing out Kant—a few brave people were found who loaned their apartments for the so-called black university. Professor Patočka continued to lecture, although there were fewer of us now. Ten, fifteen people would enter the apartment, and there would already be people sitting next to each other on the floor. I was always afraid he would call on me, because he had the habit of staring at someone and saying, "And what about you, my friend, what do you think about this problem?" As far as I remember, no one has ever intimidated me more than he did. When he addressed me, I froze up like a beetle that had been caught and made a fool of myself. I always tried to sit out of his range to avoid being invited into the discussion. But at the same time I longed to sit close to him. When he lectured, you had the feeling you were participating in the creation of his ideas. In my studies in the late 1950s and early 1960s, I had never experienced anything else like it. No one else lectured off the cuff. All the others read their

---

*From the Communist takeover in 1948, Patočka was virtually forbidden to teach, with the exception of a brief period from 1968 to 1972.

lectures and sat behind a table. What they recited to us was nonsense, and we had to repeat it.

The last lecture the professor gave was in an apartment on Kampa Island. Beneath the window, the Čertovka (Devil's Stream) was flowing. He lectured on the topic "The Spiritual Man and the Intellectual." It was like a consecration, and I understood what an intellectual is, and that I never wanted to be one. I understood what is was within me that struggled against being an intellectual, and that this inner conviction would always prevent me from straying, even if I were to consider it. It always put me back on the path where I belonged. Until this inner voice speaks, there may seem to be a place I could stray to, but in reality there is not. Like my parents, Professor Patočka represented the European spirit to me. People like him are dying out. Today there is almost no one among us who speaks three languages and reads the poetry of Baudelaire and Hölderlin in the original; there is no one who can answer questions about philosophy, history, and mathematics all at the same time. There may never again be people like him, because since his day people have become so senselessly specialized that they cannot see the whole picture. Their inability to see the whole picture and to become whole themselves is the beginning of tragedy for humanity.

I remember how the professor stood with us at one end of Kampa Island, where the Čertovka branches off from the Vltava to circle the island. Behind us was the church of St. John Na prádle (At the Laundry). It was after the lecture, during which it had struck me that the professor had talked about something we had all known for a long time, but that only he could articulate. We did not arrange a date for another meeting. I did not know how long he intended to be silent, and I did not dare ask. I stammered out a thank you for the lecture and he shook my hand. His hand was warm, living. On Kampa Island, autumn was beginning; I don't know whether it was October or November. The professor was already someone else, or maybe more than ever himself; another current had taken him up. He no longer had time to give lectures, and he had also ceased to have contact with some people.

I walked across the Legie (Legion) Bridge toward the National Theater, and I thought to myself that Professor Patočka resembled Plato. He went into internal exile and created his work. I did not suspect he had already decided to be like Socrates, that he had applied philosophy to everyday life and resolved to dedicate himself to serving. He left his students in order to give them the most important and greatest lesson—by his action, and by the death that followed.

When he died, I thought that it was a pity he had chosen to serve the cause of human rights. I thought he could have continued to lecture, write essays, and philosophize. But later I realized he could not have. I know now that only service can teach the most essential truth. When the time comes for action, nothing else can take its place. Action shifts all thought to another place, as if action gave thought new, still virgin soil, clean water, and blood. The Charter was the pinnacle of Patočka's life, as it was Havel's. But the latter still had to carry the idea further; he was morally bound to that to which the professor by his death had bound us all. For years, people asked Václav, "Why don't you write plays? Why don't you drop politics? You're only wasting time you could devote to writing."

I think that each of us is made differently, and that a writer must above all lead an authentic life, one he had created himself. If a political power opposes the way the writer chooses to create his life, the writer has no choice but to confront that power. A good writer always senses when something ought to happen and when it is necessary to see a thing through. From time immemorial, the best writers have been prophets, who have foreseen the future in their works. This is related to the ancient principle, well known in Plato, of the care of the soul as an attempt to reach clarity, to live *in* examination and *according to* examination and to be responsible to that examination. In his treatise "The Meaning of a Pact with the Devil," Patočka has the following about the universal sense of responsibility:

It is a sense of solidarity in participation and in truth, based on what makes these possible: human destiny. What then does this responsibility mean in a universal sense? To submit oneself to judgment, and to the law, and to a universal, authentic society. To want to be judged, knowing of one's complicity in everything. To want to take up and redeem one's share of the universal cruelty. Not to want to escape into a realm of privacy, games, and esthetics. To want to take part in universal justice as being the only state in which a soul like this—i.e., an existence whose Being is an up-swing out of decay—can exist.

Professor Patočka's concept of responsibility shifted in the direction of rationality—toward living in truth. I cannot leave out another quote, this time from his teacher [Edmund] Husserl, who in *The Crisis of European Sciences and Transcendental Phenomenology* seems to have answered the question directly and given Patočka his blessing. It too is a prophetic text:

The development of the future *is the business of the* living, *for their continuous creation forms the future. The future, however, is born from an unending process that is characterized by a repeated resuscitation of the spirit of dead philosophers. The future grows by appropriating works that have descended from their original meaning, i.e., from the meaning as formed by earlier thinkers, who may have departed this world as individuals, but who have a philosophical effect on the present that lasts and lasts.*

What sort of historical reflection should a philosopher of the present engage in—a philosopher who lives in an environment that is present and alive, who is no doubt certain of his free will, certain he is called to his task, but who acknowledges that philosophy is threatened by this presence? His reflection should undoubtedly have the character of radical responsibility playing itself out in his person, but acquiring nonetheless the character of communal responsibility of the entire contemporary philosophic community. [Translated by Caleb Crain]

Husserl wrote these words in the 1930s, but they may be more relevant today than when they were written. The historical situation has changed, and the contemporary state has metamorphosed. Today, the country where both these thinkers lived directly invites philosophy to set about the task of responsible thinking—to be, in fact, philosophy. Only in Europe did the intention to live in truth arise, and only here did this conviction develop in an intellectual continuum. Surely it is no accident that this conviction took root in the Czech lands in the 1970s, and that it is the philosophy of Václav Havel.

Professor Patočka collected signatures for the Charter with his old friend Zdeněk Urbánek as chauffeur. Whenever he returned out of breath from some fifth floor apartment, he was heard to say, "He didn't sign; he'll be coming to hell." Many of his friends disappointed him.

Landovský collected signatures with Jiří Němec. A thorough-going agnostic and a thorough-going Catholic—what a pair! They drove through the monasteries and nunneries, where, according to Pavel, they said, "We'll cross our fingers for you, but the papal synod does not allow us to mix in political affairs."

The Charter was Havel's baby, whether he admitted it or not. He himself visited people he assumed could take the risk, but if people turned up who had decided to sign of their own accord, he would try to talk them out of it. He would point out that they had jobs or children. Right at the outset, he announced that he would ask everyone who might be seized and questioned to tell the authorities they had received the text of the Charter from him. Věra Jirousová dissuaded a couple of divorced graphic designers with children from signing. Professor Patočka decided he should not accept signatures from students. He said that sometimes it was harder to pass exams than to sign something and get thrown out of school for political reasons, and that no one should sign the text who was not yet eighteen years old.

25 ▪ The Three Kings,* 1977

On the evening of January 5, the first round of collecting signatures for the Charter ended. Each of the signatories had signed a small piece of paper, and there were 242 pages of these in all. The exact text of the document had to be sent to the signatories by mail, so they would have it on hand. Zdeněk Urbánek wrote the addresses on envelopes containing the text of the first Charter document as Václav dictated them. They worked long into the night and Vašek was tired, so Zdeněk sent him home. Havel lived at the foot of a hill on U dejvického rybníčku Street, which was only five minutes from Zdeněk's house on Střešovická Street. Zdeněk continued addressing envelopes until morning with the help of his girlfriend, Markéta Hejná.

They agreed that Vašek would return at nine o'clock in the morning; Landovský would follow in his Saab; and as soon as the stamps were stuck on the envelopes, they would begin to distribute the Charter. First they would have to drop the 242 envelopes for the signatories into various mailboxes, in sets of ten if possible, so that at least a few of the packages would make it, in the event some of the mailboxes were being watched. Then, as a two-member delegation, they had to deliver Charter 77 to the Federal Assembly and the federal government. The document was already abroad, but with instructions about the timing of its release to prevent it from being publicized before the Czechoslovak government had a chance to act, or allow a dialogue to be held.

Václav telephoned Pavel Landovský in the morning to tell him that he could not come by car, because a mysterious troublemaker had slashed the brake lines of his Mercedes the night before. He said he would walk. He arrived at Urbánek's house, bringing Ludvík Vaculík

---

*A reference to Twelfth Night or Epiphany.

with him, because Ludvík had come to visit Havel unaware that today was the big day. They worked on the envelopes together at Zdeněk's house, and from time to time short salvos of laughter burst out of them. Everyone was already very tired, and the laughter increased their energy. Perhaps the unconscious awareness that it was a historic moment created a slightly hysterical mood. Markéta Hejná, who was licking stamps and sealing envelopes in the next room, later testified in her interrogation that she heard nothing but laughter. When they were all interrogated, they were asked repeatedly what they had been laughing about, but they wouldn't have been able to answer even if they had wanted to.

When Pavel Landovský arrived at 64 Střešovická Street, he noticed that several odd Škoda MB cars were parked outside. He told his friends inside about them. They looked out the window, but they didn't believe him. Secret police assigned to surveillance duty were always given powerful cars such as Zhigulis* or Chevrolets, but this time the police must have run out of them. As our heroes were soon to learn, for this job the police had brought in a few moderately beat-up Škoda MBs that the Ministry of the Interior had bought and installed with brand-new 1,300-cubic-centimeter race-car engines.

No sooner had the final envelope been sealed and the last stamp licked then the troika of Vašek, Ludvík, and chauffeur Pavel sallied forth. Landovský drove a short distance before he realized the MBs were following them. Then the wild chase began. In the Hanspaulka Villa Quarter, Landovský tried to give them the slip, but he realized that they had "souped up cars." At a bend in the road near the pub Na Staré Faře [At the Old Parish], the police cars collided behind them. Pavel didn't even look back, but floored it. This gained them a little time, and Pavel spotted a mailbox below Hanspaulka. Vašek managed to stuff about forty envelopes inside. Later, to everyone's astonishment, these envelopes arrived at their destinations—the police had been so completely caught up in the chase that they hadn't noticed.

---

*Russian cars.

At the next intersection the MBs drove in a left-right cross; they always drove up from two sides, and then one followed the perpetrators and the other sped off to the next intersection, where the pursuit was probably headed, and where it would take over the pursuit. The actor and playwright Pavel Landovský will continue the narration:

"There were ten or twelve cars assigned to the case, I didn't count. Originally they must have planned surveillance, that's why there were so many. You don't realize they're following you because there's always a different car behind you. There were always three or four behind me and it wasn't surveillance, it was a chase. I drove like the devil and they chased us. At the intersection where Gymnazijní Street ends, Pevnostní Street begins, and Glinkova intersects, they blocked us in. I had to stop. I reached over and locked the car doors so they couldn't get in. They tugged on the doors and beat their knuckles against the hood and roared, 'In the name of the law, in the name of the republic, open up!' During the chase, they must have received an announcement from the dispatcher saying that we probably wanted to blow up the Castle, so they were banging away dementedly. Vašek was sitting next to me and he said, 'What a pretty beginning for our fight for human rights.'

"They were beating against the hood and roaring and Vašek advised me, 'Land'ák, open up, these gentlemen might actually be from the police department.' And I said, 'I'm going to wait a little longer, until they beat their knuckles to a bloody pulp; right now all this banging would end up in our faces.' But when it looked like they were going to break the windows, I unlocked the car, hooked my elbows around the steering wheel, and roared like an ox. And then I saw—I'm not lying to you—the soles of Vašek's shoes. They sucked him out, as if with a vacuum cleaner. Vaculík was sitting in back, and he flew after him like a log tossed into the fire, and they shoved the two of them into different cars. They grabbed the bags left behind in the back seat. They were the kind of bags they use in Moravia when they're collecting sod, burlap bags with a wooden handle; Vaculík must have brought them from Brumov, and they were full of Charters. I had about thirty or forty in my bag, and Václav had the rest in his. We also had the pages of signatures with us. I'd been given orders to fetch them from Kohout in Hradčany, where he'd hidden them in a hole. I rang the doorbell, he didn't say a word, he only gesticulated and gave me the sack. I no longer remember why we had the signatures with us, maybe so we could show them if we were lucky enough to be let in to the federal assembly. Maybe it was just as well. When they took everything from us, they knew at once what was going on. Those little pages were what fascinated them the most; they kept looking at them like they were witchcraft.

I kept screaming, hooked onto the steering wheel, and people were already starting to mob together, and somebody shouted, 'Hey look, Landovský is making another film.' There was this kid with a video-camera there; we called him Visconti, and this Visconti, as you'll see in a minute, played an important role. I refused to get out of the car, explaining that I had not parked and secured the vehicle according to state regulations. In the end they saw they would have to break my arm, so they let me alone and simply sat down next to me. They ordered me to drive behind the others. We drove in line along the Chotkova highway, and this boy, this young State Security guy sitting next to me, suddenly put his pistol back in his pocket and said, 'You dope, you guys fucked it up. We've been on alert since two in the morning. These guys are gonna blow you to smithereens.' I told him that we were only bringing letters to an institute, and he said that since two o'clock everything had been abuzz. I asked where he was from, and he said from the airport, from the antidrug and antimoney-changer squad. Maybe they had learned from *L'Humanité* that they were going to run an article on the Charter, so in the morning when they saw Vašek milling around his car, they slashed his brake lines. We drove along the Chotkova highway, which has those high cement walls as you go up the hill, and I said to him, 'So look, either you promise you'll bring me toothpaste and a carton of Sparta cigarettes in jail, or I'll drive into the wall and fuck the car up. We'll both die, but you first, because the wall is on your side.'

"He promised to bring them, and he actually showed up later with half a carton of Spartas; he said he couldn't lay his hands on any more than that.

"On Bartholomew Street, I parked in a no-parking zone and then refused to get out of the car because I had to park the car correctly. They said, 'Here you can do anything as long as you do what we say, so get that into your head.' But I got angry; I continued to play Švejk.* They went through the car from top to bottom, took my bag away from me, and tried to spook me. They told me to leave the keys in the car, that nothing could happen to it here because they were in charge of everything. They examined me; this traffic cop showed up with a balloon, and the State Security guy told him to continue with the examination: he wanted me to stick the balloon in my mouth to check my blood-alcohol level. I said, 'Mr. Examiner, I refuse; this gentleman is not wearing gloves. Please read the regulations. This will not do.' The copper slunk away and came back with mittens, because he couldn't find any gloves."

Such was the fate of all three kings—i.e., Landovský, Havel, and Vaculík—and shortly, Zdeněk Urbánek, too. No sooner had he lain down to rest than someone rang the doorbell. Zdeněk opened the door, and there were two secret agents escorted by two uniformed policemen. Zdeněk defended himself and did not let them into the house. "You don't have the right," he said, but they replied that they did have the right and would supply him with a warrant from the district attorney's office, filled out, stamped, and approved, within twenty-four hours. After an hour of shouting things like "Give us your materials!" they took Markéta and Zdeněk to Bartholomew Street in a Tatra 603. The interrogation, with occasional breaks, lasted until five in the afternoon. Zdeněk refused to give them any of his "materials," so they decided to take them themselves. Searching Zdeněk's room alone took until midnight, and then he had to return with them to Bartholomew Street. They released him at about two in the morning.

---

*See note on p. 8.

They took about a hundred letters Zdeněk had received from Václav. Then, at Havel's house in Hrádeček, they seized about the same number of letters to Havel from Zdeněk and, of course, many other things that did not fall into the category of what they called "materials."

After nearly identical experiences, Vaculík, Havel, and Landovský met again that night in front of the infamous tile-covered building* in Bartholomew Street. The Saab was still in the same place. Landovský loaded up his friends and drove them home. Then he went home too. During the rest of the night, they learned that every international radio station on the air was talking about the Charter. The telephones rang. At six-thirty in the morning, the three kings were rounded up and brought to Bartholomew Street again. The authorities didn't quite know what to do with them, but nonetheless they held them until four in the afternoon. Then something happened to them, repeated in nearly the same form in all three cases. Pavel tells the story:

"At about four o'clock they suddenly came and said very officially, 'Follow the escort!' So I followed them. They brought me into a gigantic room, where there were thousands of light bulbs and reflectors. There was a T-shaped table and twelve or fifteen State Security guys standing in a circle in the Uruguayan position—hands over balls.†
On a ladder in the right corner was Visconti with his camera. I stood there, agog, watching for whatever was going to happen next, and suddenly one of them ordered, 'Stand beside your luggage.' And I looked, and there on the end of the T-shaped table was my bag, my crumpled old sack. I went up to it; the light and all the reflectors were shining on me, and Visconti was shooting. 'Empty the contents,' the next order rang out. I started to pull things out of the bag and they ordered, 'Name the contents.' So I named them: 'Thirty copies of Charter 77, . . . string, . . . pocketknife, . . .' and suddenly I came

---

*The headquarters for State Security, and where preliminary and pretrial detention cells were located.

†An untranslatable joke. Landovský is punning on *urukvajec*, the Czech word for "Uruguayan." In Czech, *u* means "near" or "at," *ruka* means "hand," and *vajec* literally means "eggs," but is slang for "testicles."

across a little cellophane envelope with aspirin inside. I tore it open, tossed the pills down my throat, and roared into the camera, 'I give my life for the fatherland!' They started to guffaw and the whole production was shot to pieces. They knew it was aspirin; they had inspected the bag quite thoroughly; after all, they had scripted the whole thing. Vašek had a similar scene with Visconti; the script was the same, only in the middle stood Colonel Dvořák, who was the top banana there."

"Did Vašek also make a joke out of it?" I asked Pavel.

"He has a different brand of humor. He has certain time-wasters, so that he can get things straight in his mind, if he needs to. When he talks about it, you'll see he watches the State Security guys as if they were characters in a play; he remembers absolutely everything, a movement, an index finger, ... He's at home in it, and he observes these people much more closely than they observe him. He's a keen judge of people and he can tell what they're thinking.

"He also has a way of starting a debate and dragging them into it," Pavel says.

"When you read Solzhenitsyn or when you read about how they treated people here in the 1950s, doesn't it seem like all of this is something out of Švejk?"

"People have to go with the situation they're given. If somebody today were to take it the way they took it in the 1950s, he'd be trembling with horror, and they'd be able to get him on his knees with methods that were actually rather mild. You have to get your bearings, see what's going on. And now and then you have to make a stink, to see how far you can go."

"I've always admired that Vašek, Vaculík, you, Magor, and others are able to hold out on the edge. To stand there like a beacon, signaling how far it's possible to go right now. And trying again and again to find firm ground further on or to extend what you have. To always take the risk that as the first, you might, during a larger tremor, be the first to fall into the abyss."

"You see, decent people would shit their pants in fear. And they

said Vašek was a decent person. He's tough and he's a good guy, and his whole life has been a conscious preparation for what happened."
"He was preparing the whole time for the revolution?"
"Ever since the fight over *Tvář*, that's what it was all about."
"I think it was all about that long before."
And at this point, Pavel laughed, the way he and the rest of God's children know how to laugh. Those who do not calculate, but simply live. He said: "I told him once, 'When they give you the Austrian State Prize for European Literature, go to Austria, go for at least a year.'
"And he said, 'I can't.'
" 'And why not?'
" 'My daddy told me I couldn't.' "

As his mother wrote in her diary, during the German occupation, little Václav admired the German regulations and decorations. There were nationalist emblems everywhere, and he ran after the German soldiers in the street. His father and mother were patriots, and they decided they had to discuss this with their son. It was not a simple thing to instruct a child in patriotism at the time; the child might mention it in school, in the park, or on the tram. As soon as his father set about the task, he decided he would lay out the essentials of the political landscape for his son, tell him how things stood, and swear him to secrecy. He spoke to him about it man to man, but hardly had he begun to explain who the Germans were, when he was peremptorily interrupted. Vašek declared he did not need any explanation, because his friend Mandík had already told him everything. This of course did not relieve his mother's anxieties; she didn't trust Mandík's explanation. Once when Václav was at home alone with her, she made him promise he would never tell anyone about what they were going to talk about. They sealed the promise with a handshake and a kiss. Then his mother described the horrors of the concentration camps, the massacres, and the wrongs the Germans committed against whole peoples. She named noted persons, friends and acquaintances, who had been victims. Václav listened to it all with great interest, and a quarter of an hour later, he summoned his mother mysteriously and whispered in her ear, even though they were alone on the floor, "Mommy, what was the Austro-Hungarian flag like?"

And Pavel adds: "Old Mr. Havel, a very correct gentleman, told him, 'Vašík, here is where you should be.' And here he stayed. His whole family upbringing was right, and this republic can rub its hands in glee that it is lucky enough to have him here."

26 ▪ What Rudé Právo Had to Say About It

I cannot refrain from quoting the official reaction to Charter 77, which was published in *Rudé Právo* on January 12, 1977.

> . . . *In this category too belongs the latest pamphlet, the so-called Charter 77, which a group of people from the class of the bankrupt Czechoslovak reactionary bourgeoisie and also from the class of bankrupt organizers of the 1968 counterrevolution delivered to Western agents as instructed by anti-Communist and Zionist headquarters.*
>
> *It is a case of antigovernmental, antisocialist, antipopulist, and demagogic libel, which coarsely and deceitfully slanders the Czechoslovak Socialist Republic and the revolutionary achievement of the people. Its authors fault our society because life here does not suit their bourgeois and elitist ideas.*
>
> *These pretenders who despise the people, the people's interests, and the people's chosen representative bodies arrogate to themselves the right to represent our people. They ask for "dialogue with the political and state authorities," and even want to play the role of some kind of "mediator in various conflict situations." The pamphlet mentions the existence of socialism in only one instance—in*

the name of the republic. It comes out of a cosmopolitan position, out of the class position of the overthrown reactionary bourgeoisie, and rejects socialism as a social system. . . . . They are concerned with certain "rights and freedoms" that would enable them once again to freely organize antistate and antiparty activities, propagate anti-Sovietism, and try again to destroy the power of the socialist state. . . . . This time the bourgeois agents have been indiscreet, and they refer to several names with which the reactionary pamphlet is connected. In a political sense, it is a jolly ragbag of human and political castaways. Among them are V. Havel, a man from a family of millionaires and a confirmed antisocialist; P. Kohout, faithful servant of imperialism and its experienced agent; J. Hájek, bankrupt politician, who under the slogan of neutrality wanted to dissociate our government from the society of other socialist countries; L. Vaculík, author of the counter revolutionary pamphlet "Two Thousand Words"; V. Šilhán, the puppet of a group of counterrevolutionary forces; J. Patočka, reactionary professor who has dedicated himself to the cause of anti-Communism; P. Drtina, spokesperson of the pre-February (1948) reaction and bourgeois minister of justice; V. Černý, notorious reactionary, famous for his statement about the "lampposts" from which the followers of socialism were to be hanged in 1968; anarchist and Trotskyite individuals of the likes of Uhl; organizers of the sadly famous K231* and KAN†; those who want to abuse religion for reactionary political purposes; and others who have been rightfully condemned in recent years for substantial antigovernment activity. . . . . In its history, the revolutionary movement has known more than one Mrva** who for blood money became a toady, informer, and flunky betraying the interests of the people. The

---

*An organization of former political prisoners.
†The Club of Committed Non-Communists.
**A police informer, named after an agent, Mrva, killed in the 1890s by members of the Prague progressive movement. Now used as a vulgar expression for someone who has spoiled everything.

international reactionary movement has depended on him and those like him for its defense throughout its history and today as well. . . . Socialism, however, is not frightened by atomic black-mail and is surely no coward before the scribblers of reactionary pamphlets.

The government and its representative, the ministry of the interior, in fact declared war against the 242 signers, as if what was involved was a conspiracy that threatened to overthrow the regime, chop off the heads of all its representatives, and introduce a new system in the country. They didn't know what kind, but they knew it would not be socialism, because they equated themselves with socialism. They were socialism, and therefore whatever anyone had against them, he had against socialism, and could be condemned for it. They demonized the conspiracy and attempted to frighten its adherents. In the first few days after the announcement of the Charter, they rounded up the signatories at work or at home, drove them to Bartholomew Street or the local police department, screamed at them, threatened them, and threw them out of their jobs. They took their passports, hunting per-mits, telephones, and driving licenses. In short, they unleashed a hell of intimidation. The Charter spokespeople* spent many hours in inter-rogations every day. After the interrogations, in the evening and at night, they met at Havel's house on U dejvického rybníčku Street, a dead-end street, running along the train line that went from Prague to Most. The apartment was on the second floor. There were houses only on one side of the street, and they had small yards. It was peaceful and quiet, but it would have been more peaceful and quiet if the Havels hadn't lived there. Throughout the seventies, a State Security car was parked in front of the house. The crew inside was rotated regularly, and sometimes the car was also switched. By the end of the seventies, guards stood in front of the apartment door. They even

---

*The first three chosen to represent the Charter as spokespeople were Havel, Jiří Hajek, and Jan Patočka. See *Disturbing The Peace* (pp. 134–135) for a discussion of how they were chosen.

installed a table and two small chairs in the hallway and set up a kind of an office there.

The apartment contained a hall, where pictures by Saudek predominated, and a pretty, tasteful, and colorful kitchen, which had a dining area and a balcony. Original artwork hung on the walls. The Havels are very fond of paintings, and so in their house there are even originals in the toilet and the bathroom, many of them prints. In the living room, which was connected with the study, my favorite was a portrait of a woman by Béda Dlouhý. I remember exactly where it was hanging, just as I remember where Vašek hung the portrait of Mikuláš Medek in the bedroom. These two paintings are among Vašek's favorites, and he brought them with him to the Castle, where he hung them in the room where he received visitors and met with his advisers and cabinet.

In his childhood, Václav loved to draw and paint. It is a pity this book is not in color, because some of his paintings have been preserved. When Václav and Ivan were young, the painter Milén painted a portrait of them at Havlov. Vašek enjoyed engaging him in professional conversation.

"What kind of pencil do you use?" he asked. "I've got one like it, or at least similar. And this is pretty paper."

One lovely evening on an observation deck which looked out over the countryside, Milén remarked aloud that it would make a beautiful painting. Václav looked at the countryside, and said, "I've tried to do the countryside too, but it didn't work out."

Milén liked Vašek's paintings very much. His mother, who was learning to draw and whose hobby and greatest entertainment was painting, consciously avoided instructing her son, so that he could paint according to his childhood fantasies for as long as possible. They went by the Souček gallery in Prague, where a Nejedlý was displayed at a price of 60,000 crowns. Vašek was offended by the "scribbling." He said that for one thing, it was a waste of good paper, and for another, it was a terribly large amount of money.

Apparently he was decisive in his opinions, and his younger brother tried to accommodate him. One New Year's Eve, when they were attending a cabaret program in the Great Hall of the Lucerna Palace, Vašek was very engrossed and did not want to go home. He cried that he wanted to stay. His mother turned to Ivan, whom she noticed was tired, and said, "Let's go home, shall we?"

Ivan looked at his older brother and in his good-heartedness replied, "Whatever Véna wants."

Sometimes he wanted to be a painter and an owner of apartment houses; at other times a businessman and a professor of natural sciences and astronomy. Ivan always insisted on being a mechanical engineer.

In the apartment on U dejvického rybníčku Street, the furniture was custom made according to the architect's design specifically for the apartment. They were polished, solidly made pieces. The furnishings of Hrádeček suited my taste better, and then the furnishings of the apartment on the embankment. It pleases me that the Havels are able to part with things they no longer enjoy. Normally, the only things that get replaced in a marriage are ripped sheets and hand towels. Usually it ends the same way it begins, but with more junk. In the apartments of my older friends and colleagues, I often see the sectional furniture of the 1950s and 1960s. There is probably nothing uglier and more impersonal. Added to that are a few pieces of antique furniture bought later, when it started to become fashionable. When they were young, antique furniture was sold for peanuts in our country, and people chopped it up and used it as firewood. But that was when they hadn't started to like it yet. This is particularly the case with the generation of svazáks and young Communists. Their world, evoked by the slogan "The old way has to go," was decorated with fiberboard and Formica.

The Havels' apartment was decorated with a First Republic respectability, but also with an impersonality that didn't seem to suit them. It was not a fitting stage for the drama Václav lived. Only the paintings were modern and exciting—some even upsetting. The apartment was always in perfect order. The books and papers were as carefully arranged as the items in the bathroom or the kitchen. Olga took care of this. Some people might consider Vašek a pedant, but it strikes me as evidence of his rage for order and cleanliness. He keeps his papers in order, and he knows what he has where. As if a person could fend off confusion in the soul by arranging everything around him, or at least everything nearby. Or as if, when a person can no longer put the world in order, he at least puts his own household in order, his own small world.

On January 14, Vašek did not return from his interrogation. Every day he had been expecting he would be locked up, because of the three Charter spokespeople, he was the youngest and most mobile. He was the only one who had and drove a car, and at first glance he seemed to be the *spiritus agens*. Clearly, those in power had to lock up someone, and they wanted it to be someone whose imprisonment would paralyze the Charter and frighten the others. To lock up one of the older gentlemen, either Dr. Hájek or Professor Patočka, did not seem right. After a few days' hesitation, the lot fell to Havel. They yelled at him, saying they knew things that would surprise him, that they were through with the little games, and the working class would put him in his place. After the "Bankrupts and Pretenders" article was published in *Rudé Právo* attacking the Charter and reprinted in other newspapers, everyone knew jail was imminent. The campaign against him was formidable; in the fifties, this kind of public accusation would have meant the death penalty. In the seventies, however, the dog barked a great deal, but no longer bit quite as often. Of course, the days of Stalinist terror were still vivid in people's memories. The irrational fear that someone could disappear and never be seen again, or could be executed without any crime ever having been proved against him, is buried somewhere deep in our unconscious minds—the fear that anything could happen, that those in power cannot be controlled. Already, our children understand words for what they are, nothing more, without the shadows the words invoke in us. When, during the last few years, the authorities rounded them up at protest demonstrations and drove them off somewhere, it did not occur to them that they might never return, or that they might be liquidated. They accepted the situation with admirable humor and great bravery. Perhaps it was necessary to wait for a new generation to arise. I think that the apprentices and the high school students were the bravest, and their parents were afraid for them.

When Havel was imprisoned, the other two spokespeople, Patočka and Hájek, worked all the more intensively. Nor were the other Chartists and friends of the Charter idle. The regime's attempt at intimidation backfired. People were tired of everything being unendingly the same, and a new energy flowed out of the spirit of change. More than anything else, this change consisted of a sense of liberation. What had long been said in secret had now been spoken aloud, and people had signed their names to it. It was an authentic human act that had kicked open the door to a new realm. A society of people who shared the same opinions and the same fate sprang up. Among the signatories there reigned the purifying and exhilarating awareness that they had done what they should have done, and that they had done it together. Their signatures brought them closer together than if they had been working together in an office or business for years. Under the circumstances, the grievances and feuds of the past seemed petty. The intimidation and duplicity only strengthened this feeling of unity. The government and its far-reaching arm, State Security, had miscalculated. Even Dr. Husák had miscalculated. As long as he remained silent and did not react, nothing could change. But every action awakens a reaction. And any kind of reaction is good, because it involves movement. The same was true of the media campaign. The more vulgar and deceitful it was, the better. In 1989, the number of people who signed the declaration "Just A Few Sentences"* grew by the thousands after every slanderous article in the press.

On the morning of January 15, 1977, when Vašek still had not returned, Olga Havel telephoned the ministry of the interior. She was told that he had surrendered to the police. A few days later he was

---

*See Chapter 48.

charged with the crime of subversion of the republic for his open letter to Dr. Husák of April 1975 and as the chief initiator and organizer of Charter 77. For these alleged crimes he was being held in custody. Later it turned out that another pretext had to be found for his imprisonment, and therefore Havel's case was attached to the case of "Ornest and Co." They tried to find a connection between the Charter and the smuggling of texts by Czechoslovak authors to the Paris magazine *Svědectví*, to show, for example, that the text of the Charter had been smuggled via the same route. It would have suited their purposes to be able to link the two things and label them both "injurious to the republic's interests abroad."

Meanwhile, Professor Patočka kept writing. On January 7, 1977, he wrote the essay "What the Charter Is and What It Isn't." Later, this essay was revised and given the title, "On the Duty to Defend Oneself From Wrongdoing." In it, he wrote:

> *Therefore, let us consider this epoch in which it is possible to sign accords on human rights as a new stage in the historical process, as a stage whose significance is immeasurable. It involves a revolution in people's consciousnesses, in their behavior toward themselves and their neighbors, since the motives for their actions no longer lie exclusively in the domain of advantage and fear but instead in respect for what is higher in human beings, and take into consideration duty, the common weal, and the necessity to accept, in this sense, the burden of misunderstanding and certain risk.*

The professor wrote the first Charter documents by hand, in his small, scarcely legible handwriting, which later annoyed the executors of his literary estate for years. The poet Věra Jirousová, Magor's wife, copied the texts out on a typewriter because she could decipher his scribbling. She relates that the old gentleman was tired, but he could not stop to rest. They locked up Havel because he was young and strong, and day after day they dragged the two professors to twelve-hour-long interrogations.

Fanynka Sokolová, Professor Patočka's daughter, recounts in her hand-written memorial volume, which she dedicated to her father on July 1, 1977: "When men cry, it should not be kept secret. I heard you cry for the last time a few days before we parted. You were not well; you were lying down. We were speaking about the lives of philosophers. I babbled something about how they were usually a little at sea in our evil world. And you were silent. Then suddenly you said, 'You know, when William of Orange had that Spaniard murdered (I've forgotten the name you told me), no one said anything. And Spinoza, that Jewish dog,' you sobbed and turned to the wall, 'went and wrote on his door: *Ultimi barbarorum.*' For a long time you were silent before turning back to face me."

The last text he wrote was on March 8. It was titled, "What Can We Expect from the Charter?" A few days before his death, he wrote:

> *Many questioners go so far as to ask: Doesn't the Charter worsen our society's situation? Doesn't it cause more repression . . . ? Let us reply bluntly: yielding has never led to any improvement, but only to further worsening of the situation. The greater the fear and servility, the more the powerful have dared, are daring, and will dare. There is no way to diminish their pressure except to unsettle them, to make sure they see that injustice and discrimination will not be forgotten, that the waters do not close over their crimes. This does not mean a call for impotent threats, but for dignified, unintimidated, and truthful behavior in all situations, behavior which impresses simply by distinguishing itself from official behavior.*

The professor died several days later.* For many people, his funeral in the cemetery at the Church of St. Margaret in Břevnov was a defining moment. There the powerful showed themselves in their ugliest and most demonic aspect. A helicopter hovered over the ceme-

---

*He died as a result of an intensive police interrogation that lasted for many days.

tery, and race-car motors roared on the other side of the cemetery walls. It was impossible to hear the priest's words over the noise. Cops sat on the graves and the cemetery walls; with videocameras, they insolently shot close-ups of people crying. Later, they threw the people they videotaped out of school or got them fired from their jobs. Everyone who attended was filmed because they had installed cameras at the cemetery entrance. As I stood there among the graves, my anger grew, and I was paralyzed by the appalling realization that there are people in the world who have no respect for the dead, and who face to face with death are capable of performing these insulting theatrics. At that moment, something inside me was broken forever, and died. I knew I would continue to live in this country, but I vowed never to have anything to do with this regime, even if the regime itself should ever attempt to reach out to me. What I had known for a long time was here displayed in a concentrated, appalling scene. It was a nightmare, but it took place in daylight, while I was wide awake.

Patočka's cop, assigned to him since the 1950s, identified with Patočka so strongly that he had forced himself into an acquaintance of sorts with the professor and wanted to speak a few words over his grave. He felt like it was the final report he would be called upon to write about the professor as his surveillance agent, and that no one was better qualified to write it.

The funeral of the beloved professor was a shock for hundreds of people. It bound his students together. His death did not call forth deadly hatred—that was not in the order of things—but it laid the seeds for the death of the regime and Patočka's immortality. The following words are also taken from his essay "What Can We Expect from the Charter?":

> But it is none of our business to examine someone's conscience; only to observe and bear witness.
> But also to observe and bear witness to internal development. To affirm that people today once again know that some things exist that are worth suffering for! That the things worth suffering for

are also the things worth living for. Without this, what people call art, literature, and culture are sheer mechanical operations, which will never lead anywhere but from the office to the bookkeeping department and from the bookkeeping department to the office. We all know this today—in no small part thanks to Charter 77 and everything connected with it.

The state police dragged people into interrogations and interrogated them for hours. They were attempting to map out the landscape, so they were interested in absolutely everything. Věra Jirousová recalls that she and Jiří Němec instructed people in how to behave when their houses were searched and during interrogations. This information also began to circulate in samizdat, including legal advice. The advice of friends who had gone through the experience was invaluable. People chose various tactics. Those who could not manage to keep entirely silent talked about something else. It turned out, however, that there was rarely any subject the State Security agents could not exploit in one way or another, and the best alternative was total silence—either to refuse to answer, or to answer "No" or "I don't remember."

For me, the basic problem was always whether or not I saw the cops as human beings. If I saw humanity in them, I could succumb to the temptation of talking to them and trying to convince them of the truth of my position, or of our position. Very soon, however, I became convinced that I was dealing with people whose nature was so different that it was not worthwhile to try to convince them of anything. This helped me and made my life and my situation easier. It did not bother me if I seemed to them to be an idiot who remembered nothing, knew nothing, and was only waiting for them to find out that she was so foolish it would be impossible to collaborate with her. It amazed them that I had been able to write books that were published abroad, and that at such a young age I had such a bad memory, especially since I was well rested, as a housewife. I remember that Petr Pithart once told me, "You mustn't let them know that something matters to you, because that's what they'll go after. I once let slip that it mattered to me if my boy could go to school, and that was a mistake." They marveled at my indifference to the fate of those nearest me. They even reproached me for it. But it did not bother me at all that these monsters should think I too was a monster—scaly with different-shaped teeth and ears. In time I realized that they made short work of anyone who was haughty and who styled himself as an intellectual. People who tried to talk about something else were always scrutinizing the interrogators' questions and their own replies, trying to discover what pertained to what, why the interrogators asked what they asked, and whether their answers were cagey enough. They always found that there was something they shouldn't have talked about, and they had pangs of conscience and fear, even when the matter at hand was of no importance.

Of course, State Security was more apt to mistreat people who were young or less well known. In the absence of witnesses, they were free to abuse them physically. They treated people from the underground with particular cruelty, because they considered them to be some sort of subhuman species, against whom any crime was permissible. They were quite surprised when respectable professors and well-known writers stood up for the Plastics. But all the same, most of the Plastics were forced to emigrate, at least. Perhaps the greatest sadist they had there called himself Duchač, although who knows what his real name was. He mistreated Třešňák and Vratislav Brabenec [of the Plastics] until he drove them into exile. Věra Jirousová claims she got the better of him, by virtue of having been the only person shorter than he was and by acting silly. Duchač was a short, greenish-looking man, with a face like a goblin's. He was fighting it out with the big boys. The more conspicuous a man was, the more he went after him. Věra claimed she didn't understand politics; she told them she worked as a professional teacher, an expert in art history. For several hours, she lectured them on art history, until they decided she was so boring they had to throw her out. However, they repeatedly threatened that they would keep her case partially open so that they could jail her once her son Tobiáš had grown up. But when he grew up, she became pregnant again. It was interesting that they rarely locked up the mother of a small child. They were constantly taking into consideration how things might look to the outside world. Olga Havel during that time coined the maxim, "During an interrogation, don't tell them anything, not even the name of your dog."

Jirousová, Němec, little Tobiáš, and many other people were constantly on the run. They borrowed other people's apartments; they slept over at friends' houses. When Brezhnev visited the country, they were on the move; on May Day, October 28 (Czechoslovak Independence Day), and November 7 (the anniversary of the October Revolution in Russia), they always had to disappear, because if caught they would have been locked up for forty-eight-hour detention.* They wrote Charter documents and declarations, and made copies of samizdats, but in order to get anything done, they had to avoid their own homes.

27 ▪ First Imprisonment

In body, Havel endured his first imprisonment well, but in spirit, poorly. In letters number 138 and 139 of his *Letters to Olga*,† he writes about an incident that occurred during this imprisonment that he considers a key event in his life. I would not like to simplify his confession in any way, but I must recount what was involved. Like a number of other prisoners, Havel wrote a request for release from custody. He thought it would end up in a wastepaper basket somewhere, because his release did not of course depend on whether or not he wrote a request for it. Nonetheless, he wrote it. His interrogators

---

*The police could detain anyone for up to forty-eight hours without giving a reason. On state holidays, they locked up potential protestors to prevent them from disrupting the official ceremonies.

†Václav Havel, *Letters to Olga: June 1979–September 1982*, trans. Paul Wilson (New York: Alfred A. Knopf, 1988).

at once understood that Havel had lobbed a slow ball, setting them up for an overhead smash. They interpreted the request as a sign of weakness and an irresistible desire to get out of prison. They added a clause to the text of his request saying that he gave up the position of spokesperson for the Charter, persuading him that the Charter had already come to an end without him, that "the guys had given up." He believed their lies and regretted it all the more bitterly later. He soon recognized that he himself had first set in motion the process that led to his shame, and that the interrogators had seized the opportunity and exploited it as far as they could. The Czechoslovak Press Agency (ČTK) published the news that Václav Havel had given up everything and turned away from the Charter.

Ruzyně prison has a gate like a crematorium's. Dark, metal, gigantic. It slides shut the way the crematorium door closes behind a coffin when the corpse and the catafalque jolt away into gloomy eternity.* On the other side of the gate, Pavel Landovský was waiting with his Saab. It was May 20, 1977, and Vašek's first words were, "You gave up."

"I said, 'What are you talking about?'

"He sat next to me and said, 'So they lied to me. Please, can you take me to Hájek's right away?' He was terribly annoyed, because he felt he had failed. We all tried to talk him out of it, but it was no use. It makes sense; he was more honorable than this incident. He couldn't forgive himself for having fallen for what they told him. He got right back into the thick of it and wouldn't stop until they locked him up a second time, and then a third time."

When Havel was released, the Czechoslovak Press Agency published a statement that again attempted to discredit him. On May 21, 1977, Havel published a declaration in samizdat and other media explaining

---

*At the end of a funeral service in a Czechoslovak crematorium, the corpse, in an open coffin, trundles out of the room on a conveyor belt, and then a heavy metal door slides shut behind it. See Chapter 11 of *The Dean's December* by Saul Bellow for a description of a similar ritual in a Romanian crematorium.

the whole affair and why he had given up the position of Charter spokesperson until he was set free. On May 26, the Charter published a communication regarding the resignation of spokesperson Havel, and declared the Czechoslovak media's coverage of the incident as "a tendentious attempt to sully the name of an honorable person." Havel himself interpreted the incident as a trial in which he had not held his ground. Trials meet us on different levels, and we engage them on different levels. What for one person is a misunderstanding, easily rationalized and forgotten, is for another a crucial moment when he stands face to face with a central problem and does not hold his ground. Our crime was that we were not wary enough, that we let our guard down. And punishment soon followed. Punishment, too, comes to each of us at our own level. One person is punished by an exterior catastrophe, another only by pangs of conscience for betraying people whose fate was linked to his.

Later, in his *Letters to Olga*, Václav wrote that in this state of remorse, he felt best in prison and directed himself there. He understood imprisonment as a necessary punishment that would allow him to atone for his misdeeds. Writing about saints, Schopenhauer said that when an adept at sainthood detects even a small misdeed, he may experience it as a mortal sin. Those around him do not understand and attempt to talk him out of feeling guilty. As Václav says in the letter, there is no way to help this kind of person. He must help himself by realizing he stands face to face with God; he will then find himself directly in God's workshop. This would not have happened to Václav if he had not failed, while it mattered little whether he failed in the eyes of the world. In the end, he was thankful for it. He understood that if his request had ended up in the attorney general's wastebasket, he would not have reached this realization, which in the end he received as grace. This trial had nothing to do with earthly justice.

Zdeněk Urbánek—dear, tolerant Zdeněk, perhaps Vašek's closest friend and confidant, who never intervenes in other people's affairs unless he is asked to, and then does it so nobly and sensitively that you almost do not understand what you did wrong—said the following when I asked him how he saw Vašek's position and future at the time:

"For him it was less tolerable than any kind of long imprisonment. I tried to tell him how difficult his decision had been; I said that everyone surely understood what had happened; but beyond a certain point, I was not able to urge him to act more circumspectly than he acted. He acted according to his viewpoint and according to the viewpoint of what was best for everything in motion at the time (the Charter, the documents, and all that). He could not do anything but provoke the police to arrest him again. Naturally, they soon found something to charge him with. It's frightening, of course, when you hear such a person—someone you've known for a long time—declare that he's going to get himself caught. You could see from the expression on his face how badly he was taking it. No other solution presented itself; there was nothing else that would have been as risky but would not have led straight to prison. His way is to give an answer, without posing the question directly. He's a person who needs to discuss a difficult decision openly, but he alone bears the unconditional responsibility for his actions."

The Charter had not been destroyed, as Havel's prison interrogators had said. On the contrary, it was then living through what may have been the period of its greatest flowering. Many things happened that had been unthinkable before. People straightened their backs; they were no longer so weighed down; they ceased to be tired; and they had the feeling that life was worth the effort and that it was possible to do something, even if it involved a known risk. Citizens recognized that they were not as powerless and the government not as all-powerful as they had assumed.

28 ▪ Paragraph 112

In 1977, while still in prison, Václav Havel filed charges against Tomáš Řezáč, who had publicly slandered him in a radio program called, "Who is Václav Havel?" Newspapers and radio stations had of course received instructions to vilify Havel as part of the fight against the Charter and the Chartists. They would have preferred to condemn the Charter and sentence its spokespeople outright. But this was no simple matter, given the worldwide response to the Charter. Tomáš Řezáč's text was a compilation of slanders and accusations aimed at proving that Havel had always been (as "the son of well-heeled capitalist bastards") against socialism and had been trying to discredit, criticize, and liquidate it with the help off his friends, emigrés, and foreign imperialist spies and headquarters. The closing paragraph of the text gives a fair enough impression of what was involved:

> *Václav Havel will continue to strive to do his share in the political campaigns of the imperialist powers against Czechoslovakia, and by the same token, against other socialist countries as well. He will continue to preach about morality, about human rights, about personal freedom; he will disparage and slander the results of the efforts of millions of people. Furthermore, Havel has never abounded in "philanthropy," and his actual opinion about democracy and freedom is sufficiently well known. He has long since become estranged from the land we live in, which is his homeland too. His pro-imperialist opinions, though they are most cleverly veiled in diverse parables about "problems common to all people," no longer have any influence over anyone in our country. Our people—the workers, the cooperative farmers, and the working intelligentsia—have already drawn the correct conclusion, already know very well who this Václav Havel and his cohort are. On the*

question of where truth and falsehood lie, no one from abroad need enlighten us. Indeed, they made it sufficiently clear what they think of Mr. Havel and the other traitors when they unambiguously condemned their pamphlet Charter 77.

From prison, via his lawyer, Václav Havel requested the district attorney for Prague District 2 to sue for slander. In his request, he stated, among other things, the following:

> . . . *In this radio program and the published excerpts from it, Mr. Tomáš Řezáč has made several statements about me personally. Among them is the claim that I have been "supported by funds from American, West German, or other intelligence services." . . . Whatever he may think, this claim, in my opinion, constitutes the crime of slander according to Article 206 of the criminal code, because it fulfills both requirements of the legal definition; what is involved is an allegation which the author knows to be*
>
> *a) untrue, and*
>
> *b) likely to threaten, to a considerable extent, my reputation among my fellow citizens.*

All the same, he could not force Tomáš Řezáč to retract his slander, and so he used all the means available to him in the émigré media and in samizdat to defend himself and communicate the message that he was not a spy.

On January 25, 1977, Havel's father wrote the following in the "Addenda to the Daybooks," which Božena had begun to write:

> *The New Year, for the time being, has not brought me good cheer. Last night the television informed me that I—and maybe Váša too—was a "multimillionaire." Two days ago, almost twenty minutes of television time was devoted to my family. There was a list of what we owned at some point during the prewar period; two employees of Lucerna Palace talked about us; I also saw the gamekeeper's lodge and the barn at Havlov, representing our summer home, and other less interesting things, all presented*

as evidence of the kind of family the writer Václav Havel came from. This was part of the unusual campaign against Charter 77, a petition that asks only that human rights be respected according to an international agreement our government has signed and ratified. Váša (without my knowledge) worked on the preparation of this Charter. And so I too, as his millionaire father, have appeared in the newspapers, on the radio, and on television several times in connection with him, not of course in an entirely favorable light—even, at times, compromised by false conjectures. No one has mentioned that when Váša was ten years old, I was no longer paying the millionaire's tax, that after nationalization I had to give up what remained of my property, and that as of January 1, 1977, having a pension of only 751 crowns, I may ride Prague public transportation for free! This is mean-spirited and thoughtless propaganda. On the other hand, however, the Western radio stations and the newspapers—even in some Communist nations—mention Váša's name in a very favorable light, and the whole action which he is taking part in has had an unexpectedly favorable response. To be sure, the human rights covered by the 1975 Helsinki Accords are at stake. Indeed, for a Czech, both human rights and the truth are at stake, and they must be fought for, if they are to prevail.

It is bad for my nerves, however, to know that Váša is currently residing in Ruzyně prison, waiting to be prosecuted for "subversion of the republic." Anyone who knows Váša knows this would be against his views. He only wants human rights to be re-established, and he does not care whether it is the current government or another that re-establishes them. He is said, however, to be "in the service of Western imperialists." Let those who want to believe it, believe it. But I do not believe it, and I know that no one who knows him will believe it either.

When Vašek returned from prison in May 1977, his father recorded this in the "Addenda":

Klaus Juncker* called me and said that Váša's plays are being performed with great success not only in West Germany and Vienna, but also in England and Paris, and they will be performed elsewhere as well. The reviews are apparently excellent, but every critic emphasizes that he does not praise the plays because V. is in prison, but for his new, impressive dramatic style for contemporary subjects.

. . . Prokůpek welcomed Váša home by jumping on his lap and shouting, "Hello, Vášek!" When Vojta learned that his uncle Vašek was locked up, he immediately asked when he would be "opened."† . . . My heart has been slightly agitated, and my blood pressure has gone up, even though at home with my family I have been shielded from excitement and kept under Dr. Fučík's care. The writing of my memoirs has gone somewhat slower; at most I have written two hours daily, although I have been encouraged by Váša from prison and by family and friends with the word, "Write!"

In London, an interview with Václav Havel was published titled, "Breaking the Ice Barrier."** Havel stated that he had been charged with subversion of the republic because he had organized and signed Charter 77 and had been its spokesperson. Other subversive acts included his letter to Dr. Husák in 1975, his contacts abroad, his publication of samizdats, the royalties from abroad, and passing a manuscript of the memoirs of Dr. Prokop Drtina (one of Edvard Beneš's close collaborators and minister of justice in postwar Czechoslovakia) to the journalist Jiří Lederer. Lederer sent the manuscript of the memoirs to his friends in the United States. When his interrogators could not find any grounds for a case based on the Charter or the letter to Dr. Husák, they were stuck with the manuscript smuggling, and they initiated criminal proceedings according to article 112 of the criminal code—

---

*Havel's literary agent at his German publisher, Rohwolt.
†Prokůpek and Vojta are sons of Ivan Havel.
***Index on Censorship*, volume 7, no. 1, Jan/Feb 1978, pp. 25–28.

i.e., "actions injurious to the interests of the republic abroad." Havel's case was attached to that of Ota Ornest and company, and he, Ota Ornest, František Pavlíček, and Jiří Lederer were accused together. Meanwhile, the original charge also remained in effect. The group— brought together artificially by the government's lawsuit—was accused of having served Czech culture by attempting to publish the writings of authors who were illegally banned at home. Thus, State Security violated Article 19 of the International Covenant on Civil and Political Rights, which guarantees citizens the right to accept and distribute information and ideas of any sort freely, without regard to borders.

When a journalist asked whether he felt any hatred toward his interrogators, Václav confessed that instead he felt sorry for them. He was not even able to get angry at his friends, actors at the Theater on the Balustrade, who went on television and disparaged their co-worker and friend in order to accommodate their director and keep their place in the theater. As Mrs. Tomíšková from the Theater on the Balustrade related, "When the Charter broke out, *Funambules* 77 was in rehearsal. There were arguments in the theater about whether the name of the performance should be changed, or at least the '77' dropped, to avoid reminding anyone of the Charter. One day the door opened, and it was the manager accompanied by a stout policewoman. He told me to show them when Mr. and Mrs. Havel had been employed and to find Přeučil and Sloup. I warned them both at once, because I suspected that the police would want to get something ugly out of them. Sloup did it. Přeučil was already in hiding; he wouldn't answer the telephone. Whenever I called him, I had to ring three times first and then hang up. When I called the second time, his grandmother would answer, just to make sure. It was a frightful chase; they looked for him in the theater, at home. I knew he was at the drama school of the Academy of Performing Arts, so in my tennis shoes and sweater I ran off to warn him. He locked himself in the toilet and that's where they got him. I told him then, "Johnny, I'll be your witness that they drove you to it." That was when they had people signing the

Václav and Ivan in March 1944 on the way to grammar school.

Summer holidays in 1949 at Havlov: the emperor and his
advisers (Ivan Havel and Jan Škoda).

Sergeant Ivan Havel and Private Václav Havel on furlough
from the army, 1959.

Olga Šplichalová, later Václav's wife, in the Cafe Slavia, 1958.

Václav Havel at the beginning of the 1960s.

In New York, April 27, 1968, at a memorial demonstration
for Dr. Martin Luther King, Jr.; Havel with his agent
Klaus Juncker (left).

Libor and Anna Fára introduce Václav Havel to Arthur Miller
in their Prague studio in 1963.

Performance of *Audience* in Andrej Krob's barn at Hrádeček in 1978; Havel is playing the role of Vaněk.

A "Garden Party" at Hrádeček in the summer of 1976.

The meeting of writers at Hrádeček in September 1989. From the left: Petr Kabeš, Eda Kriseová, Jan Šabata, Hana Ponická, Václav Havel, and, sitting on the fireplace, Ludvik Vaculík reads from his latest feuilleton.

In the kitchen at Hrádeček in the 1960s.

In the kitchen at Hrádeček with Olga at the beginning
of the 1970s.

Olga and Václav Havel outside Pankrác prison right after he
was released midway through his sentence in May 1989.

The first negotiating session between the government and the
opposition: Václav Havel meets with Prime Minister Adamec
on November 26, 1989.

On a balcony overlooking Wenceslas Square on
November 21, 1989.

The demonstration on Letná Plain on November 26, 1989.

Václav Havel jangling keys as a symbol of the Velvet
Revolution on a balcony overlooking Wenceslas Square in
December 1989.

Returning from a meeting with the government during the euphoric days of the Velvet Revolution in December 1989.

On a flight to the United States.

In the Kremlin with Mikhail
Gorbachev and Jiří Dienstbier,
February 1990.

At the grave of Andrei
Sakharov in Moscow with his
widow Yelena Bonner.

With President George Bush at
the White House in
February 1990.

With the Pope at the Castle in
Prague on April 23, 1990.

Anticharter. They threatened to close the theater on us if the actors didn't sign. No one will ever know what might have happened if. . . ." Václav says that he feels anger only when innocent people are persecuted, people who make copies of samizdats and try somehow to help him or Czech culture. Injustice to him personally does not upset him.

On October 17 and 18, 1977, in the Prague municipal court, the chief session of the trial of the criminal case against O. Ornest, J. Lederer, V. Havel, and F. Pavlíček took place. For his alleged attempt to injure the republic's interests abroad, Havel was sentenced to the forfeiture of his personal freedom for fourteen months, with a conditional postponement of three years. The decision was upheld by the Supreme Court of the Czech Socialist Republic on January 12, 1978.

During his closing statement before the court, Havel defended himself by remarking that Prokop Drtina, whose manuscript he was accused of smuggling to the West, had written memoirs that were important sources for research on Czech history and that should have been available to researchers. Learned experts had criticized the political position of the author, but they had not mentioned any mistakes or untruths the author had committed. Drtina was describing events that happened thirty or forty years earlier. "I cannot imagine," the accused man remarked, "how the interests of Czechoslovakia today could be injured if these memoirs were published somewhere, particularly if these memoirs are actually and explicitly memoirs, which do not claim to be considered as an objective historical work and nowhere attempt to appraise the contemporary development and political situation of our nation."

He invoked Article 19 of the International Covenant on Civil and Political Rights, which is part of the Czechoslovak legal code, and said he felt he was not guilty.

Although he lived under a suspended sentence, he did not stop working for the fulfillment of the Final Act of the Helsinki Accords, on which Charter 77 relied as its legal authority. He drew attention to every violation of it. At the end of October, Ivan Martin Jirous was arrested during a private viewing of an exhibition. In January he was convicted. Havel and sixty-six other citizens took his side in a complaint filed with the attorney general.

29 ▪ The Railwaymen's Ball

On January 28, 1978, the Chartists decided to attend the annual ball in honor of railwaymen. In March, after his release from imprisonment in connection with his participation in the event, Havel gave a detailed report of his visit to the ball. The police encircled the Railwaymen's House in the Vinohrady district and attempted to prevent the Chartists from entering. Every ticket the Chartists presented was inspected by the secret police, who had been assigned to the Chartists. The proprietors then had to take back the ticket and pay the Chartist a refund of twenty crowns. Meanwhile, the secret agents and the cops were swearing at the Chartists and throwing them out rather roughly. Finally they expelled them from the building early and ordered them to disperse. Havel behaved inconspicuously; he left the building early and waited on the corner for Pavel Landovský, because they had made plans to go somewhere together. When Pavel arrived, accompanied by two uniformed policemen, one of the policemen told Pavel he would have to go with them. Landovský asked Vašek not to leave him, and so Havel set out with him to the local police department in order to testify to Landovský's innocence.

After the interrogation, during which the interrogators were curious to know who had come up with the idea to gatecrash the Railwaymen's Ball and who had sold them the tickets, both of them were arrested, and Jaroslav Kukal as well, and transported to a preliminary holding cell on Konviktská Street. In vain did they and Kukal put their heads together all night trying to figure out why they were in jail, all dressed up in evening wear. It was only on the following day that the interrogators told Havel that he was charged with attacking a public officer. The charge was based on the testimony of the police's own people, and so Havel immediately filed a complaint on the grounds that the witnesses were liars. The next day, they cut his hair, washed him, brought him to Ruzyně prison, and put him in a cell. He was in prison for six weeks.

Interrogator Pavlovský rebuked Havel, claiming that in his letters to his wife Havel made fun of prison and interrogation; one letter even gave the impression he enjoyed being locked up. To this keen perception, as absurd as something out of *Švejk*, it should be added that during this incarceration, Václav was treated as a regular criminal, not as a political one, even though the whole affair was a sheer game.

After his release, Havel and his friends founded the Committee for the Defense of the Unjustly Prosecuted (also known by its Czech initials, VONS) on April 27, 1978. This committee kept track of who was imprisoned for what, passed this information on to international human rights organizations, and stirred up world opinion. It also made sure that prisoners' wives and children had enough to eat. Václav once again became a Charter spokesperson. He did everything he could to rehabilitate himself. His friends watched his hectic activity and total commitment to the cause with anxiety, knowing his efforts would lead him back to prison.

30 ▪ *Passion Plays*

Despite all the oppression, society was coming back to life. So-called black or home universities were organized in apartments. Professors who had been thrown out of schools during the purges of the early 1970s lectured on philosophy, history, law, political science, and literature in people's homes. The Havels invited people to Hrádeček, and they came, even though everything that occurred there was under police surveillance. Writers and musicians met there; philosophers held seminars. Every year, in early summer, the so-called Consultatio Academiae Catholicae took place there. Radim and Martin Palouš, Zdeněk Neubauer, Ivan M. Havel, Pavel Bratinka, and Daniel Kroupa met. For four days, they conducted an almost uninterrupted philosophical debate.

Václav's father started a guest book at Hrádeček. Everyone who came had to write in it. Whenever there were photographs of the visit, the old gentleman carefully pasted them in. Sometimes he decorated the text with pictures, the way Vašek and Ivan's mother had done in the family album. He always entered a report of his own stay at Hrádeček into the guest book as well.

In the spring of 1978, after Václav was released from his six-week stint in jail, the Passion Plays were performed at Hrádeček. Chartist Dana Němcová remembers attending with her children. The fifty or sixty invited guests arrived at Hrádeček in groups; they came through the forest and from different directions. The Plastics performed in the barn, which Libor Fára decorated. Under a tree in the orchard, Landovský read his play at a long table. The decoration of the barn was simple. Milan Hlavsa wanted a circle drawn all the way around the barn, so Fára did this for him. Fára manufactured the other decorations out of burlap. Filip and Jáchym Topol performed as the opening act. They were still children; Jáchym sang and Filip played.

In content, the Passion Plays were perhaps the best thing the Plastics ever did. Havel offered his own private space at great risk in order to make it possible. The Passion Plays hinted at the idea of a sacrifice that turned out to be in essence a victory. Horror was transformed into imperishable glory. The concert in the barn at Hrádeček was recorded, and someone smuggled the recording out of the country. In the West, it was made into an album. Paul Wilson* then issued it in Canada.

---

*The translator of many of Havel's works, he played with the Plastic People before he was expelled from Czechoslovakia in 1977. He now lives in Toronto.

Everyone who was there remembers the event with gratitude. They unanimously say it gave them the strength to carry on for a long time afterward. Václav helped the Plastic materially as well, and while he was in prison, Olga loaned them money for equipment. Dana Němcová remembers that when the concert ended, the Plastics filled the whole barn with artificial smoke. When the smoke dispersed, fellow Chartist Jaroslav Šabata was sitting next to her, overwhelmed by the experience. They both realized how the Passion Plays fit in with the menacing atmosphere of the times.

The Plastics performed for the last time in 1978 at the Kerhanec resort outside Česká Lípá. The name of the concert was "What Does It Mean to Lead Horses?" After their performance, an organized group burned down the building so they no longer had a place to play. This was the kind of risk Vašek had taken when he invited them to his house.

As was customary at the Havels', there was food and kegs of beer for the occasion. On any occasion on any occasion like this, Vašek cooked pots of soup or goulash. Pavel Landovský remembers:

"When he cooked, Vašek was experimenting on human subjects. He didn't like to cook according to a recipe; he insisted on improving or revising the recipe. He didn't believe there could only be one way to make wild hare in cream, and that that one way was the best way. Normal cooking was beneath him. He'd add vinegar or tarragon. He believed there was always a better way to do things, but there are some things that can't be done any better. I think he finally recognized this with that fence of his. That's why it gave him such unbelievable pleasure to have one picket just like the next, no experimenting. Usually the food turned out all right for him, but once he cooked cabbage, and when you ate it, it didn't hurt you, but it lay in your stomach like an explosive. He called it intensive cabbage, and that's how he presented it."

Dana Němcová remembers that after the Passion Plays, when they were setting out to return to Mladé Buky by bus or by train, there were yellow police cars circling Hrádeček. They followed some paths through the forest, and when they came to a field, one of the yellow cars came up to them and the police asked to see identification. Everything seemed to be all right, because the concert was already over. But the events of the day continued that night in a dream Dana had:

> *It was a clear, blue, sunny day, and she was walking through the forest with her children. It was summer, her children were barefoot, and suddenly a large green snake rose up in the forest path. Dana looked for a rock and found one beside the path; she shooed the barefoot children off; she grabbed the rock and threw it at the snake. It landed on the snake's back, but the snake rose up as if wounded and hissed into Dana's face: ''Citizensss' identity cardssss, pleazzzzze. . . .''*

In the summer, on the first weekend in August, "Garden Parties" were held regularly at Hrádeček. For instance, one year, they set up an exhibition of Jan Kašpar's photographs in the Krobs' barn. Everyone dressed up as high-society ladies and gentlemen, and they held a private viewing, where Anna Fárová, as an expert on photography, delivered an introductory address. Then there was the premiere of *Audience*, directed by Andrej Krob. In the barn were a table and two chairs. Landovský sat in one of them; they dragged Vašek to the other and told him he would play Vaněk.* The script was on the table so they could read it. During the sequence when the brewmaster gets up to urinate, Landovský went to the toilet, and a different actor returned. The new actor played the role until the next urination sequence, when yet another actor substituted for him. It was an ingenious idea, because it added another dimension to the play. It showed that Vaněk was irreplaceable, he was one of a kind, but anyone could be the brewmaster.

The radius of Václav's activity is broad. He knows ordinary people who sat in jail with him and then visited him when they were set free,

---

*A soft-spoken dissident, he is the main character in the play.

stagehands, workers, actors, singers, philosophers, and creative artists from the establishment and the underground. He is able to bring people together, host them, and get them acquainted with each other. A great many people know him personally, address him with the familiar *ty*,* and love him. Perhaps this is the chief reason why society has rallied around him during decisive moments, why representatives of the widest social spectrum, united by a common idea and mutual respect and trust, chose him. This was the case with Charter 77, with the November revolution, and finally when he became president.

There were 150 people at one of the Hrádeček concerts. Bedřich Fučík and Václav Černý also visited Hrádeček. People with children who had nowhere came there on their days off, and the hosts gladly accepted all of them. Many people remember Hrádeček as a happy stopping place along a meandering pilgrimage full of woe.

Every year, Olga organized a New Year's Eve party with and for their friends. Every year, the party had a different theme, and the guests chose costumes in the spirit of that theme. For example, when Havel wrote *Temptation*, the New Year's Eve party was given the name "Magical Prague," and one component of the evening was Walpurgisnacht.

When Václav was imprisoned in 1979, he asked Olga in one of his letters to dress well, have fun, and lead a social life. During his imprisonment instead of Garden Parties, there was a party for Olga's birthday in July, equally well attended. Olga learned how to take photographs in order to send Vašek pictures—of her birthday party, of a feast in honor of Vašek's birthday, of a harvest festival, of *tableaux vivants* of a hunting scene, and other group activities that he could not participate in. They did not give Vašek the photos, however, because they said there were not enough family members in them. Olga lived at Hrádeček with her mother all summer, accompanied by her dogs Ajda and Golda. The house was often full of people; there was dancing and theater; they arranged concerts, parties for children, and perfor-

---

*Like *Du* in German and *tu* in French, much like being on a first-name basis.

that people still traveled to Hrádeček as if they were making a pilgrimage. He, in turn, was in everyone's thoughts. The police followed all these activities with varying degrees of attention, and those who visited risked arrest or at least inconvenience. Nonetheless, they came. The constant presence of the police and the awareness that it could all end at any moment gave everything that happened there a deeper existential dimension and significance.

31 ▪ On the Polish Border

"Was Vašek a good conspirator?" I asked Pavel Landovský. Starting in 1977, the two of them had formed a remarkable pair, until Vašek's definitive long-term imprisonment and Pavel's departure for Austria, where they took away his Czechoslovak citizenship.

"Too much conspiracy prevents you from doing anything," Pavel answered. "An intelligent fellow and an experienced guy can solve a situation when it arises. If you have to think through everything that's going to happen ahead of time, you'll never get anything done."

Pavel's answer made me laugh, and I told him that once I had reproached Vašek for having spoken about something before it had taken place. He might have given the whole thing away. He stopped short and stared at me with his blue, ingenuous eyes. With his blond curly hair, he looked like an angel, and he asked, "But we're not doing anything wrong, are we?" I thought to myself then that the cops must have a hard time with him. He looks like one of God's blameless children, and he is, but he has sharp insight and intuition. It must have caused them a lot of trouble before they caught on, if they ever did. And he is as strict with himself as he is kind and forgiving to others.

Pavel made me laugh again when he told me a story about an adventure the two of them had while sitting in the Mánes restaurant.

Vašek had his "dissi" bag* with him, which he would look at every now and then and remind Pavel that he must not forget the bag, because there were very dangerous documents inside it. As was customary at the time, the special patrol was sitting at the next table. "Tomorrow we have to give it to Šabata for his signature," Vašek whispered to Pavel, and again reminded him of the sack's importance. He picked up the bag about twelve times and finally looped the strap under a leg of the chair. The cops could not have failed to notice that the bag was particularly important to him. Then Vašek and Pavel left Mánes restaurant and headed downtown along Myslíkova Street. They got about two hundred meters when suddenly they heard a fearful yelling. They turned and saw a waiter from Mánes rushing after them with the bag. Behind the waiter came the cops, who wanted to take the bag away from him, but the waiter was faster, and he got to them in time.

"That time we escaped jail, but Šabata went to jail in a flash when we were on our way to the second Polish border meeting.† The first one was lovely; it was in August 1978. I met this guy who had a wooden hut where he was brewing tea. I told him, 'I've got some friends from Poland here.' He invited us inside; we wrote out our statement; Michnik** sang a Polish song; and the border patrol was patrolling around outside, and the little guy crawled out every once in a while to tell them, 'I've got jolly company in here.' We wrote our names in his guest book, and out went the document. But that little guy in the mountain service ended up with the most important document, because every rascal there signed his guest book."

The second meeting took place in September and the participants signed a "Joint Letter to the Defenders of Human Rights in Eastern

---

*Dissidents were always carrying bags crammed with all sorts of papers.
†In August and September 1978, Charter 77 meet illegally on the Czechoslovak-Polish border with representatives of the Polish group KOR (Committee for Workers Defense).
**A political scientist writer, he was a founding member of KOR.

Europe." The third meeting went badly. Everyone was arrested except Havel and Landovský, and Jaroslav Šabata was sentenced to one and a half years without suspension.

The third meeting with KOR was supposed to take place on October 1, 1978, on the Czechoslovak-Polish friendship trail on Sněžka peak, not far from Hrádeček. Somehow the Polish and Czechoslovak police found out about it and arranged a joint raid. The friendship trail and all other trails leading from the Luční and Obří chalets were under surveillance. The police watched the recreational center and the platforms for the chairlift. Polish security arrested the KOR members Michnik, Naimský, and Lityński. On the Czech side, Šabata, Němec, and Tomaš Petřivý were arrested. Here is Pavel Landovský again, telling the story of how he and Havel reached Sněžka:

"Everyone was marching along like obedient tourists, and I suggested we take a short cut to the chairlift. There was a little path with a little wire fence across it to keep people out, because it was a national park. We were in a big hurry, and I said, 'To hell with the fence, Vašek.' Therefore we reached the chairlift from a direction they weren't expecting. A few school groups were standing there, so we mingled with the teachers. The cops were taking shelter behind a sausage stand, and they had already caught everybody down below at the station. We rode up to the top of Sněžka. We were riding along okay on this two-seat chairlift; it was nasty weather, misty and cold, and Vašek was wearing a knitted woolen hat Olga had given him for the journey, so Vašek says, 'If it weren't for our duty to rescue the nation, we'd never get any of this fresh mountain air!'

"Out of the whole group, we were practically the only ones to reach the top, and right away, this Polish border guard came up to us and asked for our citizens' ID cards. I asked him what he was doing here, and he said they were on double duty. When I stepped onto the friendship trail, I saw a Prague cop in the mist. I retreated into the mist and said, 'Vašek, let's go back to the chairlift.' We rode back down. Vašek went to rescue Šabata, and I went after Tonda Maněna—he was our connection in Trutnov. Either he'd already been arrested maybe the only one still free. I went to the pub, where the manager was a guy named Franta Křídlo, and I told him, 'If Maněna or Vašek show up, tell them we'll meet at midnight at my grandmother's grave.'

"At midnight, in a mad, torrential thunderstorm, I gave a whistle in the Pilníkov cemetery. Vašek crawled out of the darkness and the rain. He looked like a watersprite and he said:

" 'They're here.'

" 'Who? The police?'

" 'No. The ghosts.' "

He'd come on foot through the forest for the rendezvous. Olga deserved the credit for this. Vašek did not know the woods around Hrádeček and got lost even in familiar places. Since it was night, he had asked Olga to guide him. Bravely, she brought him to the intersection and then had to return alone. She fell over an uprooted tree and was terribly frightened.

"Vašek won't go hiking in the mountains for just any old reason," I said, remembering that several times we had wanted to bring him along with us on a hike. The mountains on the horizons had been clear and alluring, but he wouldn't go.

Pavel laughed and agreed. I saw that he was no hiker either.

"The time for that is until you're fifteen years old," he said omnisciently. "The time for games. Go kick the ball around, play a scrimmage match. Then a man has to do something substantial. So that the time he spends in this world will have a point. So he will have done something toward moving the world along. So he won't have frolicked away his time here."

32 • *Under Surveillance*

Beginning August 5, 1978, Havel was under continuous police surveillance. The police decided to harass him until he could no longer stand it and left the country, or until his nerves gave way and he attacked a public officer or committed some other rash act he could be locked up for. Vašek's patience and self-control, however, are unsurpassable. These aspects of his character are connected to his tolerance; he feels sorry for these people rather than angry at them. There was never any hatred between him and his secret policemen. He always tried to get along with them and avoided humiliating them, even when they did nothing but humiliate him. For instance, in 1978, when a police car was continuously parked in front of his home and policemen accompanied him even when he went shopping or walked the dog, he negotiated some rules for their forced coexistence. If he met someone on the street and stopped to talk with him, they checked this person's documents. Vašek therefore waved at people not to stop, to prevent them from acknowledging him. People he worked with, whom he contacted more often, he met in cafés and restaurants. The special patrol always sat at the next table. When someone new arrived, Havel introduced him to the police, so they would know who it was and the newcomer would be spared the embarrassing procedure of showing his papers.

One day, under this arrangement, he met Jan Lopatka in the U slunců pub on Nerudova Street. Vašek introduced Jan and said he hoped it didn't bother him. It took Lopatka a long time to read the text Vašek had brought him. The cops, left to their own devices, got bored and began to chat with some soldiers. When Jan went to the toilet, one of the soldiers was also there. Jan told him to keep watch out for the cops. Later, two cops walked Vašek through the Castle courtyard while another drove the car around the long way, because cars are not permitted on the Castle grounds. Vašek started discussing Lopatka with them, saying that he and Lopatka were only friends, but that Jan always got into trouble at work whenever the two of them met. In short, he tried to convince them to leave Jan alone.

"Don't you worry about that guy," they said. "He's got his own problems; today he informed on us."

When Vašek asked how, they explained that Jan had finked on them to a soldier in the toilet, and the soldier had told them about it. Thanks to the impertinence of Vašek's friends, the younger cop complained, people looked at them funny.

And the older cop said, "Are you ashamed to be what you are?"

Petr Uhl also had one of these "operatives"—as they are technically known—almost constantly while he was at large. Dr. Hejdánek, Dr. Mlynář, and Dr. Hájek also had one during certain periods. A Tatra 613 was constantly parked in front of Havel's home, and the men inside the car watched the door of the building. When Havel drove somewhere, they drove after him. When he walked, two of them followed him on foot, and onto subways and streetcars. When he went into his house, they left him alone. If he telephoned from a phone booth, they listened at the door, quite openly. When he went to the post office, they looked over his shoulder to see where he was sending letters. All of them were equipped with transmitters. They sat next to Havel in pubs, in cafés, in bars—they even sweated with him in the sauna. As I said before, there was no hatred between them; Vašek was not capable of hating anyone. I have heard that Julius Tomin tried to fight his secret policemen, and in the end they forced him to emigrate. While he had a special patrol, he ran and jogged maybe eighteen kilometers a day. The secret policemen had to run after him; they spat; and all out of breath, they snarled curses and threats:

"We're going to liquidate you, Tomin. With Mr. Havel, it's another story. With him it's all restaurants and cafés."

Vašek is a polite and essentially decent person. At least he seemed that way to me, until one day I saw him get angry. An argument arose over something that seemed to be inconsequential, but the argument opened a kind of trap door, behind which everything lay collected, as if in a vault. And then it was gone. I heard him tell a mutual friend of ours everything he blamed him for and everything he had against him. He was not mean; he said it with regret. But he chose his words so exactly that it was like something that had just come out of the oven cooling down in a pantry or cellar. I was sorry he carried that kind of burden around with him for so long. The person attacked—who naturally tried to fight back, but was so startled that he found he was not up to it—received an apology from Vašek the next day. Vašek said he had fits of temper like that only at long intervals. Once he had one in front of the closed door of a wine cellar that refused to admit him even though there were tables free inside. He started to kick the door and scream. It seems incredible, because many times before he had stood in front of the iron grille* of a closed wine cellar, just as power- lessly. Once we were in that position with our friend Bruss, a transla- tor. The head waiter stood behind the grill of the Barberina bar, looking like a Sicilian mafioso. He shouted at us that it was full and that we should leave immediately. With a pleasant smile, Vašek told him:

"This gentleman is German, but he can speak Czech," and pointed at Bruss. They threw all three of us out.

They had Havel under surveillance both in Prague and in Hrádeček. Hrádeček is out in the wilderness. Andrej Krob, who brought the Havels here, lives in the cottage that faces it, on the other side of the garden. Above Krob's cottage is a hill where there are the ruins of a castle. The Havels have a two-story cottage: downstairs is a kitchen and a large living room with a fireplace; upstairs are the bedrooms and Vašek's study. The highway curves behind the barn, then leads uphill via a maple-lined alley. From this hill it is possible to see almost all the Krkonoše mountain range and a little bit of Sněžka, which Černá Hora occludes. After 1978, a police car with two uniformed officers was stationed next to the cottage at all times. The officers were

---

*See note on page 55.

rotated in eight-hour shifts. The highway was blocked off so that no one could drive in. Whenever they removed the barricade, the uniformed officers checked the papers of all the cars that drove by, issued fines to the drivers, and from time to time took away their drivers' licenses. They warned the Havels' guests that they proceeded at their own risk, but refused to be more exact about the nature of this risk. As in Prague, they followed Havel when he walked his dog in the forest, and they accompanied him when he went to buy groceries either in the village nearby or in the more distant town.

Pavel Landovský must have gotten on the police's nerves terribly. Often they thought they had him, that they had destroyed him, and then he and Havel would turn up again in high spirits, happy and healthy. The two of them complemented each other; together they created something neither of them had on his own. They formed a pair that was intellectually and physically strong. Pavel explained to me that it was like with the heroes of the novel *In Cold Blood*. Neither one of them would have killed on his own, but together they formed a personality who killed. Therefore, they were both executed. Vašek and Pavel together were dangerous to themselves, too, as if the metabolism between them were leading to the inconspicuous manufacture of explosives. With her woman's intuition, Landovský's mother suspected this. She used to say to him, "You'll come to no good with that Howel person." Olga sensed it as well.

When Pavel talks about Olga, he speaks somewhat sheepishly, as if he had a bad conscience.

"Are you afraid of her?" I asked him. And this man, who hates cowards more than anything else, meekly nods assent.

"When I turned up, Olga always knew something was happening. She looked at me, and I was afraid she already knew what. I was an evil spirit, because Vašek used me as an excuse even when I wasn't involved at all. This was already going on in the Theater on the Balustrade. We were both absolute zeroes, and she used to protect him from me. At the same time, she knew she had to take me along with him, and that it shouldn't escalate into open conflict. She's a very clever woman. You have to be careful not to make a mistake, because she'll remember it and three days later, she'll bawl you out for it. I'm afraid I'll let something slip that she'll discover, or that I'll say something different from what I said last time. She butts in at the right moment, and you see that she knows everything. I'm permanently under suspicion; since 1963 she's known that when I come by, it's not by chance. But I couldn't live without Vašek. Back in 1968 I discovered he was the only sure thing in my circle, and my circle stretches all the way to Slovakia. He's a person I can hook up with as far as ideas are concerned. Pretty soon I started to suspect his personality was not only strong, but world-recognized, his position to a certain extent guaranteed by his renown. I'm a practical guy, and if something's going to turn out to be something, it has to start with practical things. All the others were full of gibberish; their activities were too narrow, limited by the environment or the person: Catholicism, the underground—it always ended up in some kind of utopia—whereas Václav was realistic, like hardly anyone else."

"Apparently you claim that you forced Václav to build that lovely fence, the one his neighbor Krob is jealous of? Olga says he built the fence himself, and she helped him."

"Vašek was prouder of that fence than of his plays. It's a fence with one picket just like the next. It was like when he wrote a typographical poem on a typewriter. For him, the fence was like an expanded typographical poem. A man is prouder of this kind of thing than of a few ideas about how the world is governed, and this fence made you think of a row of books lined up on a shelf."*

In his letters to Olga from prison, Vašek continually reminds Olga that his fence needs painting. The fence might be one of his greatest manual achievements. And Olga did paint the fence.

For a long time, they had noticed something sparkling in the window of a cottage on the slope of Hrádeček. This cottage was almost

---

*Literally: "this fence seemed like a library."

entirely hidden in the forest, and it was possible to see the Havels' wilderness and a section of the valley from it. From there, everything that happened around the Havels' house could be easily observed. It seemed to Vašek that it might be a directional microphone, because from the sparkling part, which had lenses that moved, a thick cable led to the ground. He had seen people going in and out, and the owner always greeted him, "Good day, Mr. Havel," but maybe there was an agreement between them. Václav and Olga were alone at Hrádeček; there weren't even any signs of life visible in the house across the way. They went to investigate. And in fact, a nine-pin connector led into the ground. Olga took the cable and began to tug it out of the ground. They went through the forest, winding up the cable. The roots of trees had been cut and the cable skillfully woven among them. It led them to the castle ruins. They went about a kilometer further, until they reached a precipice where the cable headed toward a caravan. There was no need to walk there; it was clear this was not the forest service or a water-pumping station, but Them. Olga cut the cable and carried it to a rubbish heap. Once, by accident, Václav discovered a listening device in the ceiling of their Prague apartment. They had no idea how many of them there were. A half year after he became president, they searched Hrádeček with special instruments designed to detect these listening devices. They did not find anything. In the end, a few months later, the person from State Security who had installed them revealed that there were three, and told where they were.

In the 1970s, when Václav was under police surveillance at Hrádeček, his father acted as his Prague secretary. Václav would have had trouble getting by without his self-sacrificing father. I quote from one of the letters he sent him:

> *Dear Daddy,*
>   *This time I have a somewhat larger number of secretarial tasks for you, but I believe you will be able to handle them and that they will not cause you too much trouble.*

1. My first priority is that the yellow folders contained in this package be delivered to Ludvík Vaculík. They contain one copy of a one-act play I wrote that Vaculík wants to publish in Padlock Press. He does not want me to send it to him through the mail, because he has the impression they are checking his mail. [Instructions for how to reach Vaculík follow.] . . . Don't arrange your visit to him over the telephone beforehand, because he has the feeling he's under heavy surveillance . . .

2. I am also sending you a letter to Klaus with the request that you let Mrs. K. translate it. . . . When you make arrangements with her on the telephone, do not say that a translation of my letter is involved; she is sure to understand without your saying it.

3. In the green folders is another copy of my one-act play, earmarked for Klaus. If you or Puzuk [his brother Ivan] are interested in reading it, please read this copy while my letter to Klaus is being translated.

4. Once you have the translation of my letter to Klaus (it would be better to make two copies, in case the first does not arrive), please take the following steps:

a) sign the letter on my behalf (if it is not on paper with my signature on it)

b) divide the one-act play into four parts of about ten pages each; put the letter to Klaus inside one of the parts; then place each part in a separate envelope; insofar as it is possible, mail each envelope a different way (air mail, small-size regular mail, medium-size regular mail, etc.); if you need to, make five packages.

c) in various sorts of writing (by typewriter, by hand, etc.) write this address on all the envelopes: . . . [an inconspicuous Hamburg address follows]; either don't write a sender's address at all, or write the addresses of various people from out of the telephone book.

d) have the appropriate postage put on the letters at the post office, but then it would be better to drop them in several different mailboxes.

These are all the services of an outright secretarial nature; I would be very grateful to you if you could take care of them.

And now a further, no less important item: between July 30 (or maybe 29) and August 3, we will not be here. We are invited by several friends to their summer homes and we would like to combine the visits into one trip (the Kohouts, Juráček, Marta). While we are gone, would you like to come here—in addition to your regularly planned stay—for a week's excursion to Hrádeček? . . . It would help us because somebody would be watching the house, and the animals. We would pay for the bus fare. . . .

And this is definitely my last request: the writers' conference Zdeněk is coming here for was shifted to July 15. . . . we would be grateful if you could send us the following items via Zdeněk:

a) 300 Millers [Tuzex crowns*]

b) from the Tuzex shop, coffee (it's hard to believe, but we're going to run out soon), two bottles of soy sauce, and one instant cocoa.

c) conceivably, some exciting vegetable, like last time, if you run into something—but this is not in any way particularly necessary.

As you see, today I have really burdened you with a list of tasks and subjects for consideration; I trust you'll know what's what and you'll somehow manage.

I would appreciate it if you could acknowledge the receipt of this package with a small note. . . .

Havel's father received a letter with tasks and instructions nearly every week; sometimes they arrived more often with fewer tasks.

When Václav and Olga then drove to the Kohouts' place in Sázava,

---

*Tuzex crowns were vouchers that could be used to buy luxury or imported goods in special Tuzex shops. One could purchase Tuzex crowns with hard Western currencies or—at a highly disadvantageous rate and in limited quantities—with regular Czechoslovak crowns. In black market transactions, Tuzex were preferred to regular crowns.

Vašek got lost, as he often does. The police passed Vašek's car, stopped him, and said, "Mr. Havel, please, this isn't the right way. We'll show you how to get there; follow us."

On another occasion, when there was ice on the roads, the police skidded into a ditch and Vašek towed them out with a rope. Sometimes they complained to him about their degrading jobs, and said that one day their bogus degrees would no longer be worth anything. Their complaints got on Vašek's nerves.

33 ▪ House Arrest

In October 1978, Havel wrote an extensive essay while at Hrádeček with the title, "The Power of the Powerless," which he dedicated to the memory of Jan Patočka. The essay quickly spread around the world and in our country circulated in Xerox copies. As he had in the letter to Dr. Husák, Havel analyzed the contemporary state of society and the causes of its decline and the rising sense of self-awareness. Jan Lopatka read "The Power of the Powerless" in Valcav's father's apartment. Vašek did not want to have the text on him, because he did not want them to confiscate it from him. He waited in a restaurant on Mikulandská Street for Jan to come tell him what he thought of it. Jan praised it.

In November, Havel once again accepted the position of Charter spokesperson. State Security initiated the next stage of its "operatives' surveillance." He was put under house arrest. The policemen moved a small table and two chairs into the hallway in front of his apartment and would not allow anyone into the apartment except Olga. They only let Vašek out once, then arrested him in his father's apartment, where he had gone to visit, and locked him up again at home. The police amused themselves by ringing the doorbell and then threatening Havel when he answered the door. Of course, they never did this when civilian witnesses were present. Vašek and Olga decided to return to Hrádeček. They were surprised to discover that the police had settled in for the long haul. They were now stationed in a peculiar little shack on insect like legs, positioned so that they could see all the roads that led to the house. Vašek christened the shack Lunochod, because it reminded him of the Soviet lunar module. They would not let anyone into the house, and they only sometimes let Vašek out to walk the dog or to drive to the grocery store. They always had to radio the operations officer in Trutnov for permission first, who would then ask the regional headquarters of State Security in Hradec Králové. They hung around the house and looked in the windows. Apparently every police officer in the district served a stint. When Havel went to the grocery store, they walked through town at his side, trying to hold a friendly conversation with him in order to avoid being conspicuous. Nonetheless, the citizens of the town and the neighboring villages noticed this strange phenomenon. The police's activity aroused not only puzzlement and smiles but also anger—all this was at the expense of working people. It outraged them that such a done-for nation could permit itself this kind of luxury.

Before Christmas, Václav bought a little tree that had, as Olga said, about four twigs. With the tree and a plainclothes policeman, he went into the tobacconist's, where Olga was buying cigarettes. When Olga saw the tree, she started to laugh. The young policeman also simpered. The tobacconist asked Olga if he was their son.

The lady in the butcher's shop slipped Olga meat under the counter. In various ways, people made it clear they were sympathetic and they knew what was going on. The plainclothesmen and the State Security men who always accompanied them made themselves at home at Hrádeček. When they were bored, they played fetch with Ajda and Golda, the Havels' schnauzers. Olga found this particularly hard to stand. She preferred it when the dogs attacked the police when they came to search their house. Then she liked them even better.

All the neighbors were warned not to have any contact with the Havels or help them in any way. For people who live in the mountains, this was particularly humiliating, because they are accustomed to helping each other out. If they violated this prohibition, the police threatened that they would be fired from their jobs, their children would not get into any schools, and so forth. And to make the couple's existence total hell, "unknown perpetrators" very carefully slashed the tires of Havel's car and broke his windshield. If you do not know what it is like to try to find auto parts in Czechoslovakia, you do not know the meaning of inconvenience. They knew quite well what it was like. They thought up annoyances that bordered on sadism. They dumped cubes of sugar in the car's gas tank. After a long absence, Hrádeček's owners returned during a cruel cold spell to discover that the heat did not work. Someone had severed the electrical contacts to the boiler's burner; the water pump was stuffed with wool; and all the traps of the drainpipes from the bathtub and sinks were filled with a peculiar resin, which couldn't be removed. They had to dig out the walls and change the water pipes. It was difficult, because no one was allowed to come to the Havels because of the police threat, and nothing they needed was available.

At the close of the eventful year 1978, which had begun with the Railwaymen's Ball and Vašek's arrest and ended in strict house arrest which practically amounted to prison, an incident took place which gives an excellent glimpse of what life in the dissident movement— or, to put it in more human terms, in our ghetto—was like at the time. Every year, on St. Nicholas' Day, Jan Lopatka played the devil. In 1977, dressed as a devil, he stopped by Mánes restaurant, where Havel, Věra Jirousová, and Jiří Němec were sitting. Vašek liked it immensely, and, as is often the case with him, decided he wanted to do it too. Jan promised that next year Havel could go as an angel. So on this St. Nicholas' Day, the devil and an angel visited the Chartists' children.*

On December 5, 1978, they met at the Lopatkas' house in Vlašská Street. Nikolaj [Andrej] Stankovič dressed up as St. Nicholas, Lopatka

---

*Even though Havel was under house arrest, it wasn't consistently enforced, and sometimes he was able to shake the constant surveillance. And, as described earlier, he was able to go to Hrádeček.

as a devil, Havel as an angel, and with them was a cohort of junior angels and devils, twelve in all. They had three cars. Pavel Landovský drove one of them; his leg was in a cast, so he couldn't play a role. Nikolaj has no idea how to talk to children, nor does Vašek. Neither of them has any children of his own, only the devil has three. But the devil, according to the tradition is not a role for speaking, but for frightening the children. Vašek was wearing a bath towel over his face and his head, and he resembled Yasir Arafat. Jan was the chief devil, and he had a police truncheon and a sheriff's star. He had horns like a bull's and a cow chain that he clanged. They spent a long time getting into their costumes, and when they crawled out in front of the house, policemen who were frozen stiff were standing there. To avoid having to show the police their papers, Havel introduced St. Nicholas, who said nothing, and the devil, who went, "Blrblrblr." Some of the policemen laughed; others remained stiff and grim. Our actors got in their cars and drove off, followed by the special police patrol. When they got into the apartments, the parents gave them pieces of paper informing them how naughty the children were. At the Bendas, they even got the white book of good deeds and the black book of sins. Nikolaj never quite got his bearings; he was a little drunk and his hat kept falling down so he couldn't read. As I said, he was not good at speaking with small children, and so gradually he limited himself to reproaching all of his victims with a long speech about nose-picking. The last stop was in Lázeňská Street in the Malá Strana (Lesser Town) district. The family's four-year-old boy wanted to fight with the devil, so the devil carried him outside into the snow. While he was tossing the child about and everyone's attention was diverted, the angel crawled into Landovský's car and Landovský into Havel's. The police did not notice and they followed Pavel. Thanks to this, Vašek drove undisturbed to Most the next day, where there was a trial he wanted to participate in. The following day he was put under even stricter house arrest.

The winter of 1978–1979 was dramatic and cruel for Pavel Landovský as well. On Legie (Legion) Bridge, at that time Mayday Bridge, an incident took place that to a certain extent determined the rest of his life. Pavel was waiting outside the National Theater for a streetcar to take him across the river to Újezd, when a half-insane man approached him. Apparently this man had already thrown someone off a steamboat into the Vltava. This dangerous man, who worked for State Security, provoked Pavel, wanting to fight with him. The streetcars did not seem to be running, so Pavel decided to cross the bridge on foot. The man waited beside the stone balustrade of the bridge and then attacked him. They started to wrestle. He wanted to throw Pavel over the balustrade of the bridge, so Pavel hooked his leg around the balustrade. The man jumped on his leg and broke it. It cracked like a branch, Pavel says. Because the man was pounding Pavel's face with his fists, it was clearly a matter of life or death and he thought he would have to kill the man. He took out a knife he always carried and knocked the man out with the shut knife. Blood spurted out and the body of the State Security man slackened. At that moment, a woman ran out of the darkness—it was his moll, who had been hiding somewhere—and dragged him away. Pavel crawled across the bridge on all fours to the Smíchov district side. It is because of this incident that on St. Nicholas' Day he had his leg in a cast and acted only as a driver.

After this incident, of course, it was clear that Landovský could not stay. The police accommodated his request for a one-year stay in Austria, where he had a contract with a theater. Before he left, he and Vašek made a recording of *Audience.* Then Pavel brought Vašek and Olga to the train station, because they were going to Hrádeček. It was terribly cold. Pavel put them both on the train and complained that he still had somewhere to go. Vašek took off his T-shirt. Sparks shot off it in the dark, since it was made from artificial fibers, and Pavel put it on under his jacket. It was still warm. He said, "God bless you," and left. The train pulled out of the station. They did not see him again for almost eleven years. It was January 5, 1979.

34 ▪ Imprisonment

On March 3, 1979, Havel wrote a letter to Dr. Jaromír Obzin, minister of the interior of the Czechoslovak Socialist Republic. In it, he wrote the following:

> . . . This house arrest, meanwhile, is becoming worse: for example, not long ago I was at least allowed—albeit with complications, in a limited way, and under a police escort—to shop for basic necessities. As of yesterday, i.e., March 2, 1979, I am forbidden to leave my house even to purchase something to eat. The police officers who guard my house even told me that they did not care if I starved to death in my home. They said they would be happy to supply me with a coffin when this happens. (They did not, of course, say this before civilian witnesses, because as I have noticed, they only say these—and worse—things when no one besides me is present who is not a police officer.) . . . I only know that I am not breaking the laws of this country, but that those who ought to uphold these laws are breaking them more and more openly and conspicuously. . . . Therefore I sit in my apartment, at liberty and also in solitary confinement, and I am sad. Not because I cannot bear solitude, but because I am saddened by all the things that are possible in the country I live in, which I love and do not want to leave.
>
> P.S. It is characteristic of the situation that I had to smuggle this letter out of my confinement with quite a bit of difficulty. I did not succeed until the second attempt; on the first attempt, your employees confiscated it.

Václav felt they would jail him soon, because the longer the peculiar hunt lasted, the faster and more cunning it became. On May 28, they looked for him at Hrádeček and searched the house while Olga was at home. It was a gorgeous warm day, summer already, and Olga had an odd premonition.

The Committee for the Defense of the Unjustly Prosecuted (VONS) functioned until May 29, 1979. At five in the morning, the police launched their attack. They held sixteen members of the committee in custody and searched all their homes. They were Rudolf Battěk, Otta Bednářová, Jarmila Bělíková, Václav Benda, Jiří Dienstbier, Václav Havel, Ladislav Lis, Václav Malý, Dana Němcová, Jiří Němec, Luděk Pacovský, Jiří Ruml, Gertruda Sekaninová-Čakrtová, and Petr Uhl. Albert Černý had been in prison since March, and they arrested Jan Tesař in Chrudim and transported him to Brno. Nine of them were placed in pretrial detention and charged with the crime of subversion of the republic according to article 98 of the criminal code. The lower sentencing limit for subversion of the republic was three years; the upper, nine years. They seized Václav at his apartment in Prague. Olga learned about it at Hrádeček, where the weather was still beautiful. A crane came and carted away the Lunochod. She knew that Vašek would be away for a long time, perhaps several years.

Václav dated his first letter from prison June 4. In it, he wrote:

> It appears the astrologers were right when they predicted prison for me again this year and when they said the summer would be a hot one. As a matter of fact, it's stifling hot here, like being in a perpetual sauna. . . . [June 4, 1979; Letters to Olga, p. 23]

On June 19, he wrote:

> . . . I'm taking this imprisonment neither as tragically as I did the one in 1977 (then, of course, things were a lot worse and I was also new at this and frightened out of my wits), nor as a joke, like last year's; this time I'm being more fatalistic about it, and treating it as something I've long been destined to go through. After those two odd, false starts, it seems that only now—the third time—the inevitable has finally happened. If it hadn't, I'd proba-

bly have grown more and more nervous, because I would have been subconsciously expecting it at any moment. When this is over, I may finally be more at ease with myself, and this will have a calming effect on things around me as well. . . . [June 19, 1979; Letters to Olga, p. 25]

These letters begin the book of all the letters Havel wrote from prison, collected under the title, *Letters to Olga*.*

On July 22, 1979, Vaclav's father died. His son had been in prison for two months when, to everyone's great surprise, his jailers brought him to his father's funeral. Nothing like this had ever happened before.

On October 24, 1982, his brother, Ivan, wrote him a letter in which he copied out a portion of Ludrik Vaculík's *The Czech Dreambook* that describes the funeral:

> *On Friday I attended the funeral of the senior Mr. Havel at the crematorium in the Strašnice district. When the side door of the hall opened, Václav Havel entered along with the other survivors of the deceased. He sat with Olga, his brother Ivan, and Ivan's wife in the first row; the rest of the family sat behind them. A safe distance was maintained. There were no guards in sight, but they must have been present, clothed in the deepest mourning, including black ties, because the only others to wear a tie were Stanislav Milota and Dr. Kriegel. Who would deliver the eulogy?*
>
> *The door opened again, and a cane appeared, followed by a gray-haired lady. She spread out her papers and began unhurriedly to recite a biography of the deceased: what he was like, what he did, that during the First Republic he initiated the construction of a temporary student dormitory which then was in use for fifty years, that he organized the construction of this sturdy dormitory and had it built and entirely furnished in two years, that with his brother he founded the neighborhood and film studios of Barran-*

---

*See note on page 134.

dov, that he built the Lucerna Palace. . . . The work of Václav Havel endures to this day; we all know that. He raised his two sons as honorable people.

This dry report, delivered in the direction of the coffin, filled us with tension and awe. There was music, a violin, and even a hymn: "Saint Václav, prince of the Czech land." When the crematorium door and curtain closed, the usual receiving line formed. When he shook my hand, Václav Havel whispered a short sentence in my ear, but unfortunately I only caught two words: "our controversy."

Outside, I asked Dr. Kriegel who the speaker had been. It was Dr. Anna Kavinová-Schustlerová; he introduced me to her, and I thanked her. Two policemen got out of a car parked in front of the crematorium gate, approached the young Kyncl and Bednář, and confiscated the film in their cameras. If I know those young fellows, they had already changed the film, and the police confiscated empty rolls. . . . Everyone pondered what this generous gesture could mean. Their consciences have been aroused, said some. They'll use it as a psychological weapon against Václav, proposed others. In short, they're acting more cleverly, yet another group proposed. Only Madla* considers it quite normal; for that matter, she had known he would be there. Do we still want to complain about something?—Yes, they did it for Madla. But this is all right; it is necessary to see the silver lining on every cloud. But I have my own theory for it: the world improves only so fast and only to a certain extent. . . .

Two years before, the sons had arranged for their father's eightieth birthday party. It was a show of all their love for him. They invited sixty-four people, their father's friends and their own. Everyone dressed up in an elegant and festive way and enjoyed themselves. No one got drunk. The old and the young enjoyed each other's company.

---

*Ludvík Vaculík's wife. She always tended to see the very positive side of everything.

It was another instance of communion between the era of the First Republic and the present day. Václav's father even danced a waltz. He sat enthroned like a patriarch, surrounded by gifts and flowers, and was happy. He could not, however, stop thinking of his poor Božena, nor could he believe he was really as old as he was. His parents died in their sixties, and he did not know why he deserved such a long life. Landovský says that it was one of the nicest parties he remembers, and it lasted from five in the afternoon until three in the morning.

After the death of their father, Ivan wrote to Vašek in prison:

> *As I go through the archives, I discover that something like a "family spirit" exists, something that is transmitted from generation to generation. It is impossible to characterize it, because these generations do not have to be comparable in any way. . . . From the documents, I definitely see that when one person departs, the survivors bear something away from him and after him, and that the cultivation of this spirit is always important to at least one person. From the first, I thought of Father's memoirs above all as a therapeutic device (and by the way, an excellent one) that gave him something to fix on and helped him avoid the feeling of emptiness in old age. Now, suddenly, I have the feeling that his project should be continued further (perhaps our Pupa* will take it up).*
>
> *If there is not any yet, in the future there surely will be greater interest in authentic testimony about this or that period from the pen of participants, rather than interest in abstract historical studies written by mere spectators. The perspective that the spectator assumes is frequently an illusion, if not an outright falsehood.*

In his eleventh letter to Ivan, on October 6, 1979, Václav writes:

> *As to the matter of the "family spirit": I also feel that it exists, and am glad it exists. I feel, however, that the spirit's practical*

---

*Ivan's son Prokůpek.

business sense clearly will fall to you—for various reasons, among them, that I am repeatedly imprisoned. Maybe I enrich the "family spirit" with new values.

In mid-August 1979, while Václav was still imprisoned at Ruzyně, the head of the bureau of the ministry of foreign affairs offered Havel the opportunity to travel to the United States. The offer was genuine, and the credit goes to Miloš Forman and, above all, to Joe Papp. Joe Papp, a world-famous New York director and a divinely good American, produced Havel's plays in the U.S. and was also concerned with the fate of their author. He offered Havel a position as dramaturge and tried to help him. It was not easy. Perhaps he was sorry to hear that Havel did not accept his offer. Havel refused to act on the suggestion in any way and said that he was not going to change his life on account of a few years in prison. During a visit, Olga agreed with his decision.

She could still send Vašek choice goodies. She tried to think up ways to prepare the food that were as cheerful and clever as possible. For example, she bought several kinds of small fish and layered them between onions. In October Václav's trial came with unanticipated speed.

35 ▪ The Trial

The trial took place on October 22 and 23.* The governmental power had prepared for it well. It was the greatest political trial since the 1950s.

The trial sessions were ostensibly open to the public. In the morning, before the day's session began, friends and relatives gathered outside the courthouse, but most of them could not get in. There were about

---

*By the time of the trial four of the original ten detained had been dropped from the indictment. These that remained were, in addition to Havel, Otta Bednařova, Václav Benda, Jiři Dienstbier, Dana Němcová, and Petr Uhl.

150 friends, diplomatic representatives from eight nations, foreign journalists registered in Prague, other foreign journalists, lawyers, representatives of Amnesty International, the International Federation of Leagues for Human Rights, the French trade-union organization CGT, and representatives of the January 5 Committee for a Free Socialist Czechoslovakia.

Dr. Kašpar, the chief justice of the tribunal, had chosen one of the smallest courtrooms. There were only eighteen seats in it for the public. They only let twelve people in, however. Three of Dana Němcová's children—Dana is the mother of seven—were not allowed inside. Dr. Kašpar refused to give them entrance tickets, even though they had been guaranteed to them. Nor did he give an entrance ticket to Otta Bednářová's sister; he told her they had all been given away.

There were therefore only twelve family members in the courtroom. Some relatives got as far as the corridor to the courtroom, but they had to pass through a quadruple security check. When they led the accused to the chamber, they were at least able to see them up close and greet them. Five seats in the courtroom remained empty. During the session, various gentlemen came, sat for a while, and then left. Jiří Hečko, the editor of *Rudé Právo*, sat there the entire time.

By the afternoon, there was still a group of people clustered in front of the courthouse who did not want to disperse. The police tried to break up the group, and when they refused to leave, they rounded up about forty people, whom they locked up in preliminary detention cells for forty-eight hours. The same thing happened to Anna Šabatová, the wife Petr Uhl, who was taking notes during the trial. Two of the people arrested were beaten, and six of them had their hair cut off. Several Frenchmen arrested by the police were transported to the border and thrown out of the country. It was an international scandal. When Jiří Bednář, Otta Bednářová's son, was leaving the courthouse, they arrested him and searched his person; they said he had a weapon on him. The same thing happened to Jan Dienstbier. They were looking for notes of the proceedings in order to confiscate them and make sure nothing was carried out.

Thanks to the Bednář brothers, Zuzana Dienstbierová, and Pavla Němcová, a transcript exists. The proceedings took place in a very tense, argumentative atmosphere. The judges knew they actually had nothing to judge. The entire suit was fabricated, and this gradually became apparent during the proceedings. Here is an authentic extract:

> *Chief justice to the public: "You there, in that white sweater, come here! And bring what you're writing. All of it!"*
> *"These are just blank pages."*
> *"Bring all of it; come closer. What's your name?"*
> *"Ondřej Dienstbier."*
> *"Show me your notes!" The chief justice inspects what he has written.*
> *"Why are you doing this?"*
> *"We have other relatives and an old mother. So that I can inform them about the course of the trial."*
> *The chief justice dictates into the record. "The notes of Ondřej Dienstbier were confiscated and placed in the records." Then he informed the participants that they could only take notes during the trial with the consent of the justices. Anna Šabatová, Petr Uhl's wife, raised her hand. The chief justice called her to the stand:*
> *"What's your name?"*
> *"Anna Šabatová."*
> *"How can we help you?"*
> *"I would like permission to take notes."*
> *"Taking notes during the trial is not permitted. Consider this to be a warning. If the standing order is violated again, you may be excluded from this session."*
> *"I believe that at a public trial I have the right to take notes."*
> *"The justices after consultation exclude Anna Šabatová from the courtroom until the conclusion of this trial."*
> *"I'm not going."*
> *Anna Šabatová returned to sit in her chair. The chief justice declared a five-minute break, during the course of which two*

uniformed officers dragged Anna Šabatová out of the courtroom.
She went limp and let herself be dragged out. She was then detained
for thirty-eight hours.

The entire case was a fabrication, as I said. We ought to remember that the founding declaration of the Committee for the Defense of the Unjustly Prosecuted was issued in April 1978, and that the attorney general received it in April, too. The government initiated proceedings in March, a year later, and this for the crime of subversion of the republic. If the activity was in fact as exceedingly dangerous to society as the accusation alleges, the attorney general, who knew of it, should have prosecuted it in a timely fashion, as the law directly enjoins him to do.

The charge against Petr Uhl, Václav Benda, Jiří Dienstbier, Václav Havel, Ottá Bednářová, and Dana Němcová read as follows:

> . . . *from the spring of 1978 to the end of May 1979, in Prague District 2 and elsewhere, out of resistance to the socialist governmental organization of the republic and with the intent to support anti-Communist foreign propaganda and intentionally to call up hostility among the residents of the republic against the socialist governmental organization of the republic, they founded an illegal organization, the Committee for the Defense of the Unjustly Prosecuted, and after a statement of the organization's program and allocating tasks in mutual understanding with other persons and several agents of seditious foreign headquarters, they gradually prepared a great quantity of writings, in which by coarse means and with the help of fictitious or intentionally distorted allegations, they crudely attacked the security organs, the attorney general, the courts, and prison staff. They circulated these writings in the Czechoslovak Socialist Republic and put them at the disposal of foreign anticommunist headquarters, which used them for attacks against us in the Western and emigré press and in the programs of several seditious broadcasters, such as Radio Free Europe. Thus, out of hostility toward the socialist organization of the republic's*

society and government, they engaged in subversive activity against the republic's social and governmental administration and against its international interests, committing this crime in collaboration with foreign agents and on a large scale.

For these reasons, all of the accused have have been charged with the crime of subversion of the republic according to article 98, paragraphs 1 and 2, letters (a) and (b) of the criminal code.

In the closing argument for the defense, Václav Havel's lawyer, Dr. Josef Lžičař, drew attention to the long gap of time between the inaugural declaration of the Committee and the initiation of prosecution proceedings. If the charge was conspiracy, this had been attained merely by the inaugural declaration—which, by the way, seventeen people had signed, and only ten were being prosecuted. At the end of his statement, Lžičař attempted to prove that subjectively, his client was innocent, and objectively, his guilt had not been proved either directly or via a chain of indirect proofs. For this reason, he urged that Havel be acquitted.

Václav Havel supported this in his own statement before the tribunal: "In my case, then, it turned out that the police and judicial organs had committed a mistake. I realized how easy it was to find oneself in a situation of being unjustly prosecuted, and that in such a case, an effective defense was possible. This led us to the idea for the Committee for the Defense of the Unjustly Prosecuted (VONS)."

The chief justice interrupted. "Your experience does not interest the court. Speak to the point."

V. Havel: "I only wanted to explain my opinion as to why those in power decided to take steps against VONS. Those in power start with the a priori assumption that governmental organs never act unjustly. The judicial decision-making process is considered to be infallible as a matter of principle."

The chief justice again intervened. "Mr. Havel, prosecution is nonetheless something quite different from the judicial decision-making process. Please continue, but be brief."

V. Havel: "I want to emphasize that this assumption of infallibility is very dangerous. Whoever casts doubt on the state is automatically considered an enemy and all his behavior is labeled as hostile. From the point of view of the prosecutor, if the governmental organs cannot commit mistakes, then anyone who criticizes their actions is logically commiting slander, calumny, and the like. And why is he slandering the government? Out of hostility, of course, and if this is the case, he must be collaborating with foreign hostile and antisocialist powers. . . . If the prosecution were to allow an analysis of the evidence, it would actually be allowing for its own fallibility. And those in power are very sensitive about their infallibility; therefore the establishment of proof is not based on the material content of our communiqués. Our communiqués only contain basic allegations, quotations of documents, and specific activities for which people were prosecuted. If someone were to write that gymnasium student XY typed an extra copy of a feuilleton by Václav Havel and gave it to a fellow student to read, this would not sound anywhere near as frightening as if one were to write that student XY duplicated and by illegal means distributed an antistate pamphlet by a right-wing exponent. . . . In the text of the accusation, certain words are repeated that can be singled out for their sharpness: for example, subversion, lies, malice, illegal organization, anti-Communist headquarters, hateful slander, and the like. But when we look to see what lies behind these words, we discover there is nothing behind them."

The chief justice again interrupted Havel. "But Mr. Havel, briefly, and to the point."

V. Havel: ". . . The question arises—is VONS an organization? If so, then an organization is any team working together, an artistic group, an orchestra, any essentially random group of people brought together by a common task. . . . In addition, I would like to point out that aside from membership in VONS, this court has proven absolutely nothing against me. . . . Finally, I would like to mention one more thing. A strange thing happened to me. About two months ago, two people visited me in prison and offered me the chance to travel to the United States. I refused to consider this offer until my friends and I were set free. I do not know what might have happened if I had accepted the offer, but it is possible that right now I would be somewhere in New York and would not be standing before this court. Therefore, it is to a considerable extent my decision that I am here. I think this decision proves I am not behaving out of hostility toward our country. On the contrary, it proves that I continue to have faith in the cause of justice in this country and that I have not lost this faith.''

In his defense statement, Petr Uhl added:

''. . . It troubles me that Czechoslovakia is today probably the only country in Europe where this sort of trial could still take place. I suppose that we will be found guilty and that we will be sentenced—all together, maybe to several decades of imprisonment. I am not a nationalist, but I love this country; I am not indifferent to its fate, and I want to live here.''

At this point Petr Uhl was also interrupted by the chief justice. ''The court is not for discussions. It is here to render a verdict on your criminal behavior.''

P. Uhl: ''I do not in any way consider you to constitute a court that could judge me. I know that you, your honor, will not render any verdicts. Those decisions have already been made in other places.''

Chief justice: ''If you do not consider this to be a court of law, then you needn't express your opinion.''

P. Uhl: ''Yes, you're right; it's pointless.''

In the course of the trial, no guilt was established for any of the points put forward in the accusation. It was not confirmed that VONS was in fact an organization. On the contrary, all the witnesses and the accused showed that what was involved was a citizens' initiative, issuing from the right to petition guaranteed in article 29 of the constitution, as well as from other legal rulings. This was already obvious from the fact that VONS communiqués were regularly sent to official organs and it never used conspiratorial methods. The fact that their work had lasted more than a year and no one had ever intervened strengthened VONS members' conviction that it was legal. The justices did not allow individual VONS communiqués to be quoted, so it was impossible to demonstrate the supposed falsity of the data they contained. All of the accused declared that they did not feel themselves to be guilty. Also, all the defense lawyers requested their clients be acquitted, except for one, who stated that he acted thus at the request of his client. Nevertheless, after a very quick, two-day session, the justices returned to the courtroom shortly after eight o'clock in the evening on October 23, and the chief justice, Dr. Kašpar, announced the verdict. The accused were found guilty as charged of subversion of the republic and received the following sentences:

Petr Uhl—five years
Václav Benda—four years
Jiří Dienstbier—three years
Václav Havel—four and a half years
Otta Bednářová—three years
Dana Němcová—two years, suspended for five years. . . .

It is sad that the members of VONS were condemned for their good deeds. People who had received financial assistance while their relatives were in prison testified against them.* The members of VONS had arranged support for these people from international organizations such as Amnesty International, the Charter 77 fund, and not infrequently out of their own pockets.

Part of the reasoning for the court's decision, it seems, was that the defendant Václav Havel had come from a bourgeois family. The text reads as follows:

---

*They testified because either they were threatened by the secret police or were frightened for themselves and their families.

According to the report of the District National Committee in Trutnov, between 1958 and 1969 he took an entirely reactionary position and has remained faithful to that position to the present day. At the cottage he purchased in the district of Vlčice, he is in contact with persons of doubtful reputation. The District National Committee's bureau for internal affairs also issued a warning to him.

The mass media in Czechoslovakia covered the trial and the accused very sketchily. Only a few extracts from the district attorney's speech were published, and they reported a few of the points falsely. For example, they claimed that VONS defended terrorists.

The trial provoked an enormous reaction abroad, in part because State Security had committed so many outrages in connection with it. To foreign observers, it appeared to be a willful violation of the Final Act of the Helsinki Accords. Individuals as well as organizations protested, including religious institutions, trade unions, members of parliament, several governments, and political parties, including Communist ones. Around the world, the trial was considered as an act against lessening international tension. Who, therefore, was injuring the republic's interests abroad? Who was agitating?

According to an earlier understanding, Havel's signature was added to a "Statement of Fellow Citizens" in late October 1979. The statement protested the government's decision to revoke the citizenship of the Czech writer Pavel Kohout. Kohout was forbidden to return to his country. The same thing later happened to Pavel Landovský and to Jiří Gruša. All three left Czechoslovakia because they had received a grant or a short-term appointment in the West. The Czechoslovak government took advantage of the opportunity and refused to allow them to return. Havel rejected every offer to travel. Because he was a nuisance to those in power, they wanted to get rid of him, but they did not know how to. When they imprisoned him, such a wave of protest rolled forth around the world that he was even more conspicuous and more famous than before. He was more dangerous in prison than free. What could they do with him? This is why they offered to let him move to the United States. If he had agreed, they would have let him out of prison.

In December 1979, at the initiative of the organization AIDA (Association internationale de défense des artistes victimes de la répression dans le monde—International Association for the Defense of Artists), the Paris theater Cartoucherie performed a dramatized reconstruction of the Prague trial of the six members of VONS. Two months later, the reconstruction was produced in German in Munich. German and Austrian television broadcast it as well.

Nor did European theater forget about Havel. On November 17, the Vienna Burgtheater produced his play *Protest* together with Pavel Kohout's one-act play, *The Pedigree Certificate*. On May 23, 1981, his play *The Mountain Hotel* premiered at the Akademietheater in Vienna. On November 21, 1981, Warsaw's Mala Scena Teatru Powszechniego produced the three one-act plays *Audience*, *Private View*, and *Protest*. They played until martial law was declared on December 13, 1981.

On December 20, 1979, the Supreme Court of the Czech Socialist Republic considered the appeal of the case of Petr Uhl and Co. Havel delivered a prepared statement for the defense. He emphasized that no hard evidence had been presented that demonstrated that the VONS communiqués were in fact false and distorted, as the verdict claimed. It had not even been demonstrated that VONS members made their communiqués public. The court had not managed to show that VONS was an organization, or that as such it was illegal. The fact that VONS acted publicly did not exceed the right of petition ensured by the constitution. The claim that VONS arose through mutual agreements with foreign agents or organizations was not substantiated, nor did they even substantiate the fact that VONS had gotten its resources from abroad. The convicted man further complained that they had not even demonstrated his participation in a single meeting. He himself had answered that he was a member of VONS and that he agreed with its activity right at the start of the criminal proceedings, and despite the court's finding to the contrary, this was the only fact that had been securely established during the trial.

The reasoning given by the court to justify the verdict of guilty was that Havel had written several articles and letters that had been published in the foreign press. For one thing, the articles and letters had no connection to VONS, and for another thing, it was never demonstrated that he had published them or had given permission for their publication. After the closing argument for the defense, Havel made this statement before the appellate court:

> *Esteemed court:*
>
> *Among other reasons, I have appealed this verdict because I have serious reservations about the course the trial took. I did not have the impression that the goal of the trial was the factual uncovering of the truth, as the law demands, but rather the quickest conviction possible. The evidence offered was not objectively investigated; remarks by the accused were disregarded; it was usually impossible for them to deliver their defense statements without interruption and in their entirety, although they did not digress from the essence of the matter at hand. The trial lasted twelve hours on the first day and thirteen on the second; these conditions did not contribute to an atmosphere conducive to an objective investigation into the truth.*
>
> *If I ask the Supreme Court of the Czech Socialist Republic to overturn the verdict of the Municipal Court, I take this step not only because in my opinion this case does not belong before any court and I consider the charge to be a fabrication, but also because I consider the decision of that court to be null and void, and I believe that the acts against the regime that were alleged were not proven.*
>
> *Your honors, the ability to repair these wrongs, which are a disgrace to Czechoslovak justice, lies in your hands.*

The court, however, upheld the earlier verdict.

On January 7, 1980, Havel was transported from the Prague prison

to the prison in Heřmanice outside the city of Ostrava, where he began
to serve out his sentence.

36 ▪ Serving His Sentence

While Václav was in prison, his family turned out to be his salvation.
His brother Ivan's letters to Heřmanice made it possible for him to
philosophize. His brother inspired him, posed questions for him to
answer, and engaged him in polemics. Olga and Ivan gave Vašek's
letters to Zdeněk Urbánek, Zdeněk Neubauer, Radim Palouš, and Jiří
Němec to read, and copied down their ideas, suggestions, polemical
remarks, and observations for Vašek. Ivan copied into his letters not
only his own philosophical treatises, but also Heidegger's lectures; in
installments, he copied out E. Levinas' essay "Without Identity" from
the book *The Humanism of the Second Man*; he collected reading material for his brother that was appropriate to the Advent and Christmas
seasons. He copied out Rouyeur's study on expressivity and Edith
Stein's biographical sketch *Plant Soul—Animal Soul—Human Soul*.
Last but not least, he copied out his own essays, for example, "Philosophic Aspects of Artificial Intelligence" and an essay about para-
doxes.

He collected and copied out poems by Vladimír Holan and Daniela
Fischerová and English poems for Vašek to memorize, to help him
learn English. He translated the reviews of Vašek's plays when they
were performed abroad. He shared everything that he read and that
interested him with his brother, including what he himself was writing. He reacted to every inaccuracy in Vašek's letters, even spelling
mistakes. It is great good fortune to have a brother like this, I said to
myself when I read *Letters to Olga* and discovered what had inspired
it. It was a constant, weekly flow of ideas, thoughts, and inspiration,
hundreds of densely typed pages.

From Ivan and Olga, Václav received impulses from the outside world that he integrated into his own world; he dwelt on them all week while he worked, expanding on them, and they raised him above the misery he found himself in. He could philosophize, thanks to his brother, his friends, and his wife, with whom he had long ago begun a dialogue, which he now continued despite all the murderous obstacles. These spiritual packages in the form of letters were as important as the packages with vitamins and spices thrown in as something extra. They were also more frequent. The soul comes first; the body takes second place. When the soul sickens, the body also withers. Ivan's and Olga's letters, which their friends collaborated on, were injections of salvation and love. But Vašek also wrote in letter 155 on December 18, 1982:

> . . . it is simply the joy of communication, of being understood, of being appreciated—that is, a pleasure that somehow returns to me through my echo in others, and reinforces my own identity, or in which my efforts find support. [trans. Caleb Crain; letter not included in Knopf's edition of Letters to Olga]

The only thing left to him as a writer was the private letter he could write to his wife once a week on four sheets of standard writing paper. Otherwise, he was strictly forbidden to have paper and a writing instrument or to make notes. He was even punished when they discovered rough drafts he had written for the letters he was allowed to send home. The only opportunity left was for him to write a censored letter once a week. In his letters, he resumed his old subject of human identity, but treated it in a different way than he had in his plays. And on the theme of responsibility and of the horizons toward which our being reaches, and so forth. Many letters were confiscated with the explanation that they should only deal with family matters, but then somehow the censors grew accustomed to the writing. Věra Jirousová remembers that once Ivan Havel asked her to write a letter in his place. She mused for a long time over what she could write Vašek, and then she wrote him a letter inspired by her reading of Carlos Castaneda. It was full of Castaneda's allegories and magical imagery. This letter, too, had to fit into the prescribed format. When Václav received the letter, so much of it was blacked out that he had no idea what it was about. The prison goons must have thought they were dealing with a particularly dangerous and mysterious conspiracy, so they made sure he could not figure out anything.

Olga thought up ways to send Vašek as much sensory stimulation as possible—the most exciting colors, people, and objects. Since they were allowed to send him family photographs, they dressed up as colorfully as possible and piled up a lot of different objects around them, so that in conjunction with the family photograph Václav could see as much as possible.

Vašek liked it when Ivan interlarded his letters with essays about physics—about quasars, black holes, and antimatter—and when Zdeněk Neubauer, through Ivan, discussed biology. He insisted on knowing what his friends and his brother thought of his letters and his philosophizing. The letters renewed Václav's continually eroded and splintered identity; they gave a meaning to his stay in prison and to his life. Again and again, they lifted him above the ingenious system of humiliation and cultivation of all base and low aspects of human nature on which life in jail is based. The visits Olga and Ivan made four times a year were of course also uplifting; Václav prepared for them by making notes and writing down questions to ask, and the answers he received sustained him for a long time after.

Perhaps Ivan quoted philosophers in order to hide the shyness he felt toward his brother. All of us know what it is to feel embarrassed by the suffering of those near to us, and it is our siblings, after all, to whom we never say the most essential things directly. Something like a family shyness exists, which conditions love and is a component of it. We live next to each other our whole lives, and as a punishment, we do not tell each other what is most essential. We have better luck with other people.

In his letters, Ivan did not describe his life, his problems, or his cares. Sometimes at the end of a philosophical letter, he observed that someone had or was going to have a birthday, that someone had been born, that there was a party and so-and-so attended, or that someone had left the country forever. Around 1980, there were many people who left forever because they could no longer stand the persecution. They were missed sorely and for a long time; some of them will always be missed.

In 1981, charges were filed against Ivan M. Havel and he was prosecuted, although he was allowed to remain at large during the course of the proceedings. There is no mention of the affair in his letters to his brother. It was in connection with the seizure of a French truck which was bringing banned literature and magazines across the border. On this occasion, the Prague police made a big raid and arrested 233 people. Olga and Ivan were incarcerated for four days and charged with subversion of the republic, under Article 98, for publishing Expedition Edition. At the time, all three were in jail at once, which in effect amounted to the liquidation of the family.

Olga says that afterward they went on a visit to Heřmanice prison. Vašek told them that if the two of them were ever again in danger of imprisonment, he would just as soon they emigrate. Olga and Ivan told him they would stay no matter what the circumstances. A stone seemed to have been lifted from Václav's heart.

During the raid, the authorities also made a thorough search of the Havel's home. Mostly they took unpublished Czech literature— Hrabal, twenty-four copies of Bondy, etc. No sooner had they carried the writings away in burlap sacks than the doorbell rang. Olga opened the door, and there stood Fanda* Pánek, who with a smile offered her his new poem. At the same time that they were carting literature out of the house, more literature was being gathered.

They also took a lot of printed material from Ivan.

Olga says that during the visits to Heřmanice which were permitted four times a year, the authorities emphasized that they were only allowed to speak about family matters. Nonetheless, they spoke about

---

*Diminutive for František.

everything, because the police did not actually know what they were talking about. Olga always tried to dress as colorfully and prettily as possible and she always wore make-up. Vašek asked her to. Olga and Ivan tried to bring as much colorful, lively light into the gray prison as possible. I would like to quote part of a letter now. It is a regular letter Ivan sent during the last phase of Vašek's imprisonment, when the prison goons had already resigned themselves to the philosophizing they did not understand. Paradoxically, one of the freest exchanges took place in this letter. It shows that it is possible to express everything through the language of philosophy and it is not necessary to use allegories. On January 14, 1983, in his ninety-second letter, Ivan wrote:

Hi Véna,

Amidst a flood of events, it is only now that I take up your letter number 160 (the "melancholy" one) together with 161. Of course I am giving both to ZN [Zdeněk Neubauer] to read. In addition to his comments and to ZU's [Zdeněk Urbánek's] reaction, which Olga probably already has written to you about, here are a few of my observations.

It is characteristic of the variation in human sensitivity (including intellectual sensitivity) in your and our conditions that a by and large innocent suggestion [ZN's commentary to 144] calls up a surprisingly strong "pre-Christmas melancholy" in you—and that in turn your (however unpleasant) clearly transitory and apparently not at all unusual melancholy causes us surprisingly strong concern here. In order for it all to stand out in sharp relief, because of the natural delay of the mail you receive and will receive our consoling and reassuring letters only when your spirits are already refreshed. (It seems to me we should pool our resources and put together one universal letter of consolation, which we would send you at regular intervals—maybe then we would hit the right moment from time to time.)

Right now I have no intention of trying to console you. Nonetheless, I would still like to make a few remarks about these matters. (By the way: note that—whatever the cause of your melancholy might be—your "August melancholy" came when you were writing [a rough draft of] letter 144, and your "pre-Christmas melancholy" came when you read a commentary on the same letter.)

I have the feeling that your letters are not only a diary based on your experiences (ZU), but at the same time *essays—and well thought-out essays at that; it's even possible to say they are philosophical treatises—and* at the same time *dramatic formations in a literary style, and* at the same time *poems in prose, and thus their multigenre nature makes and will make them the particular thing they are. It is not necessary to see them from all sides in the same way at the same time. One person reads them one way; another, another; all of them meanwhile could be reading them the right way (for example, in his commentary, ZN was reading as a local reader, but now there's another ZN walking among us, a global reader, who, as he confided to me, now sees the letters from many other angles—you will learn about this eventually). I don't share with Zdeněk U. the need to defend your right, while trying hard to capture your experience, to "borrow terms from specialized fields" in which you may not feel yourself to be "at home as a professional and an expert." Not that I think you do not have such a right, but simply that I don't think there are any such "terms." There are only words, words, words, (originally the word* naopak *["on the contrary"] was borrowed from natural speech) which the course of time and the incoherent efforts of various thinkers cram full of a certain deeper philosophic significance. That significance, among other things, is first given shape by the feedback from these words, ...*

. . . it is exactly the inequality of the situation from which both characters speak that gives this play its particular meaning. It is a play *whose moves are not only the moves the pen makes across*

paper, but also a new experience provoked by the play, including melancholy (which it approaches, I have the feeling, from both sides!).

Thanks for pointing out that book on people's experiences of clinical death. Evidently even in your present surroundings it is possible to find out about interesting news in the world. . . . I ran into your classmate Lojza at the airport again. He was full of interesting stories from your younger days together.

Now once again I will defer to Levinas, continuing his third essay, "Subjectivity and Vulnerability."

He continues with several densely typed pages of Levinas. Ivan also sent Vašek news about "An Evening with Václav Havel" in Avignon:

As part of a world theater festival, an evening in honor of the imprisoned Czechoslovak writer Václav Havel took place on July 21 in Avignon. The organizer AIDA invited playwrights around the world to write scenes for Vaněk, making it possible for this character from several of Havel's plays to live on while his author is in prison. For the six-hour program, ten scenes were chosen, interspersed with singing by the Czechoslovak émigré singers Jaroslav Hutka, Karel Kryl, and Charlie Soukup. On an improvised stage under the ramparts of Urban V's palace, Hutka opened by singing the song "Havlíček, Havel,"* whose meaning was translated and explained for the French audience. In a vignette by Jean-Pierre Faye, "A Seat," opportunities for betrayal and capitulation were offered to Vaněk, with the chance to sit down in a chair as the reward. In a monologue, Arthur Miller mused on the fate of the imprisoned writer and considered the West's inability to understand the Eastern intellectual's situation. In "Catastrophe," Samuel Beckett presented a director who with the help of

---

*The song links Havel's protest and punishment to that of Karel Havlíček-Borovský, a critic of the Hapsburg regime.

an assistant manipulates a character tied up on stage. The audi-
ence had to decide whether they were seeing a rehearsal for a play
or preparations for an execution. In addition to other vignettes, a
montage of the work of Pavel Kohout and Pavel Landovský was
performed.*

*Tickets cost sixty francs, which is expensive; nonetheless, the
show was sold out. In the end, the organizers let in everyone who
wanted to see the show, so hundreds of young people were sitting on
the grass, the ground, and the ramparts. During the performance,
several hundred postcards were sold that could be sent to the Czechoslovak authorities to ask for Václav Havel's release. In the course
of the evening, a letter of support from the French minister of
culture was read aloud and at the conclusion, a letter of thanks
from the writer's wife, Olga.*

I remember that Olga used to let any friends who came to visit read
the latest letter from Vašek. Generally, the first person to read the
letters after Olga was Zdeněk Urbánek, who stopped by U dejvického
rybníčku Street almost daily. Andulka Freimanová-Krobová remembers that at Hrádeček, Olga would open the window and shout "Letter!" out across the orchard. And everyone would immediately come
running to listen.

In July 1982, Ivan sent an atypical letter, which I would like to
quote from. He signed it, but it was in fact a letter from Jiří Dienstbier,
who had been set free:

Hi Véna,

*In order to relax in the fresh air and cope with the trouble I
have breathing—as the years go by, panting my way up to the fifth
floor is a less and less enjoyable task—I sallied forth to Northern
Bohemia for a while. I wandered among the meadows, and I felt*

---

*In Beckett's script, as published in *Living in Truth*, the Protagonist is standing
passively on a plinth with his hands in his pockets, but there is no mention
of him being tied up.

like writing you a kind of tone poem, something that would for a while raise us above the usual debate about meaning and horizons, and would remind us that the world is not only a battlefield in us or outside us, but also many other things. This letter, therefore, does not belong to the regular series and I do not know whether I will continue these sorts of attempts, though perhaps I will.

As Hanička [Anna Šabatová] said, ''the saddest thing was that they jailed the kind of guys who like life, girls, good food, and drink.'' Nevertheless, it occurred to me that this is exactly your good fortune, that what helps you maintain your good spirits is the awareness that you haven't wasted your time on anything, the way a lot of people waste their time on endless preparations for a life they never attain. Therefore you really haven't lost anything, and after this pause, you can continue naturally, no poorer, in fact richer for the widening of your field of vision. Only a few minor adjustments, maybe, and well, there's no denying that the increase in age, with the physical consequences it brings, can annoy us, but we're already learning to manage that. . . .

. . . More than a month ago, I went through Prague on a Saturday afternoon. It seemed battered and decayed to me, and the clincher was that dead pigeons, killed by chemicals, were lying here and there along the sidewalks and roadways. Nobody paid any attention to them. There wasn't a soul in sight, except from time to time a pedestrian would blink by in the distance or a car would drive through. The desolate Saturday town, which everyone had fled in order to tinker with their country cottages. I stopped by to visit Vlasta and Standa [Stanislav Milota and Vlasta Chramostová], whose electricity is being converted to 220 volts. They gave me a warm welcome amidst the ruins of their apartment, of their disassembled theater. In the evening, some of our dearest friends came over, and everything became clear to me. Our anchor is not in the unsettled mud at the bottom of a stream; it is in those who are close to us, who will find their place in any kind of stream.

This is a boon that no one can take away from us, no matter where
we are at any given moment, let the swamp waters toss as much
as they like. . . . That's all for today; I will continue later. . . .

During Václav's long imprisonment, the Burgtheater in Vienna produced *The Mountain Hotel* with Peter Palitzsch as director. The play
had lain in a drawer for five years. Ivan Martin Jirous, alias Magor, a
sensitive critic, one of the best, who later understood *Temptation* and
did justice to it in an ingenious way, one of the most truthful people
I know, wrote this about *The Mountain Hotel*:

> *We are the zoo of the West, the terrarium of the West. Havel*
> *speaks about it clearly in "The Power of the Powerless," when he*
> *points to the "rebirth" of the "dissident." In his case, of the*
> *"dissident" who writes plays in his "free time." At least right*
> *now, the pseudopoliticized West does not understand that for us*
> *art is the most important thing in the world. That before every-*
> *thing else is the play, and only then comes its interpretation. It is*
> *with pain that we recognize that many of the things we do would*
> *not be accepted in the West were they not banned at home. (This*
> *is not the case with Havel; I am talking about other artists. Václav*
> *Havel is one of the few whose work has been understood as a*
> *universal human situation.)*

Havel wrote a commentary for his play, just as Poe wrote one for
"The Raven." Critics who did not understand his play too well generally quoted what the author himself had said about it in the program
notes: that it was about nothing for a long time, and then suddenly
about everything. And that it was actually a fugue. The reviews also
talked about the loss of identity, which is a theme in all of Havel's
plays, about the absurdist rondeau of characters who because of alienation sank to the level of marionettes and played parts in a repeated,
cyclical performance. The critics praised the finely finished, precise
compositional form and the expressive compactness of the play. However, *The Mountain Hotel* also received unfavorable reviews, which

claimed that the play was running on empty, that it was an unplay, a bad play—all straw and no manure. They said that solving its riddles was like kicking in an unlocked door, and that its cheap stereotypes were as easy to explain in the East as in the West.

As a political prisoner, Vašek acted as a parish priest, a judge, a counsellor, a consoler, and a psychologist to his fellow prisoners. He wrote love letters, advised fellow prisoners about whether they should divorce, he settled several disputes, and talked some of them out of committing suicide. They trusted a political prisoner; they knew he would not inform on them, and so they told him everything. He always had to be ready, always in good shape. In Heřmanice, Láďa Sobas agreed to act as his bodyguard (Jiří Dienstbier and Václav Benda also had bodyguards). Václav talked to him about literature and the theater and actually brought him back to life. Láďa is a child from an orphanage. He stole cars until they locked him up. Since his release from prison, he has lived a clean life; he is married and has two children. He is now a spokesperson for miners and is concerned about their health.

Václav befriended priests who held a secret mass at Bory prison; they also gave him strength.

A prison goon asked the librarian at Heřmanice to work out the answer to his final exam question on Marxism-Leninism. In fact, it was Václav who did the assignment. In exchange, the librarian smuggled a message to Olga in Prague. They met at the train station.

He kept up all these friendships when he was set free. Whenever his fellow prisoners announced themselves at Hrádeček or Prague, Václav always gave them priority over friends he had not done time with. Spending time together on the inside is a bond that lasts one's whole life.

37 ▪ Letters to Olga

Jan Lopatka—the literary critic, Václav's friend from *Tvář*, and a collaborator in the publication of Expedition Edition—received the original letters to Olga—i.e., the handwritten manuscripts—in the autumn of 1982. They were written in a small, careful, legible hand on small pieces of paper that had been crammed with writing from the upper left-hand to the lower right-hand corner. The author had wanted to get as many of his ideas down on paper as possible. Indeed, all week, while working at the sanding machine, he would look forward to Saturday afternoon, when he would be permitted to sit in the common room—where the others played cards, amused themselves, and shouted each other down—and lay out on paper the thoughts that had occurred to him throughout the week, which he had been sorting and arranging day and night. Lopatka had the job of turning these letters into a book. Václav refers to this in his letter to Olga dated October 2, 1982:

> *Whatever kind of chapel it is, it must now live its own life, exposed without my protection to all the winds, which will blow against it and may even crush its masonry . . . . In general, please don't take me too much at my word, but follow the general "sound," impression, sense, expressivity, ethos, etc., rather than the factual-logical-semantic "information." I haven't heard from Jan Lop for a long time. I missed his face in the photos of your birthday party. I would welcome it if he were to collect my correspondence and share with Ivan the task of putting it in order; I have an uncommon faith in Ivan's feeling for these matters. . . . When Ivan has it all completed and safely stowed away, please let me know at once— only then will I have the joyful feeling of completion—and I will toast the occasion with a mug of English tea and eat a bar of Tuzex*

chocolate. [Not in edition published by Knopf; trans. by Caleb Crain.]

Lopatka received these instructions from Bory prison. Soon after, he received a briefcase of letters from the pretrial detention at Ruzyně prison, the letters Václav continued to write after his transfer to Heřmanice, and the most recent letters from Plzeň-Bory. The author's original idea was that the editor, Jan Lopatka, would select the passages that were consistently philosophical and discard the parts that were private, intimate, technical (such as what should be included in a package etc.), and organizational (such as details of an upcoming visit). Lopatka comments:

"When I read through the letters, I started—as I realized in retrospect—to work systematically *against* this tendency. I was afraid that if we published the philosophical parts without presenting a vivid picture of the circumstances in which they were written, without the delicate and complicated structure that determines this kind of writing, that makes it necessary to think about what can be sent in a package and how to communicate what is most essential, how to learn something without provoking the head censor into confiscating the letter— I was afraid that this kind of writing was pretty damned different from writing an essay with a library at hand and access to information and data. Therefore, I started to heap together everything that would give a vivid picture of what was characteristic of the shaping of these letters.

"I didn't want to scribble on the letters, and more important, I didn't want to have them in my house. If the police had come, they could have taken them from me. The letters were only safe with Olga. I brought them to a secret place, where the most inconspicuous typist took them, and once they were copied, I immediately returned the originals to Olga. From autumn 1982 to mid-February I edited this transcript. In February, Ivan Havel called me to say that they had released Vašek from the Pankrác prison hospital and brought him to the Pod Petřínem hospital. We and Petr Kabeš went there the next day. Vašek was ill; he had a high temperature and hardly knew we were there. I asked him if it still made sense for me to edit the book if he was finally free, and he said, 'Of course,' "

They sent him from a prison hospital to a civilian hospital because they were afraid he was going to die in prison. He had a bad case of pneumonia. Every day, several dozen friends visited him at Pod Petřínem hospital, and every day he felt a little better. The doctors tolerated the visits. Olga brought him *laskonkas** the first day, and Václav declared he had not eaten anything so good in four years. She also brought him a bottle of *myslivecká*† so that he would have something to offer his guests.

Meanwhile, Lopatka worked diligently at *Letters to Olga*.

"I scribbled on the copies and proofread them against the originals. At first, Vašek was against including the more private stuff, but he quickly got used to the idea. I asked him if the people who were mentioned in the letters would allow it, and he said they would have to. In mid-April I had a definitive manuscript. Vašek added notes for the points that still were not clear to me, and then we made a clean copy. The *Letters* came out in May 1983 without a publisher, and we started to work out a new format for Expedition Edition.

"We met with Vašek, Ivan Havel, and Zdeněk Urbánek four times a year. Josef Danisz signed on to be our typist, but he only wanted to type poems with short lines. He wanted us to pay him for the poems at the same rate we paid for prose. Over the years, Martin Palouš and Tomáš Vrba were added to our number, and we called ourselves the Admiralty. Vašek was the admiral, and we had this wooden doll, a kind of monster, that was named Trejdl (pronounced "TRAY-dull"). We were always saying: 'Trejdl did it,' 'Send Trejdl there,' 'Trejdl screwed it up again,' etc. We pretended someone named Trejdl was sitting with us in order to confuse those bugging us. We referred to a book in the works or in an unfinished state as a 'Bulletin of the Museum of National Literature, Strahov courtyard number such-and-

---

*Czech pastry.
†Literally, "huntsman's liqueur." It resembles Jaegermeister.

such,' and then a slash followed by the year. On one occasion, they confiscated the bulletins when they attacked a vehicle en route to Hrádeček."

During this confiscation, Olga also had two copies of Charles Bukowski with her. State Security stopped her car in the vicinity of Vlčice. In their report, they wrote she had been transporting pornography, and at the Vlčice Municipal National Committee they fined her 500 crowns.

38 ▪ *Dear Vašek*

On January 11, 1985, I started to write a letter to Václav Havel, and even at the time the date struck me as a very good one. I no longer remember whether I mailed the letter to him or delivered it by hand. There have only been two books by living authors that have inspired me to write a letter to the author as soon as I finished reading them. They were Ludvík Vaculík's *The Czech Dreambook* and *Letters to Olga*. My letter to Ludvík was later printed in *Response to "the Czech Dreambook"* and my letter to Vašek appeared in the monthly journal *Obsah*, which we were publishing in samizdat at the time. Today I reread my letter and it seems to me that I could not now express what *Letters to Olga* means to me any more exactly than I did then:

> *I spent the end of last year and the beginning of this year with your book, and it will remain forever linked with the intense conclusion of 1984 and the liberating start of 1985. As the year ended, everything that had been a hindrance throughout the year and had been overcome with great pains reappeared, and I was forced to confront it. From the beginning I also had a difficult struggle with your book. On New Year's Day, I felt relieved, and this is a good sign. It seems to me that this year will be better than the preceding ones, that from somewhere, perhaps from outer*

space, grace is wafting toward us, even though there is no evidence of this; in fact, the evidence points in the opposite direction. A cleansing, perhaps, as if your book had prefigured it. Perhaps I felt good on New Year's Day because I had already reached the point in the Letters *when you became more and more relaxed. Before this point, I had to set the book aside several times; I could not stand the tension, which you are able to control by holding down the lid with all your strength. You keep guard over your homesickness, your pain, tears, anger, all your human emotions, and you work at your task: a superhuman, or perhaps inhuman, self-control. The time trickling away tortures you, and because you must somehow make it valuable, you use it by making an experiment on yourself. To share in this experiment was almost too much to bear. And your being in a divided world, which slices even you in two. In spirit you are still outside with those close to you, in places you cherish; you hold onto them tenaciously; and at the same time you are*̇*irreparably and without appeal inside, where it is as if there were nothing.*

How much time must pass before you begin to leave behind life on the outside, before you free yourself from it, knowing that nothing will take its place? You realize that you are left alone with yourself—a realization that reaches a climax somewhere during the description of your good and bad moods. For me, it was as though you had dug out an eye in front of me, turned it on yourself, and used it as a magnifying glass to scrutinize what is supposed to compensate you for the loss of the whole world. This is not a complaint; the reader must bear what the author bore if the author allows him to live through his trial. But I have probably never read anything so unbearable, by virtue of its absurdity, its horrible and painful senselessness, yet through it we reach the meaning.

It is a cleansing thing to read. Your demands on yourself and your frankness force people to bring that eye near themselves and inspect whether or not they are slipping into existence-in-the-world,

whether or not they are lying about themselves or about others.*
After that failure, *it is as if your eyes were suddenly opened; your
meditations become more and more consistent and brilliant, and
suddenly all your reflections revolve around the meaning of life and
of the "absolute horizon." Until it seems to me that some higher
power is governing you, a power that returns you inexorably and
logically to the place where you ended or from where you escaped,
and forces you to start over again. You cannot certainly remember
what you wrote a year or two before. I remember that once during
a visit with Vendulka Halounová you said that you seemed to be a
medium through whom certain messages were channeled.*

*You return to your experience of unity with "the absolute hori-
zon" and this forms the central image and the summit of your
meditations. You described this feeling, if it is a feeling, beautifully;
it is almost indescribable. I had this experience for the first time,
undeservedly, at age nineteen, and later I learned how to return
to it. All the same, however, I cannot manage to remain in this
state; each of us must hit rock bottom and stand up again several
times in the course of our lives. It has to be this way for us, unless
we step beyond the limits, aims, and rights of our existence-in-the-
world, which, to the extent that we are able to realize them and
fulfill our ideas, definitely prevent us from finding our identity once
and for all.† This threshing will purify us, until we are all grain,*

---

*". . . we are constantly exposed to the temptation to stop asking questions
and adapt ourselves to the world as it presents itself to us, to sink into it, to
forget ourselves in it, to lie our way out of our selves and our "otherness"
and thus to simplify our existence-in-the-world." [*Letters to Olga*, p. 320.]
"Existence-in-the-world is, after all, a temptation and a seduction: it drags
one down into the world of things, surfaces, frantic consumption and self-
absorption . . ." [*Letters to Olga*, p. 338.]
†"For succumbing to existence-in-the-world is in fact surrendering to the 'non-
I.' In renouncing the transcendental dimensions of his 'I,' man renounces
its paradoxical essences, disrupts that fundamental tension from which its
very existence, subjectivity and ultimately its identity all stem, dissolves
himself in aims and matters that he himself has defined and created, and
finally loses himself in them entirely." [*Letters to Olga*, pp. 338–339.]

no chaff. At good times it seems to me that life itself lives through me, that I cannot influence it much, and as long as it flows freely, it is good. But when, out of my own limited will, I lay some impediment before it, when I long for something and want it, I am badly off.

Everything in your book speaks to me. The dispute carried out in its pages does not permit the reader to give up—it holds onto him tightly. The dispute between the head and the body, or the soul and the body. Intellectuals often feel that the soul is in the head. In his introduction to Stendhal's essay "On Love," Arthur Breisky wrote that men are "martyrs of their brains," and he felt this applied to Stendhal, who wrote about love with his head and was an analyst of love. Just so. The head produces thought; it wants to have everything named, appraised, and explained. And the soul, which sits condemned in the head, dreams about mystery, which the understanding refuses to allow to come true.

Perhaps the experience of God is the experience of the whole body and with the head. I say perhaps, because you work toward contact with the absolute horizon by means of thinking. By rational reflection you attempt to master the irrational. It is a difficult route, but it shows that it is possible, that there are many paths, if I think that Einstein perhaps reached God through calculation and Ladislav Klíma through drink.

Do you know what I am sorry about? That several times, you use as a point of departure a meteorologist caught by surprise when the sound fails on television or the question of whether to pay the fare on an empty streetcar at night. I wonder why you do not draw from the life that must be colorful, noisy, and pressing all around you, yet you seem not to notice it. Perhaps you are not allowed to write about it: Aha, you may not, you say. And perhaps it is also not appropriate to write home about these people who are exposed and powerless before you, and yet you have the privilege that you know how to write. Writers often behave immorally toward the people closest to them, toward those who are naked before them.

In your writing, everything is filtered through a screen of modesty and refinement, even when you write about your bodily functions. If you could write what you chose for as long as you wanted, perhaps the tension of the unspoken would disappear, this tension that gives the book space and purity, from which nothing can be pared away.

Letters to Olga, *like* The Czech Dreambook, *is an event in the life of Czech literature. Everyone is talking about it and wants to read it. It makes me very happy. It has also occurred to me that my beloved philosophy has found a way to return to life. Almost no one reads philosophy today; people don't have time. But if meditations come with the exciting packaging of a famous writer in prison, they read them, and maybe they understand what they would not have understood from Heidegger or Patočka. What may seem to you to be naive and unoriginal philosophizing plays a part whose impact is, I hope, beyond our estimation. The revelation of the truth has often reached people by means of those whom they consider to be martyrs.*

This book, therefore, is important, and when I imagine that it stands on bookshelves beside the obscene and bloody novels with which people revive their frozen instincts and passions, then there is still some chance, some hope for this world. If only people began to consider meditation, reflection as their salvation, as you were driven to in prison. I am afraid even to think about it.

I want to thank you for wanting me to share your trial with you, and for writing so well and so candidly that I believe everything you said. As I write, I am aware of the horrible concreteness of words. Every word ought to have shifting meaning that begets new meanings, but I am afraid that soon there will be no words that have meaning that do not depend directly on experience. What will happen to philosophy without the experience of loss and without solitude? And can there be such a thing as art, in which life is not what matters?

I pray that in all your actions, the strength that fills your letters will sustain you.

39 ▪ Free Again

In early March 1983, Václav was allowed to go home from the hospital. About three days later, we went to a meeting of writers in Moravia, one of the meetings that took place regularly four times a year. When Pavel Kohout was still in the country, he hosted them at his place in Sázava. Vašek also hosted them when Hrádeček was not under systematic surveillance. When Pavel left for Vienna and they imprisoned Vašek, the meetings took place at various places, either at the homes of writer-participants or of other good and brave people. I would like to say thank you to all those who welcomed us during those years, taking on a risk that some of them later discovered they could ill afford.

At the end of his novel *The Czech Dreambook*, Ludvík Vaculík beautifully describes, as only he can, one such trip; actually, he creates one trip out of all our trips to Moravia. I too, though with less talent, could describe several of these trips. In particular, I remember the trip we took with Vašek when they released him.

We always took the same train. It left at nine in the morning from Prague Central Station—long ago and now once again called Masaryk Station. We sat in a compartment; I think there were eight of us. I sat next to Vašek, and he was telling me how he wanted to write a play, but nothing had come to him. He had dreamed that an owl sat on his shoulder and hooted into his ear that it was a singer, and then its head changed into a woman's head. He asked me what it meant, and I did not know. Karel Pecka sat in the corner beside the door and smoked. Meanwhile, through the half-open door, he watched the corridor to see if the conductor was coming.* The same conductor had traveled on that train for years. He was an ogre whose shadow filled the entire door frame. It seemed like he could not scrape through, but would instead reach out a giant hand and drag out the culprit who provoked him. Another ogre had also traveled on that line for years, selling newspapers and magazines. Maybe both of them still travel it today, yoyoing back and forth between Prague and Nové Zámky. Although we still hold meetings, we have not taken that train in a long time. Today all sorts of people would be happy to attend our meetings, but Ludviík Vaculík has issued strict instructions that only those who attended while it was dangerous may attend now; the circle will not widen. He has started to call it the Literary Archive.

On that occasion, then, Pecka was smoking, and Vašek would have been glad to light up, but he was afraid to. I told him he should smoke too, since Pecka could. He objected that as soon as he lit up, the conductor would come. Karel laughed when he heard this, with the superiority of an insider who had spent twelve years in a Stalinist concentration camp. Vašek then pulled out his pack of BT ["Bulgarian tobacco," a brand name] and lit a cigarette. He smoked about half of it, when Karel announced that danger was approaching. Vašek stuck the cigarette in my hand, and I held onto it—I don't know why. Then it occurred to me I should throw it on the floor and stamp it out. At that moment, the compartment darkened, because the ogre's shadow had filled the doorway. He gave a few powerful sniffs that swelled his nostrils. He looked at us one after the other, and we all looked back at him. We looked him in the eye, and with his thick eyebrows and fleshy lips he looked like Brezhnev or Stalin.

"Somebody here is smoking!" the orge said. Again he looked us over one by one, and his glance alone convicted us. As writers who had learned how to be silent or to lie during interrogations, we shook our heads to deny we had been smoking. And the ogre selected a victim, rested his glance of justice upon him, and said:

---

*Smoking is not allowed in the train compartments.

"You were smoking!"

I looked at Vašek and saw that his eyelid was twitching and he was blushing terribly.

There was silence for a moment. The ogre savored his victory, and I knew then that Vašek is like Schopenhauer's saint, who is punished for peccadillos the way other people are punished for great sins. As soon as he does anything, he gets slapped. There was nothing he could do. The conductor, moved by Vašek's inability to lie, bent over and said:

"I don't want a fine. Just promise me you'll never do it again."

We learned later that the fine was only thirty crowns, which Vašek could easily have paid. But he would not light another cigarette. Pecka, the old hand, smoked merrily all the way to Kúty, where we got off.

At the time, it seemed that Václav would never again be able to be happy. He was constantly thinking about his friends, about his fellow prisoners, about Petr Uhl, who was in solitary confinement at Mírov prison, and about Magor, who was in a class three prison at Valdice—one of the most frightening prisons. Out of the last seventeen years before the fall of the totalitarian regime, Jirous spent almost nine in jail. But he wrote one of the most beautiful books of that era, *Magor's Swan Song*, and thus is everything always redeemed. I saw Vašek when he left prison, and I saw Magor, too. They both had open wounds; their fellow prisoners were always with them, as reproachful shadows that made everything difficult. Vašek thought about Rudolf Battěk, who was in prison in Opava and was sick; about Jiři Gruntorád, who was imprisoned for having made copies of books and essays by banned authors; about Jaromír Šavrda, who did the same; about Ladislav Lis, who was in prison in Litoměřice. He was on the outside, but was finding it difficult to adapt. It is easier to adjust to prison than to release from prison and existence outside. They call it postprison psychosis. Vašek did not think of his jailers with hatred, but he could not rid himself of them. Mainly, he had to always be doing something that would lead to getting his friends out of prison. Once again, he threw himself into politics, he wrote, and he gave interviews, even though he knew they could come for him at any time because he had not served his whole sentence.

During this period, Western journalists and Central and Eastern European specialists found the Charter 77 movement small and insignificant compared to Poland's Solidarity. Havel says that every nation gets the Charter it deserves. The Charter had many silent sympathizers who took its side but were waiting to see how things turned out. As before, signing the Charter meant losing one's job, manual labor, financial distress, police chicanery, and persecution of one's family members and children. The Charter had about a thousand public supporters. It was important because it formed an opposition that constantly caught the regime red-handed at its crimes, criticized it, and at the same time, offered to engage it in dialogue. There were a thousand people who, in the spirit of Patočka's words, understood that some things were worth suffering for. VONS still existed and did not cease to function, even though they locked up its members one after another. New people always appeared to take up the work. In the Western press and via foreign radio stations, VONS published the names and fates of people who were unjustly prosecuted. Even this was quite important. State Security was bolder toward people who were unknown and whom no one cared about. Drawing constant attention to the violation of human rights in Czechoslovakia provoked a large response in the West and gradually discredited the Czechoslovak leadership.

In an interview Havel gave in April 1983 to the French daily newspaper *Le Monde*, he described how the atmosphere in the country had changed. It is the astute perspective of someone who has spent time away and then returned. He saw that underneath the thick crust of inertia, history had actually moved forward in only four years:

> *The pressure exerted by the political apparatus on the official culture, which until recently had been safely in its grasp, would appear to be growing, and that is a sure sign that it is again beginning to mean something: I even get the impression that in*

some sectors this seemingly "safe" culture is getting out of its control. They have been banning plays, theatres and, in particular, numerous rock and jazz bands which not so long ago they had lavished praise on. Many people today no longer know which culture they form part of—whether the "official" or the "other"—people who are still "all right" appear on the same platforms with banned ones, everything seems to get mixed up. It also seems to me that even some—of course only a few—official artists have changed their attitude toward us. They don't seem so afraid of us anymore; perhaps they realize that they might at any time find themselves in our ranks and that there is no longer any sense on in pretending. . . .

To some extent, all this reminds me of the early sixties, when the process of self-realization and spiritual liberation likewise began somewhere on the borders between official and unofficial culture, in that strange area in which the authorities prohibit one thing only for another to crop up a little way off, unnoticed by the censors. This process, of course, culminated in 1968, when the powers that be were forced to acknowledge, could no longer ignore, the true condition of our society, of its soul.

As regards political matters, it seems to me that the authorities today are facing all the economic, social, political, and cultural problems more hesitantly than it appeared to me while in prison. . . . ["I Take the Side of Truth," Open Letters, trans. George Theiner, pp. 245–246]

40 ▪ Largo Desolato

It was not until a year after his release from prison that Vašek was able to write a full-length play. The title came from one of the movements of a composition by Alban Berg. Apparently the original title was *The Flag-Bearers*. Václav wrote the play during four days in July 1984 at

Hrádeček, at a crazy, unprecedented pace, as if it had suddenly ripened inside him and had to come out at breakneck speed. Not only did his manner of writing change—earlier it had taken him a year to write a play, and he would revise it several times—but his subject matter also changed. *Largo Desolato* is his best play. It is, at the same time, his most autobiographical play, because it describes—with literary hyperbole, of course—the situation of an author who has returned from prison. It is a play about postprison psychosis, but at the same time, about how far a person can manage to get by means of his own and others' hard work. No character in the play is good or bad, and every one of them is laid bare. It is true drama, with characters who do not act as they would like, but as they must. Their fate is punishment for the mistakes they made and for misunderstanding their own situation, punishment for failure. It is a great drama, played in an intimate setting.

An author who is not allowed to see his play performed on a stage in his own country and who imagines that somewhere abroad, without his oversight, his play is being ruined, simplified, the higher and lower levels removed, gets into the habit of writing into his play commentary on the characters, situations, and actions in a desperate attempt to save his play. How powerless is the playwright who cannot take part in the staging of his play! He has saved his work from the police, from theft, and perhaps from destruction; he has smuggled it to safety; and now he is trying to protect his play from erroneous interpretation, which could easily ruin everything. Above all, he is afraid of ambiguity, because he feels he has written quite an exceptional play, and he is afraid interpretation could reduce it to a thesis.

Havel was right to hurry with the writing and concealment of his play. In August, State Security fell upon Hrádeček. They broke into the cottage and searched the house without a warrant. The State Security investigator justified the search as the start of criminal proceedings in preparation for a case of incitement. Without interrogating Václav or explaining to him what was going on and what they were looking for, State Security started to search for a certain document.

Not finding it, they seized a number of books, letters, magazines, various documentation and archival material, cassette tapes, photographs, personal correspondence—in all, 215 items, some of which contained up to 70 sub-items. They seized family photographs, recordings of songs sung in public, and a philosophical essay. Olga, as a co-owner of the house, was transported to Trutnov, where she was held illegally for twelve hours.

Jitka Vodňanská, who was at Hrádeček, remembers the search. She was awakened by a State Security agent, who broke into the room where she and her nine-year-old son, Tomáš, were sleeping. He forbade them to leave the room, even to go to the bathroom. Later, when the State Security agent left them, Jitka discovered that fifteen to twenty people were milling around inside the house, and that the house was surrounded. She put a scrap of paper with a message in Tomáš's boots, and he smuggled it to the Krobs. That evening, foreign radio stations broadcast the news that the Havel's home had been searched. Vašek was calm and impersonal; he looked at it all with detachment. The State Security agents made great big parcels of the books and writings, which they tied up with rope. When it came to the cassettes, Václav asked them if they could leave him the cassettes, because they were recordings he would never be able to come by again. They took one of the cassettes, jammed it into the tape recorder, and for an hour and a half, they listened to a lecture Havel had given on how everyone can change, how it is never too late for anyone.

"It was an intense moment," Jitka says. "The lecture was something a parish priest might deliver, and they listened patiently and seemed to be interested. In it was Vašek's generosity, affection, and an offer of forgiveness. Just as they were ransacking his house and taking away his books and music, the things you can't replace."

There were dozens of cassette tapes to choose from. How did they come to choose that one? It could not have been mere chance. I do not know whether Vašek attracts extraordinarily absurd—and therefore deeply truthful—situations by writing absurdist plays, or whether his life is this way, and therefore his plays are too.

Václav wrote a letter of protest to the attorney general, in which he asked him to look into his case and investigate whether the search was in accordance with the constitution and international pacts on civil rights. He wanted to know whether breaking these rules might possibly constitute the crimes of violation of domestic freedom and abuse of the authority entrusted to a public official. The whole affair, he noted, aroused the impression that the police may do whatever they want in this country and need not obey the laws.

41 ▪ A Trip to Slovakia

In 1985, Václav decided to undertake a journey across Czechoslovakia and visit his friends. From Hrádeček, which was now under surveillance from a cabin which the State Security agents had built to replace the Lunochod, I received a letter announcing that he would arrive at Želiv on August 12. I baked some cakes, and a day before his arrival, I heard on Voice of America that he had been arrested at Ladislav Lis's apartment and jailed. Jitka Vodňanská says that a car was already following them as they drove out of Prague. Václav stopped, the car also stopped, and Vašek asked, "Excuse me, are you mine?" They answered yes.

Ladislav Lis's house was the first planned stop. The house sticks out from a rocky face; they call it Hell. The downstairs part of the house, is actually like hell—it's smoky, and cats and dogs live there. Above this is purgatory—one white and one black room. And all the way at the top they have heaven—two delightful little rooms, one pink and the other light blue.

When the police, who attacked Hell, dragged Václav and Ladislav to an interrogation on Bartholomew Street in Prague, Alena Lisová and Jitka tidied up—i.e., they took all the dangerous writings and books, stuffed them in plastic bags which Lis was manufacturing at the time, sealed the bags, pulled them through nettles and shrubs, and hid them under the railroad tracks. The next day, the whole group retrieved Václav's things and stuffed them in his car. Later, when the police arrested him in Bratislava, they seized everything Vašek had not given away during his trip.

He showed up in Želiv twenty-four hours late. He arrived with Jitka in the afternoon, and I was very happy to see him.

"Don't be too happy," he said at the door, "they're at the bridge. They promised me they wouldn't come in." I looked out the window, and I didn't see anyone. We ate lunch. Vašek said that at Ladislav Lis's house, the cops had sat in the room with them and taken part in their soirée. They did not drink or eat, but they listened to everything that was said. Then they searched the house, which they justified by saying they were looking for a Charter document to be issued on the seventeenth anniversary of the 1968 invasion. They did not find the document, but in fact at the time they already had it, because they had confiscated it from Jiří Dienstbier. They dragged Václav to Bartholomew Street. They interrogated him about what he knew about the forthcoming document and what the purpose of his vacation trip was. He told them his excursion had nothing to do with his political convictions or his Charter activities. Nonetheless, he was suspected of preparing to commit hooliganism and locked up for forty-eight hours in a preliminary detention cell. As he later discovered, the same thing happened to Ladislav Lis and Jiří Dienstbier. Forty-eight hours later, they released Vašek and he continued his journey. He said that three plainclothes policemen accompanied him everywhere, even to the grocery store. If he was having trouble finding an item, they told him where to look for it on the shelf. In general, he said, they were polite and had no intention of preventing him from continuing his trip. They had nothing against the trip; they were simply following him everywhere in a Tatra 613, which was now parked near the bridge.

Since it was hot, Vašek and I decided to go swimming. Vašek said he would have to drive his car there, because he had promised he would not try to lose them or leave our house without their knowledge. I have always been impressed by the way he keeps his word even when it would be easy to find many reasons not to keep it. It turned out I could not get in the car with Vašek, because it was full of stuff. I took my bicycle. A strange procession wended its way along the forest path beside the river stream. I went first on my bicycle; Vašek followed in his Volkswagen Golf; and the black Tatra 613 brought up the rear. When we rode through the village, people ran out of their cottages; and when we parked on the bank of the lake, the swimmers could not believe their eyes.

We changed into our bathing suits and swam across the lake. The water was warm and velvety. On the opposite bank, we sat out on a warm rock. Raspberries drooped down to touch the water, and the fireweed and dropwort were in bloom. Blue dragonflies fluttered just above the surface of the polished, unmoving water, which silently reflected the forest. It mirrored everything faithfully. We chatted, and then I saw that on the other shore, one of the men was testing the temperature of the water with his bare foot. Soon, two of them in bathing trunks slowly and cautiously submerged themselves, rippling the previously undisturbed water. The sun was scalding hot. We crawled back into the water and swam to the dam. It felt ugly to me. Not because they were so close—that was hardly exceptional—but because they were in my favorite place and swimming in the same water we were. I brought Vašek to where the water crosses over the dam and forms a waterfall. We swam under it, held onto the rocks of the dam, and let the water beat down on us, deafening us. We shouted through the water's roar, as if we had extremely important things we had to say to each other right there. Suddenly, someone dove off the dam into the water. I was frightened because the water there was less than six feet deep. We stared at the water; it waved, foamed, and bubbled. No one rose to the surface. We began to think he had drowned, when at that moment I felt someone grope at my feet. Cold hands grabbed me, pulling me down. I held onto the rocks tenaciously and saw the polished head and body of the "shadow" emerge from the water; he grabbed me around the waist, then groped about for the wall, sank his fingernails into the water moss, and scraped the moss off the rock as the water roared and fell. He fell once more into the white foam and then finally found a solid grip. Saved, he stood among us. We laughed.

When they left Želiv, I stood at the bend in the road beside the bridge and waved them off. Vašek's Golf drove off first; the Tatra 613 fell into step behind it. I waved at the Golf, and suddenly I could not believe my eyes. All three of the men in the black, coffin-like car were waving back at me. I dropped my arm to my side.

Vašek and Jitka then visited several more friends. They had to skip some, such as Milan Šimečka in Cyrilov, because they had lost two days and had to stick to Vašek's plan. He even showed me his map, where he had penciled in his route and circled the places he was going to visit. Napoleon would have stuck little flags on the conquered territory.

Milan Šimečka later told me what he heard while he was standing in line at the grocerymobile* that morning. The village was full of police cars; the village green was surrounded by them. People said they were looking for some criminal who had escaped from Leopoldov. Milan smiled, but their talk saddened him.

Václav's pursuers escorted the Golf. They knew the route beforehand, and better than Václav did. When he got lost, they showed him the way. They checked the papers of the hitchhikers he picked up. Once they inspected his car—both its roadworthiness and the luggage inside.

The finale took place in Bratislava at Miroslav Kusý's house. They arrived, Václav and Miro greeted each other, and about ten minutes later, the doorbell rang and the house filled up with police officers, equipped with a search warrant. Once again, Václav was arrested. He was imprisoned in the ministry of the interior building. It was the second time he had been arrested that week, and the interrogation closely resembled the one he had received on Bartholomew Street

---

*A mobile store that travels to rural areas.

in Prague. Again, they wanted to know about the Charter's August document and the purpose of his trip. This time, however, the charge was not hooliganism but incitement. On the basis of this article of the law, they locked Vašek up for another forty-eight hours. He protested by holding a hunger strike. Miroslav Kusý was also locked in a cell; when his house was searched, the police seized items that had no connection to the Charter or to the declaration about the 1968 invasion by Soviet soldiers. Tomáš Petřivý, who had been visiting the Kusýs, and Jitka Vodňanská were also detained.

Jitka was locked up one cell away from Václav, but she did not know this. She did not know how to behave or communicate in prison. When they were taking her to the interrogation room and Vašek back to his cell, they met in the corridor. He had not known that Jitka was also in jail, and he made a gesture that said everything: she should hold on, she was above these matters, it would turn out well, they could not win. His gesture gave meaning to the situation: it was not vain, the situation was neither entirely ridiculous nor entirely tragic. He was and remains capable of this: to make himself understood with a glance, a gesture, to deliver a speech without a word. Jitka was later sent to Prague by train with a police escort, although the keys to her apartment were in the car. The car was subjected to another search, and the police seized *Letters to Olga* (a book they had already looked over as carefully as possible in prison), cassette tapes of Pink Floyd and John Lennon, and the map on which Vašek had carefully traced the route of his journey, now definitely aborted.

After forty-eight hours, Vašek was released. In front of the ministry of the interior, an old gray-haired man asked him, "How long since you were last in Bratislava?"

"Twenty years," he answered.

"Then don't show your face here for another twenty years," this old man advised him sharply. "And pass the message along to your friends."

As confirmation of the man's words, an escort column followed

Vašek to the border of Slovakia. There the Slovaks delivered him to Moravians, who in turn delivered him to Czechs, who escorted him to Hrádeček, where they delivered him to his regular guards.

In a letter to the attorney general, Václav wrote the following about his trip:

1. *My trip, directly or indirectly, and for varying lengths of time, employed—according to my rough calculations—three hundred police officers. This alone (not counting the cost of gasoline, etc.) cost the Czechoslovak government at least a hundred times more than it cost me.*

2. *My trip was somewhat spoiled, but not entirely: I will surely remember it for longer than I would have if it had proceeded normally.*

3. *All the groundless and senseless interference with my trip, which the police emphatically linked to August 21—above all, the fact that during the trip, I was in prison twice, and five other citizens were also jailed—once more drew attention at home and abroad to a forgotten anniversary and to the kind of techniques used by the regime that the Warsaw Pact's intervention installed in our country. Of course, the interference also multiplied the publicity given to the August document of Charter 77. It was actually the first time the document received the proper amount of attention, and it was supplemented with colorful documentation (which I myself, by the way, became familiar with via foreign radio only after my return home). Thanks to a few elements in the ministry of the interior, the eyes of the world community were fixed on our country once again, in a manner that surely brought our country no glory.*

4. *The police had many opportunities to deter me from my journey. It would have been easy, and yet the police did not take advantage of them. Inevitably, this circumstance calls up in me the impression that someone—for reasons I can only speculate about—*

thought it very important to draw attention to these provocative confrontations.

42 ▪ Temptation

Václav had pondered the theme of Faust for a long time. It first occurred to him in prison in 1977, in the prison where he wrote a request for release and State Security took advantage of the opportunity to slander him. At the time, it seemed to him that he had been directly tempted by the devil. It was not by chance that it was also in that prison that he stumbled across Goethe's *Faust* and then the novel *Doctor Faustus* by Thomas Mann. This kind of literature is not commonly lent from prison libraries. Ideas about the relativity of truth had already occupied him. Stated in a certain manner and under certain circumstances, a truth can become a lie. Several times after his release, he began to write his own *Faust*, but because the right time had not yet come, he always gave up on the project.

In autumn, nature is quiet. Nothing disturbs people; nothing interrupts them, because what is happening is hidden. A tree, for instance, sheds its leaves, and on its stems it has already prepared buds, the germs of new leaves. In autumn, people also make fewer visits than in the summer. People are more likely to burrow somewhere; it is a time for self-collection. I remember that Václav borrowed some books on magic from me. I had perused them while I was writing *A Bat's Clavicle*. The rituals of alchemy bewitched me—during the repetition of a certain act, the essence of a substance changes; matter rematerializes. In reality, what is involved is not a change of matter—i.e., an outward change—but rather a change in attitude. All the Eastern techniques of self-discipline are founded on patient and endless repetition.

Vašek read the magic books and meditated on the topic for a few months. Only when he was alone at Hrádeček did an idea finally come to him. Like a general preparing for battle, he then drew graphs of the individual actions, sketched the sites of the battleground and the sequence of scenes, represented the characters graphically, and drew in dots that determined the length of their future speeches. Vašek first writes his plays in a sort of musical score and then, when he sees that they have structure and rhythm, rewrites these scores into words. He did not write *Temptation* as quickly as he wrote *Largo*; he wrote *Temptation* in ten nights. One scene per night. When he finished the play, he was so physically and psychically drained that he fell down the stairs at Hrádeček and cracked his head. He came down with a fever; he lay in bed, shivering with fever chills, without so much as a bottle of aspirin. He was not able to drive anywhere for medicine. In the end it even snowed; the highway was impassable, so he did not have anything to eat.

When he returned to Prague, he said that he had slipped away from the devil by the skin of his teeth. In *Temptation*, depths open that unsettle and tempt every one of us. This is how great literature should be: it does not forgo witchcraft; it is witchcraft. The writer has purloined something from a treasure hoard guarded by angels or devils. He has entered the forbidden cave, and no poet escapes punishment if he enters this cave. To write a genuine work is a hard experience for a writer. Once the writing is complete, there follows a loss of meaning and a feeling of emptiness. They had to watch over my beloved Virginia Woolf whenever she finished writing a book, to prevent her from harming herself. Once they did not watch over her. She filled her pockets with rocks and walked out into the water until she drowned.

In October he wrote the play, and in May it had its premiere at the Burgtheater. But it was as if the devils were conspiring against the play's production to take their revenge on Václav for having slipped into their workshop and wanting to give away their secrets.

I remember how he despaired when Pavel Landovský, who was play-ing the role of the Director, passed along news about how the re-hearsals were running. No one understood the play, except perhaps the actor who played Fistula. Apparently he did not ask questions and therefore was the best. The others dissected the play looking for the prime mover. Instead of rehearsing the play, they discussed it, trying to explain everything. I remember that the director wrote Václav a letter in which she wrote down her conception of the play and asked him as the author to explain a series of niggling and ridicu-lous details.

Among other things, this play is against psychologizing and the false humanities, against scientism and the abuse of everything natural— but what it stood against became its fate. In the Burgtheater, they dismantled it piece by piece. They mixed in psychotherapy and psycho-analysis because the play was too deep for them and they were fright-ened by its depths; they really did not know what to do with it. Only Landovský and the Austrian who played Fistula knew that an actor does not have to understand a play but must feel it and play it out of his own depths. Through the actor's depths, the depths of the play pass to the audience. Then the spectator can plant himself inside the play and become a character. Jan Grossman wrote somewhere that the hero of Havels' plays is the spectator. But in this case, the actors and the director wanted to force their understanding of the play on the spectator. They intellectualized it because they were afraid of it. I too am afraid of Kafka or Nietzsche, and it is no help to me that hundreds or maybe thousands of people make a living by ruminating over and explaining them. I am ashamed for these people. They always stick in my craw. How can anyone be so conceited and brazen as to analyze Kafka or psychoanalyze Hermann Hesse—dead long ago? These people are so light-fingered they disinter mystery and desecrate it. But it is the author who knows best why he opened the crater and how far to illuminate it. In the end, the director had to step down because the actors rebelled against her.

The night of the premiere arrived, but Václav understandably did not see it. The reviews followed, from glowing to devastating. Václav made a very nice recording of his play on cassette tape, and this quickly spread from household to household. I only understood it, however, when I saw it on videotape at Hrádeček. Andrej Krob shot it with stagehands and night watchmen—a three-hour performance by nonactors. Ivan Havel played Foustka. VONS member Jarmila Bělíková and Charter spokesperson Petruška Šustrová also performed. They worked on it for two years, because they were seldom able to meet.

I figured out that the play is based on fear. Fistula, a greasy, soiled Czech devilkin, does not even want a soul that badly, and Foustka, a Czech Faust, is afraid for his position in society, which he confuses with life. He is a coward; he offers everything to Fistula himself. Fistula cannot take him seriously; he is a devil, but he is also Czech, raised in a henhouse somewhere, plastered with chicken droppings. Foustka is a fallen Faust, an apostate from Marxism who secretly engages in psychotronics. When he calls up a devil, he does not recognize that it is a devil he has called up. Foustka is a white collar worker, not an exalted scientist trying to tap into what inspires all motion and progress. Nothing is sublime in this play; everything is discredited, common, and devalued. Besides, I liked Fistula, because at times he seemed like a devil; at times, an angel. His face expressed shiftiness and innocence at the same time, and he had such a hard time with Foustka that I was sometimes sorry for him.

I watched Havel's and Krob's *Temptation* for three hours, and when I finished, it seemed like no time at all had gone by. In the meantime, a mutual friend of ours had gone for a walk in the forest, because it bored her and set her teeth on edge. As the author says, it is an unsettling play.

I was a little afraid. Not even I can see to the bottom of its depths. I do not know what the play means or whether it is an evil omen. The final vortex warns us against a horrible and unmanageable end. Vašek is skillful at representing this vortex—the vortex that Jiří Voskovec signaled in his preface to Havel's *Plays*—but it is beyond even him, its author.

On January 22, 1986, the Erasmus Prize (Praemium Erasmianum) Foundation in Amsterdam announced that Václav Havel had received the Erasmus of Rotterdam Prize for 1986. In March, Václav wrote his acceptance speech. Naturally, he was unable to go to Holland.

The theme of his speech was that each of us, no matter how insignificant or powerless, is able to change the world. It sounds unbelievable, but each of us can move the globe a little forward. You must start with yourself, gather courage, and be a fool in the spirit of Erasmus, for only a fool would take on the power of state bureaucracy with no weapon but his feeble typewriter. As the West is realizing to an increasing extent, there is only one Europe. The West has been making it clear by taking sides with the Eastern fools and putting them under its wing. Thus, gradually, we are seeing a revival of the heritage of Erasmus, a great European who personified European integrity.

The Charter 77 spokespeople sent a letter of thanks to the Erasmus Prize Foundation, because the prize was also awarded to the Charter in recognition of its work. On November 13, 1986, the award ceremony took place in Rotterdam. Havel's acceptance speech was delivered by his friend, the actor Jan Tříska. On the occasion of the award, a book was also published, edited by Jan Vladislav, another friend in the émigré community. It was titled, *Václav Havel, or Living in Truth* [subtitle: *Twenty-two essays published on the occasion of the award of the Erasmus Prize to Václav Havel]. Rudé Pravo* reacted to all these events with an article that need not be quoted; the title alone will suffice: "A Fat Pay-off from Holland." On February 7, 1987, at a party held at the home of the Dutch ambassador, Havel received a certificate bestowing the Erasmus Prize on him.

He was tugged further and further into politics and had no time for writing. When foreign affairs ministers and other political figures from the West came to Prague, they met with the government's official representatives but they also met with the opposition—Havel and

Charter spokespeople and representatives. The police tried to prevent these meetings by putting Václav and the spokespeople under house arrest or detaining them for forty-eight hours, until the visit had concluded. But often the police did not succeed, either because they were not well informed or because they did not react quickly enough. The representatives of the Western governments began to understand that their interest in contact with the opposition in Eastern European countries was important for the development of democracy throughout Europe, as if the heritage of the great Erasmus was really beginning to be fulfilled.

In September 1987, Havel became a member of the editorial board of the samizdat monthly *Lidové noviny*, published by Jiří Ruml and Rudolf Zeman. The opposition now had its own newspaper, and it was not painstakingly transcribed by typewriter but photocopied. Havel wrote an editorial piece entitled, "What We May and May Not Expect."

43 ▪ *O Divadle*

Temptation caused Havel's friends to start Fausting with him. This led to a collection of essays which was dedicated to Vašek of his fiftieth birthday and published by Expedition Edition in 1986. Perhaps the time-honored theme of a pact with the devil had a mysterious and intrinsic connection with the intellectual return to Europe, with the need to find old and common roots, to return to the archetypes that linked Western culture with the cosmic experience of humanity, as it was put in the prologue to *Fausting with Havel*. There are only a few European archetypes of this caliber: Saint George, the Holy Grail, and the Golem, to mention three. As on many previous occasions, Václav was the first to recognize what was in the air. He has a gift for looking at individual events from a bird's eye view, seeing them all at once, describing the links between them, and giving meaning to the whole.

The Faustian theme was hanging in the air and he was the first to feel it, grasp it, and bring it down to earth. Otherwise, why would so many people have been concerned with Faust? Why would they have been attempting to understand it anew from the perspective of our contemporary experience? Perhaps the Faustian theme was compelling because European society had also been on the verge of a new era when the theme first arose. In his play, Václav wanted to show that we had reached a time of great change in thought and action. As is often the case, his play was not understood on the continent. They understood it better on the stage of the Royal Shakespeare Company in Stratford where it premiered on April 30, 1987. Vašek said that the English saw Krob's amateur staging at Hrádeček and liked it. Apparently, they said they were tempted to steal from it.

Once again, Václav was able to come up with the thing that everybody felt was approaching but no one could identify. His version of *Faust* presents the fallen nature of contemporary man and the contemporary era—when, as Ivan Havel says, even the devil is reduced to tears by his balance sheet, and Faust is no longer an alchemist or even an initiate to the mysteries. Today, all of us encounter embarrassing replicas of heaven and hell in our daily lives.

Fausting turned into a reason for founding the magazine *O Divadle*. The philosophers Ivan Havel, Martin Palouš, Helena Webrová, Radim Palouš, Pavel Bratinka, Daniel Kroupa, and Zdeněk Neubauer—the members of the yearly Catholic Academy at Hrádeček—put together the anthology. Others, such as Ivan Jirous (whose Faust-playing pleased Vašek the most because he seemed to have grasped the intent of his play the best), and Sergej Machonin, also wrote out their thoughts about the play. Olga Havel was afraid the essays would get lost, and so she thought it would be a good idea to found a magazine. A meeting of all potential editors and contributors convened at the Havels' apartment on U dejvického rybníčku Street. In attendance were Sergej Machonin (my source for this information), Karel Kraus, František Pavlíček, Ivan Klíma, Josef Topol, Vlasta Chramostová, Stanislav Milota, Zdeněk Urbánek, and Milan Uhde. They discussed the concept of a theater review. Karel Kraus was appointed editor-in-chief; Anička Freimanová, managing editor; and Olga Havel took charge of the finances and production. Věra Dvořáková assisted them. Gradually they came to the conclusion that it would be a good idea to devote each issue to a single theme. It took a long time to come up with the theme for each issue. They debated; they thought up a framework; and then they found authors for the individual articles. They wanted all the writing to relate to questions of theater, which is a search for the meaning of human existence that goes beyond the personal. Surprisingly, they soon found that some of the *strukturáks** were willing to write for an illegal magazine under pseudonyms, and thus they avoided the danger that every independent magazine is prey to: the danger that authors will repeat themselves. *Strukturáks* expressed their critical opinion on the position of theater in a totalitarian society. *O Divadle* soon became popular among people from official theaters and introduced new ideas, misgivings, and a slightly different, less fawning spirit. Even in official theater institutes, such as the Institute for the Study of Czech Theater at the Czechoslovak Academy of Sciences, the magazine had its adherents, and gradually more and more people came forward and joined them, attracted by this new intellectual center, which naturally formed a magnetic field around itself. In an apparently immobile society, a new locus of motion arose, an intellectual and social center. Přemysl Rut played a significant role at the magazine, becoming executive editor and deputy editor-in-chief. Václav knew how to attract people and blend them together, young and old, dissidents and *strukturáks*, reform Communists and the underground; and this was of paramount importance. He crossed the border between the forbidden on the one hand, and the permitted or tolerated on the other. He widened and diluted the borders of the ghetto, which in time would have declined, both intellectually and socially, if it had remained closed.

For security reasons, the editors knew almost nothing about the

---

*People in officially recognized cultural organizations.

physical production of the magazine. Olga and Anička gathered the manuscripts and brought them to the typist. The typist had quite a lot of work, because the review was a thick tome of 350 to 400 pages. *Strukturáks* secretly photocopied the typed issue on machines that were kept under guard and whose use was registered. There is no need to explain what kind of risk they were taking. Eva Lorencová proofread the magazine, and then Olga, Anička, and other volunteers transferred the changes into all the copies, of which there were one or two hundred. The pages were strewn everywhere in the Havels' apartment—on the floor, on the couches, chairs, and tables. You were not allowed to open a door or window suddenly or the pages would fly out of order, and no one was allowed to interrupt. The volunteers went from one page to the next, correcting. Thanks to this process, *O Divadle* was one of the few magazines that was error-free. It was common in makeshift magazines to find that pages were missing or transposed; they often teemed with typing errors and spelling mistakes. Olga is one of the most conscientious and patient people I know. Zdeněk Urbánek took care of binding the magazines. A carload of the "print run"—not unlike a carload of firewood—was then sent out, and the magazine was distributed to the subscribers. Each subscriber then loaned his copy to a dozen other people interested in reading it. It was difficult to get on the waiting list.

Theater people were curious to know what *O Divadle* wrote about their performances, and gradually a new critical community grew up parallel to the official critical establishment. It had the important effect of renewing the art of criticism generally, because during the years of normalization, criticism had been one of the first things to die out. No one took official reviews seriously, and in the unofficial culture, people often praised each other merely because they felt sorry for each other. All this synergy of the official and unofficial cultures and movement that crossed the bounds between them climaxed in a meeting between the illegal magazine's editors and collaborators and *strukturáks* at the Vyšehrad Gate. People from the Theater on a String, HaDivadlo, the Realistic Theater, and the Prague Theater Institution were present. It seemed to be a revolt of everything that was alive against what was regulated and indoctrinated. It was a revival of Czech theater, a reunion after many years, and in fact a preparation for the November revolution. People stopped being afraid. In the fifth issue of *O Divadle*, there was not a single pseudonym. It was also the final issue, because while the sixth issue was in preparation, Václav was imprisoned.

In October 1987, in between meetings with foreign ministers, vice chancellors, and human rights advocates, Havel managed to write his final play to date, *Slum Clearance*. He was also busy writing petitions and texts for special occasions and enduring the police's ongoing harassment. It is a play about the pseudorenascence, or perestroika, that those in power were trying to simulate. In the play, no one believes anything the authorities say anymore, and furthermore their plan does not work. *Slum Clearance* returned to the subject matter of Havel's earlier plays—i.e., those before *Largo Desolato* and *Temptation*—but it was as if the absurdity of life had overtaken the absurdism of his plays.

On September 3, 1988, Václav appeared at a podium in public for the first time in years. He looked like he had crawled out from underground as he blinked at the cameras at a folk music festival in Lipnice. In an interview with the master of ceremonies, who had invited him there and who later got into heaps of trouble because of it, Havel said that the last time he had stood at a podium had been exactly nineteen years and three months ago. He had not changed at all; he was just as nervous this time as he had been then. The audience exploded with joy. Later they surrounded him and asked for autographs. If only he could have suspected that soon a whole square full of people would be awaiting him.

For years that same folk music festival had taken place at Lipnice, but the following year it was canceled. The authorities had forbidden it. The same thing happened to the Bratislava Lyre, a musical festival, in the capital of Slovakia, where Joan Baez sang and, speaking in Slovak, praised Charter 77 and Václav Havel, who was in the audience. A standing ovation followed, and that was the end of the Lyre. When we went to the Sokol Hall in Okrouhlice for a performance by *Jasná Páka* (a Czechoslovak punk band), Václav asked them not to talk about him from the stage. He did not want to be the cause of the liquidation of every cultural establishment he visited.

In September 1988, we were supposed to meet at Hrádeček for our regular quarterly writers' meeting. Zdeněk Urbánek, Petr Kabeš, and I drove together. When we reached the first turn-off that leads to Hrádeček, we saw a large white disk with a red border* in the middle of the road. It was brand new, propped up by a kind of sawhorse quickly patched together out of wood. We drove to the next access road, and there was another sign, exactly the same; just beyond Mladé Buky, we ran across yet another. Milan Jungmann, Sergej Machonin, and Eva Kantůrková had stopped in front of this sign in their Škoda MB. We agreed that Zdeněk and Milan would take the cars into Mladé Buky, so they would not have to park them out in the field, and the rest of us would walk toward Hrádeček, just a little more than a mile away. A few mushrooms pickers had also stopped their car. They did not know whether or not they were forbidden to pass the sign. They said they figured it was on account of that poet who lived somewhere in the forest nearby. We wanted to tell them they could go pick their mushrooms, that the sign was not for them but for us; it seemed wiser, however, to leave them in the dark.

Petr, Eva, Sergej, and I set out across a field of corn stubble. Since we thought that State Security would have set up a patrol on the other side of the hillock, we did not travel along the highway. In fact, we were later able to see them from our position on the hillside. They were standing at the fork in the road on the other side of the hillock along with one police car and one plainclothesman. It was a crystal-clear September day; a white cloud stretched across the sky; there was a good kite-flying wind; in the distance were the peaks of Sněžka and Černá Hora, and in the foreground two little figures were moving, our

---

*This road sign means "Do Not Enter" throughout Europe.

reconnaissance men—Zdeněk and Milan. They reached the police, were frisked, showed their citizens' ID cards, and then gestured for a while, arguing. Then a policeman got into the police car and remained there for a while, calling someone on the radio. When he returned, there were more gestures and then they slowly walked back along the highway to Mladé Buky. We were standing on the hill and knew exactly what had taken place.

Hrádeček was off limits; they were not going to allow us in. But we did not feel like giving up before we had reached our goal. They did not have us yet; we continued to go on. When we reached the highway, lined with maples, I confided to Eva that I had Petr Placák's *Medorek** on me. It belonged to Vašek, and I did not want to lose it. Eva said, "Let's make a 'drop' for it." We wrapped *Medorek* in a plastic bag and laid it in a hollow tree.

We continued to walk along the highway, when Olga and her dog Golda appeared. She said that Hrádeček had been surrounded since the night before and that they had taken Jiří Hanzelka and Miroslav Zikmund to the police station in Trutnov. I showed her where the "drop" was, and asked her to recover the book as soon as it was convenient. Olga suggested that we go through the forest to Hrádeček, and she entrusted me with leading the way, since I had hunted for mushrooms in the forest and was familiar with it. She said she would leave open the door that led from the back yard to the study, and that the house seemed to be guarded only from the highway side. So we went through the forest, and I had a terrible feeling that we would get lost. It was like the scene with the smugglers in *The Kiss*,† and so Sergej sang, "Onward, onward. . . ."

In the middle of the forest, which was so thick that the sun's rays lit up only golden streaks, Petr suggested that we could have a picnic. If they arrested us when we left the forest, we might be held for forty-eight hours, and in that case it would be a good idea to have had

---

*A banned book, published as a samizdat.
†An opera by Bedřich Smetana.

something to eat and drink beforehand. So we laid out our reserves. Sergej had Jungmann's pan of roast pork. I had a plum cake in a baking tin, which in the forest proved to be a very unwieldy piece of baggage. I also had a bunch of carrots, radishes, and asters that I had bought along the way. (In addition I had on pumps, and in the cornfield I had worn down the heels until the wood was showing through.) With Eva's nail file, we sliced the meat and pie and opened a bottle of wine. We feasted for about an hour, laughing constantly. When we finished and stood up, Petr said, "If nothing else happens, we still had a good time, and that's enough."

We managed to wander out of the forest at a point near the beehives, as Olga had said we should, and we reached the Havels' back yard. The roof of the much longed-for building jutted up about a hundred meters in front of us. We stood indecisively in the orchard, not protected by the forest. Anyone could have spotted us, but there was no one in sight. We sent Petr out to reconnoiter, and before five minutes were up, he returned with purple-faced, sweating police officers tramping behind him, followed by plainclothesmen. They surrounded us and asked what we were doing there. Eva said we were looking for mushrooms, but they did not laugh. They looked as grave as if they had been arresting the assassins of the first secretary of the central committee. They demanded our citizens' ID cards, collected them, and told us that they would be returned to us in Trutnov, because we were under arrest. They then led us and the rest of the cohort around the house. Olga and Vašek ran out. We embraced and I gave them the flowers and carrots.

"And what am I supposed to do with all the goulash?" Vašek said.

"Quickly, quickly; don't delay," the police shouted. On the highway, they shoved us in a car and did not seem to know the way to go. I asked them where they were from. They turned out to be from Moravia. To guard an area around the Havels' house whose diameter was at least four miles, three days must have required a great number of police officers. And it must have cost a great deal of money.

They brought Vašek to Trutnov after us. Then they took us in for interrogation one at a time. They asked me what had been in the works at Hrádeček. I said I did not know about anything special. Then they asked if it bothered me that my writing would not be published until after my death. I said that every writer had to take that into account. Then one of the two bearded pretty-boys in checked shirts asked me if I would go to a bar in Prague with him. I told him no, and so it went for about an hour.

That evening we met in a pub, and when we headed off to Prague, a police car accompanied us as far as the county line.

44 • *Democracy for All*

In October 1988, the manifesto "Democracy for All" was prepared. There was more discussion about it than about any other petition. It seemed to many dissidents that it was worthless for the same group of people to continue to sign manifestos while the rest of Czechoslovakia only watched. For this reason, many who had signed similar petitions in the past did not sign this one. They felt that the tension between the general population and the authorities was growing, and that this rising popular movement ought to be connected in some way with the opposition, but they did not know how. I remember speaking about this with Petr Pithart at the time. He was musing about a declaration that would be acceptable to people in the establishment. It should not be worded the way the Charter was, but at the same time it should not be toothless. The bravest declaration was written that summer by Ivan Jirous, or Magor. It was called "Enough is Enough." In it, Jirous accused the Communist Party and its government of specific crimes they had committed over the course of the last forty years. Both of them were imprisoned; Magor was in jail until November 1989.

On August 21, 1988, the twentieth anniversary of the Soviet army's occupation of Czechoslovakia, riot control police took action against demonstrators in the streets of Prague.

The manifesto "Democracy for All" was much sterner than the Charter. At the outset, this ruled out the possibility that people would join it en masse. In this manifesto, the Movement for Civic Liberties* (also known by its Czech initials, HOS) said for the first time in years that the Communist Party did not have the right to hold a leading role in the government. It was an important thing to say, and somebody had to say it. About 260 people signed the manifesto. This may not seem like a lot. Foreign reporters, anyway, expected there would be more. In the spirit of perestroika the authorities made a lot of speeches about democracy. It was expected that on October 28, 1988, there would be a demonstration, and the police would react much more harshly than before. People were ominously silent. They watched as the Communists forbade them to go out in the streets and the large squares in the city centers to celebrate the seventieth anniversary of the founding of the democratic republic. The authorities did not hesitate to threaten that they would attack anyone who was moving through the streets. They would use any means. They even gave notice that they would shoot. Parents locked their children up at home. They dragged them by force to their cottages in the countryside so they would not be able to demonstrate.

The tension grew and intensified every day. On October 26, criminal proceedings were initiated in the matter of the "Democracy for All" manifesto. They descended on the signatories in their homes and transported them to various places, in fact to various cities, where they were held for forty-eight hours in preliminary detention cells. On October 27, they searched Václav Havel's Prague apartment and his cottage in Hrádeček. In addition to many books and writings, his computer was also seized. Václav was not at home at the time, but

---

*Founded on Oct. 15, 1988, a loose association of movements and clubs representing a wide political spectrum.

they hunted him down that evening and held him at Ruzyně prison until October 31. About five thousand people gathered in Wenceslas Square and later in Old Town Square on that holiday afternoon. They chanted slogans and sang a hymn. The riot control police, armed with helmets, shields, and truncheons, streamed out of Old Town Hall on command and started to beat the defenseless and peaceful crowd heedlessly. They took cameras away from people and smashed them on the ground. Water cannons struck from Dlouhá Street. Ruthlessly, the water knocked over mothers, children, and pensioners who had gone for a walk and become mixed up in the demonstration.

The superintendents of the buildings around Old Town Square had received instructions to lock their buildings so that people would have no escape route. When someone managed to fight his way to a building, the police would beat him in the entrance or arrest him. They transported those under arrest in buses. Many people were wounded, but surprisingly no one was wounded fatally. Many people, however, were lethally angry, because the police action was excessive. Armed officers beat innocent people. The young people decided they would not give up. They accepted the police provocation and decided to continue the uneven battle. The police had carried out actions of this sort in August, but in October the police were raging wildly. It was said that Miroslav Štěpán, the Prague Communist party boss, had directed the whole action. The incident clearly showed—and the message was later spelled out explicitly—that the authorities would not allow any meddling and would not hold talks with anyone. It also showed that although the bureaucrats had their mouths full of democracy, the Czechoslovak version of perestroika did not mean the democratization of public life, but only further and more marked oppression. The demonstrations in August and October proved the authorities to be guilty of bad faith. They proved that the restructuring was only another of the notorious, oft-repeated pseudorenascences, well known not only from Havel's plays but also from real life.

It seemed that the authorities would not scruple to use any means necessary to hold on to power, even if this meant imprisoning or interning all its enemies and launching a crusade of terror in the country. They outlawed a symposium called Czechoslovakia 88, which was openly set up by independent groups. The representatives of the groups informed Prime Minister Ladislav Adamec of this beforehand. Havel discussed the symposium with the Presidium of the Communist Party while it was being planned. Historians, politicians, and journalists who were interested in Czechoslovakia and its history were invited. On November 10, Václav managed to hold a symbolic opening ceremony for the symposium in the lobby of the Paris Hotel. He was arrested at once before the eyes of all the participants. He was released on Monday, November 14. The police were only waiting for a pretext to lock him up for a longer period of time. A parallel symposium was held in Vienna. Václav telephoned and apologized to the participants for the unsuccessful meeting in Prague.

The government was now hysterical. The more they pretended they were restructuring and democraticizing society, the more they attacked it. In March 1988, they had damaged streetcar tracks so that people would not be able to take streetcars to reach a festival in honor of Saint Anežka (Agnes of Bohemia),* in Saint Vitus' Cathedral. The subway was not allowed to stop at the Hradčanská station nearby. More than half a million people signed a Catholic protest petition. Its author, Augustin Navrátil, was sentenced to a stay in a psychiatric hospital. In Hungary, Imre Pozsgay had already declared that the leading role of the Communist Party would not be guaranteed by the new constitution, and in Czechoslovakia, criminal proceedings were initiated against people who signed their names to the similar plea contained in the Movement for Civic Liberties's "Democracy for All."

Havel wrote about these matters to the French president before his official visit to Czechoslovakia. And *voilà*, in early December 1988, three weeks after his release from Ruzyně prison, he and the leaders

---

*A major national celebration.

of other independent initiatives had breakfast with François Mitterrand. The next day Havel spoke at the first authorized demonstration, in Škroupovo Square.

On December 10, something happened that for a while derailed and partially divided the opposition, because opinions started to diverge; fortunately this divergence was only temporary. That day was the day the first authorized political demonstration took place on Škroupovo Square in Prague. Václav Havel, Ladislav Lis, Václav Malý, Rudolf Battěk, Vlasta Chramostová, Jana Petrová, Petr Placák, and Jan Urban spoke. Marta Kubišová sang and people publicly signed a petition on behalf of Magor. Stanislav Milota held people's feet while they spoke, to keep them from falling off the podium.

Some radicals in the opposition opposed participation in the demonstration. They felt that it was not a good idea to respond to the concessions of the regime. Instead, they argued that the authorities should be left in isolation because they had so badly discredited themselves. The regime was already dying—no negotiations, they said. This disagreement soon blew over, however, as in January the regime again showed its real face.

At the time the demonstration in Škroupovo Square seemed like a partial victory. Of course it was only a small retreat before a further attack, which came in the form of Jan Palach week in January 1989.

45 • Jan Palach Week

On January 2, 1989, thirteen representatives of independent civic initiatives sent information to the Department for Internal Affairs of the District National Committee of Prague District 1 regarding plans for a memorial ceremony for Jan Palach. The Department for Internal Affairs forbade the memorial action. The civic initiative groups then decided that according to the law, memorial ceremonies were not subject to any authorization process; in fact, the law did not even require them to notify the authorities. In violation of the District National Committee's prohibition, they met briefly near the Saint Václav monument and laid down flowers. Petr Placák represented Czech Children; Tomáš Hradílek, Dana Němcová, and Saša Vondra, Charter 77; Heřman Chromý, Stanislav Penc, Jr., and Ota Veverka, the John Lennon Peace Club; Ondřej Černý, Jana Petrová, and Miloš Zeman, the Independent Peace Association; Petr Bartoš, Pavel Jungmann, and Bedřich Koutný, the Society of Friends of the U.S.A.

On January 9, Václav Havel had received a anonymous letter. It read as follows:

Dear Mr. Havel,

We fully agree with the activities of Charter 77, which is a light in these dark times and defends human rights, the freedom of expression, and the freedom of religion. A group of us students has resolved to support your praiseworthy work with decisive acts and to achieve the concession of political rights for your efforts. As a fulfillment of these words, on the afternoon of January 15, 1989, where St. Václav sits on his horse at the top of Wenceslas Square, another human torch will shine. We firmly believe that this act will awaken the whole nation from its social and political lethargy and rouse all citizens to the kind of public openness and public expressions of national identity that took place exactly twenty years ago.

> *On behalf of the Organizational Council*
> *for the Return of Collective Suicide,*
> *Torch#1.*

Václav consulted his friends about how to react to this peculiar letter, which had arrived in the mail, was written in block letters, and could have been police provocation. He decided he had to use all available means to dissuade the unknown young friend from committing the act he had in mind. He wanted to write him a letter and publish it, because he hoped the letter writer would respect Havel's opinion; he hoped that he was waiting to hear what Havel thought. He telephoned Dušan Macháček, the editor-in-chief of the television news program, who took Havel's telephone number and said he would call him if he needed to. He never called back. (Later, in court, he testified as a witness for the prosecution that he had consulted with the head of the television studio, and had been told it was not recommended that he work with Havel.) When Václav received no answer, he turned to the Czech language programs of Radio Free Europe and Voice of America. The stations broadcast his letter to the young friend. In his letter, Václav asked the writer to remain alive because we needed people like him alive. He invited the young person to come to Wenceslas Square, but without combustibles.

On January 9, Václav gave his letter to State Security; they thanked him for his foreign radio appeal. He was therefore at ease during the radio interview that followed and did not hesitate to mention the memorial that had been scheduled to honor Jan Palach. This, however, was a snare set by the police; ultimately, it became the basis for the first point of the accusation against him at his subsequent arrest—inciting participation in a demonstration. What should he have done? As his defense lawyer, Dr. Josef Lžičař, pointed out, if he had not answered the letter writer, he would have committed a much graver crime, because he would have failed to prevent either injury or death. In our legal code, any action intended to avert the danger of death of another person has special protection.

On the afternoon of January 16, as demonstrations continued, Václav went to Wenceslas Square to take a look. He stood in front of the House of Fashion and watched as his friends laid flowers at the pedestal of the patron saint of the Czech Lands. The police rounded up everyone; the process was slow and clumsy because they did not have enough cars. When the police had taken them away, Václav crossed to the House of Food on the other side of the street, where he continued to observe the situation. A cordon of policemen began to force people down and out of Wenceslas Square. Several times they repeated their call that the citizens should disperse; otherwise, they said, they would use their truncheons against them. Václav crossed Wenceslas Square because he had heard the announcement and had decided to go home. The moment he entered the Alfa passageway, two State Security agents dashed out of the crowd, pounced on him, and put him under arrest. One of the agents was Major Petr Žák. Major Žák, who later spoke as a witness in the trial, described everything that Václav had done in the square and simultaneously refused to admit he had been shadowing the accused. He even presented the court with photographs of Havel at various places on Wenceslas Square. These photographs were supposed to be proof that Havel had ignored the order to go home. This was the grounds for the second crime on which the charge was based—that he had impeded the execution of safety measures, i.e., the evacuation of Wenceslas Square, and prevented a public officer from carrying out his duty.

Havel drew attention to State Security's pointless attack on people who only wanted to lay flowers at a pedestal in silence as a mark of respect. It was the police who had turned people who had come peacefully into a protest mob by preventing them from remaining on the square. The proud authorities would not allow people to honor the memory of a dead man, and by this they had done more to revive his memory than Havel could have if he had spoken, and perhaps more than a new human torch could have done, if one had been lit. Face to face with truncheons, people felt even closer to Jan Palach, who had intended his death to be a warning against this kind of violence. As if by a miracle, the years all merged together.

A week of demonstrations in Wenceslas Square followed. The police beat people and rounded them up, but these people came back and others joined them. The police pulled young people off a train on their way to the Všetaty cemetery.* They were going to honor Palach, whom

---

*Palach was born in the village of Všetaty.

the police had transferred there from the Olšany cemetery because they did not want his corporal remains to stay in Prague, in the hope that people would forget about him. As the events of January showed, not only had people not forgotten about him after twenty years, but young people who in 1968 were not yet born had taken the memory of Jan Palach to heart.

Václav's fate had been decided beforehand. While he was walking along Wenceslas Square, Major Žák had been following him, looking for a pretext for arresting him. When he could not find one, he pounced on Václav at the last minute as he was leaving to go home. All of this suggests that the letter too was a trap designed to catch Václav. In short, they did not want him at large.

46 ▪ *In Prison Again*

As Václav says, he got on their nerves, so they locked him up. The events of the trial, which took place on February 21, 1989, back up his assessment. The magistrate and militiawoman Helena Hlavatá presided. David Kabzan was supposed to testify as a witness for the prosecution that Václav Havel had incited participation in the demonstration. When he testified, however, he also said he was "the only one of those incited who had not been incited to anything," because, as he told the court, he was not in Wenceslas Square at the time. Later he told reporters that he had initially been forced to testify by violent means, and he filed a complaint about the police officers' methods with the military prosecutor in Prague. Witness for the prosecution Kabzan was dismissed after several minutes, because he threatened to undermine the seriousness of the court.

Witness Žák, the major in State Security who arrested Havel, could provide no reasons for the arrest other than that the defendant had been standing on the sidewalk. He had spoken with no one and organized nothing. His only crime was that after he heard the police's commands, he failed to go home quickly enough.

Managers of several stores on Wenceslas Square testified that they had closed their stories of their own free will, because they were afraid the crowd would push its way inside. These cowards claimed they had no idea what was going on outside in the square. But events did lead to a dip in the daily revenue and disruption of traffic on Wenceslas Square. This was also attributed to Havel and mentioned in the verdict.

In his speech for the defense, Václav Havel said the following:

> *As a citizen for whom it is important that our country develop peacefully, I firmly believe that in the end, the authorities will learn a lesson from what has happened and establish official dialogue with all sectors of society, a dialogue from which no one will be excluded because they have been designated as "antisocialist." I firmly believe that in the end, the authorities will stop behaving like an ugly girl who breaks a mirror because she believes it to be guilty of what it reflects. For this reason, I also firmly believe I will not be once again groundlessly condemned. I do not feel guilty; I have nothing on my conscience. If I am sentenced, however, I will accept my sentence as a sacrifice for a good cause, a sacrifice that is trivial in light of the absolute sacrifice of Jan Palach, whose anniversary we wanted to commemorate.*

The verdict declared Havel to be guilty on all counts—every one of which had been refuted in the course of the trial. Václav Havel was sentenced unconditionally to nine months in prison and assigned to class two imprisonment "because he had already been imprisoned for a similar offense." He filed an appeal through his lawyer. Olga and his brother, Ivan, also filed appeals.

47 • *The Release of Václav Havel*

As soon became clear, Václav's imprisonment was full of significance, because it spurred society into action and brought the *strukturáks**and dissidents together in a united front against the high-handedness of the authorities. As Sergej Machonin says: "Three women stepped forward into history. One morning Anička Freimanová came to the Machonins' apartment, still fired up over a debate with Mrs. Kačírková†. . . . —the topic of their debate had been society's scandalous silence in the face of Václav Havel's arrest. Anička then continued the debate with my wife, Drahuna. They concluded even more energetically that something had to be done. Then they came, with some input from me, to the idea that there should be a signature campaign and that the magazine *O Divadle* should initiate the public protest."

Sergej called Zdeněk Urbánek and Přemysl Rut, and two days later Karel Kraus called a meeting at his apartment. They wrote a short and easily intelligible text and immediately apportioned out roles in the campaign. During the first few days, the prospects seemed dark. With difficulty they collected twelve important names, and Zdeněk Urbánek broadcast them on Voice of America and Radio Free Europe. "After broadcasting the first few names, the ice cracked," Sergej wrote, "and signatures started to flood in. There was a steady stream of people at the signature collectors' apartments and at the homes of the magazine's editors. Signatures began to be collected at private viewings, theaters, and other gatherings. Suddenly there were hundreds of signatures. They were all brought to general headquarters at Kraus's apartment, usually in the evening or at night. Karel Kraus, his wife, Ludmila, and other helpers worked until they dropped. They complied

---

*People in officially recognized cultural organizations.
† A film editor from Barrandov and a friend of Václav Havel's.

individual batches for broadcasting, carefully classifying the names by social strata. The spark had clearly crossed over from theater workers, writers, and all sorts of intellectuals to all groups of the population. A small signature campaign turned into a national and federal avalanche."*

In April, the quarterly writers' meeting took place in Slovakia at the home of the writer Kadlečík. Jiří Křižan, a screenwriter, came for the first time, brought by Petr Kabeš. Eva Kantůrková approached Křižan and proposed that together they organize a petition for the release of Václav Havel at the halfway point of his sentence—i.e., in May. They had not quite a month. Jiří was supposed to collect signatures from *strukturák*s, and it turned out they were willing to sign. They appointed an eighteen-member council, and the campaign took off with enormous and surprising speed. Soon they had 3,800 signatures. They filed their proposal with the district attorney and the head of the prison, and Jiří was officially invited to a hearing, something that had never happened before. At the hearing on May 17, Václav was allowed to go home. That day, a party was organized at the Havels' to celebrate. Vašek was a wreck. Chartist Jiří Wolf was even more of a wreck. He had been released the same day from Valdice after six years.

Vašek said that this time he had had a stylish jail cell. They had not wanted him to fraternize with the other prisoners, and they could not put him in isolation because that was a special punishment. For this reason, they put two Communists in his cell and gave them a television. These fellows were serving long sentences for embezzlement they had committed as managers of state enterprises. Still, they could not understand why they were doing time with a criminal about whom they had read such horrible things in *Rudé Právo*, or why he had only been given nine months. Thanks to him, however, they had it good. They were surprised, too, that the prison manager came by every so often to ask if Havel needed anything.

---

*In March 1989, one thousand intellectuals signed a letter demanding Havel's release. The appeal was rejected but his sentence was reduced by one month.

48 • *Just a Few Sentences*

About a thousand people passed through the "Coming Back" party, and Jiří Křižan was the man of the hour. His first campaign had worked almost immediately. Jiří and Kabeš sat on the Havels' balcony, and people kept bringing Václav out to meet them. People told Vašek, "This is Křižan. You have to meet him." Jiří, who had already been introduced to Vašek several times before, had the feeling that Vašek still did not remember who he was. The next morning, Vašek phoned him and said, "Mr. Křižan, many people have told me that you organized a petition for my release. I think we should meet. What about going somewhere to have a beer?"

They went to the restaurant Na rybárně [At the Fishmonger's]. As it turned out, Václav already had an idea he had come up with in prison. He had evaluated the situation, looking for what was new. And what was new was that the *strukturáks* were willing to sign petitions and make demands; they were ready to join something— something that had not yet been formulated. All that remained was to put it in words, and Václav and Jiří set out to do this at once. Of course, it should be noted that Václav had been set free on the condition he not engage in any political activity.

"We went to the toilet," Jiří says, "and there we began to call each other by our first names. Then Saša Vondra came in, and when he saw me, he said, 'At last we have a decent guy; all those others are anemic.' "

Václav wrote out the text of the petition,* and Křižan and Vondra helped him. They were his advisers at the time—Václav says today that they were then his left and right hand. Jiří thought up the title;

---

*The seven-point petition asked for democratic reforms and religious freedom.

he thought it would be a good idea if it resembled "Two Thousand Words,"* and so he suggested "Just A Few Sentences."

As soon as they had the text in hand, it was decided that Saša would circulate it among dissidents and Jiří among *strukturáks*. They ran the text by several people, collecting pointers and suggestions. Then they met in the Paroplavba restaurant and made a final version, which Zdeněk Urbánek also had a hand in. The text was ready. Now the question was when. The summer holidays were coming, and no one would be around. Would it be better to leave it until September? They decided to go ahead with it immediately. First they would hunt down the signatures of popular actors, such as Jiří Bartoška, Suchý, Kratina, and Čepek. In the meantime everything would be secret. They would make the manifesto public when they had three hundred signatures. Vondra and Křižan added their names and addresses to the text, so that people would know where to turn in the signatures.

Then they began to search for signatures. The most important were the *strukturáks*, workers, and Communists. In addition to name and address, they asked for the signer's occupation and whether or not he was a member of the Party. To their great surprise, on June 29 they had not 300 but 1,800 signatures. When I offered them my signature, they grinned and said, see if you can find someone who hasn't signed a petition before. I tried everywhere, in Czech villages. I made the rounds of people who had sworn at the Communists for years, but I had no success. One young person said he would have to ask his father. Then he came back and told me that his father forbade him to. He explained to me what his father had explained to him: they had so many stolen things at home they could not take the risk of signing anything. What if the police came to arrest them?

Vašek of course had thought through and sketched out a plan for the campaign. He had precisely planned goals: when this or that

---

*A statement written by Ludvík Vaculik in 1968, a manifesto that was one of the pretexts for the Soviet invasion.

should be broadcast on Radio Free Europe or Voice of America. Evidently, State Security received a copy of the plan through an informer at one of the foreign press agencies, and a facsimile was printed on the first page of *Rudé Právo* along with commentary. The artillerymen at *Rudé Právo* let fly a salvo of their bullshit. Every time they ran one of their articles, however, the number of signatures that came in jumped up to several times the average—and this average was growing week by week. Pavel Rímský of the Realistic Theater brought in hundreds of signatures daily. The campaign in *Rudé Právo* and other media helped, particularly when it was emotional and hysterical.

On July 28, the authorities lost their nerve altogether and initiated criminal proceedings. State Security officers went to Líšnice, where Jiří was staying at his cottage, and searched his house. They only confiscated what he was working on at the time, because everything else was hidden. He managed to give his keys to a friend, who went to his Prague apartment and tidied up. When State Security continued their search in Prague, they found nothing. This infuriated them, and so they began to search through his laundry and personal and private things. Saša Vondra's home was also searched; in fact, they searched eight homes at once, as was their custom.

"My mailwoman was splendid," Křižan says. "Her manager forbade her to, but she heroically delivered letters to me nonetheless. And the number of signatures kept growing. We already had more signatures than the Socialist Party had members, and soon we had more than the People's Party too. At the end of the summer, they started to crack down on people collecting signatures, so in September we started to collect money to pay the fines, through Petr Uhl and Anička Šabatová. Money also came in through Petr Burian, whom Olga worked with. We put it in a pitcher at Vašek's house and once a week we counted it and put it in the VONS strong box. The money that was left over when the persecution was over was given to the Civic Forum Foundation."

In early autumn, the Bridge was formed, an initiative originated by

Michael Kocáb and Michal Horáček. Havel, Křižan, and Vondra were in contact with them daily. Křižan wrote Prime Minister Adamec a letter requesting a dialogue on the basis of the success in gathering signatures for "Just A Few Sentences." Adamec seemed willing to act. At least his secretary Oskar Krejčí gave that impression. Through the Bridge, he announced that the prime minister did not want to deal with Havel, but would speak with Křižan. He canceled several dates until finally D-day arrived, when the prime minister was to receive Křižan. Jiří dressed in the suit he wore to funerals, and because he had gained weight since the days of his youth, the suit was too small for him. His dachshund Ferda was sick, and someone had to take him to the veterinarian. Jiří put on his tie, picked up Ferda, put him in the car, and sat down behind the steering wheel. The car would not start. After several attempts to start it, he discovered that the battery had died. In the heat and in cramped clothes that stuck to his body, he pushed his Škoda MB along Navrátilova Street until he reached a hill. There he started the car and drove to the Charles Baths, where a bus right in front of him got into an accident. The street was blocked, so Jiří sat in the car, smoking and dropping ashes all over his suit. He thought he had blown it.

He arrived at the Presidium at the Straka Academy about an hour later. Kocáb and Horáček were standing on the sidewalk, smoking nervously. Then Oskar Krejčí came across the courtyard to the entrance and said that the prime minister would not talk with Křižan that day. He wanted a guarantee that the petition would not be published on Radio Free Europe before they were able to have a conversation. Jiří promised to embargo the petition for ten days. He kept his promise, but in the meantime, Krejčí phoned to say that Adamec still would not meet with him.

Even at the last hour, no members of the government or the central committee of the Communist Party could decide to act, could make a decision.

At the end of September, Saša Vondra had to serve out the rest of his sentence, six weeks that he had not served in prison in January. They declared that he was not living the orderly life of a working person nor had he given up his political activity, which had been the condition sine qua non of his release. "Just A Few Sentences," meanwhile, had been signed by forty thousand people. The entire spectrum of society was represented; Slovakia had joined, notably Eastern Slovakia. The weekend before November 17,* Křižan, Saša Vondra (freshly released from prison), and Vladimír Hanzel, Havel's personal secretary, went to see Václav at Hrádeček in order to prepare for Human Rights Day on December 10. In coordination with the signature collectors, they were considering organizing a meeting of the "Just a Few Sentences" signatories on Palacký Square for that day. But they were afraid the square was a little big. There is nothing more irritating than a small number of people in a big square.

A few days later, there were over a half million people on Letná Plain.

I remember that sometime around October 28 I went to the film club with a French reporter who wanted to interview Křižan. She asked him why the opposition was not larger. The forty thousand people who had signed the "Just a Few Sentences" manifesto did not seem like a lot to her. We tried to explain that it was more important what kind of people had signed it, what kind of sample it was. But she had a point. On Alexanderplatz in Berlin, a million people had already demonstrated, and here on October 28, they were still beating the same five thousand people while the rest were silent, waiting.

---

*The day of the officially permitted demonstration commemorating the fiftieth anniversary of the student anti-Nazi demonstrations in 1939, and of the death of Jan Opletal, who was killed in the demonstrations.

49 • *November 17*

On Friday, November 17, 1989* we marched past the Havels' house in a procession of students. People started to shout, "Long live Havel!" It surprised me that they knew where Havel lived, and it reassured me. I remember that once during the summer he had despaired because as he crossed Charles Bridge, people had cried out, "Long live Havel!" "I'm done for," he said. "They already recognize my mug."

The weekend of November 17, he was away at Hrádeček on purpose, and Olga was in the march with us. I looked up at the windows; they were dark. Five writers ran out on the balcony of the Writers' Club nearby. I did not know them. One of them made a V with both arms and someone in the crowd shouted, "Long live the writers!" And then someone—better informed about the kind of people who would be standing on the Writers' Club balcony—shouted in a voice just as loud, "May they go to hell!"

On Saturday, Václav came to Prague, as did Křižan, Vondra, and Vladimír Hanzel. When we had seen how exhausted Václav was that summer, we had been afraid for him and had asked him at least to take a secretary. Vladimír did not know what he was getting himself into when he accepted the position. He continued to be Václav's secretary after the revolution, and it was absolutely draining.

---

*On Nov. 17, as many as 20,000 students held an officially sanctioned demonstration in Prague. When about 1,500 students entered Wenceslas Square, which had been declared off bounds, security forces intervened and used truncheons, tear gas, and attack dogs to disperse the students. At least 100 demonstrators were arrested, over a dozen hospitalized, and one student was reported killed, but that later proved to be a false rumor.

50 • *Civic Forum*

On the evening of November 18, at the Realistic Theater, people from the theaters held a meeting to propose a strike. Václav had been in contact with the younger generation for a long time, and he was friendly with Karel Steigerwald, Daniela Fischerová, Jan Foll, and Jan Rejžek, as well as with people from the Theater on a String, HaDivadlo, the Dramatic Club, and the Theater on the Balustrade. When he returned from his long imprisonment, he began to go to the small theaters, chat with people in the lobby, socialize. They were no longer afraid of him, and he no longer had the feeling that his presence threatened them.

The whirlwind in the Realistic Theater took place without Havel's participation. The older theater staff were more cautious. They wanted to limit the length of the proposed strike, or at least to perform now and then and read a statement before the performances. The young actors and students, however, rebelled against the opportunists and shouted them down. "That's enough of that! Let's go all the way!" And they declared a strike.

Then they drove to the other theaters and announced the strike.

The visual artists joined them immediately.

Křižan called Ladislav Kratina of the Dramatic Club to ask if their theater would be available on November 19. Kratina went to ask for permission and called back in a little while to say it was possible. Several hundred people met there. The little theater was full to bursting. Here, Civic Forum was founded. Many people saw Václav Havel for the first time on this podium. As they told me later, he seemed too sweet-tempered and not very dangerous. He was not a good speaker, nor was Charter spokesperson Saša Vondra, who introduced him. But they could tell he knew what he was talking about and that he had a program all thought out.

Havel was proceeding according to a strictly prepared script, in much the same way as he was accustomed to setting up his plays ahead of time, sketching out the skeleton and a diagram of the important entrances and exits. Here too he had a program ready, and the small stage filled up with the people who had come with him. He put words to what everyone had felt for a long time, what they also thought without being able to formulate it properly or recognize what they should do first and what later. He united people who held different opinions and gave them a joint program. He had done this several times before in his life, and he was always pushing everything further, into unfamiliar territory, where no one had yet dared to go either because it seemed impossible or because the risk seemed too great. This revolution, which began here in a theater with a playwright as its leader, had a motto that we repeated over and over, sometimes out loud, sometimes quietly: Is this really possible? Or, as Václav summed it up, politics is the art of the impossible.

He announced here that anyone who felt he was a member of Civic Forum, was. Whoever agreed with our demands* was one of us. Debate mainly centered on the question of whether it still made sense to hold talks with the representatives of those in power, whether they still had the right to affect events if they were capable of massacring a peaceful, empty-handed crowd.

On Monday, the people were in the streets again. The police and militia closed the bridges. Students set up strike committees and occupied their schools. All the colleges were postered with declarations and slogans, and the Czechoslovak flag flew above them. It brought to mind the strike in January 1969, but the atmosphere was different. At that time, something was coming to an end, but here something was beginning. Nobody was able to forecast what it was. As Havel had earlier predicted, it was as if history had balked. Suddenly it was clear that "enough was enough," as Magor had

---

*Havel demanded the immediate resignation of President Husák, Communist Party leader Miloš Jakeš, Interior Minister Miroslav Stěpan, an investigation of the police action on Nov 17, and the release of prisoners of conscience.

written in the summer—yet for writing that, he sat in prison until November 29.

On Monday, November 20, in the evening, there was a meeting of the members of the council of Civic Forum in the Realistic Theater. It was clear to everyone that someone would have to speak to the crowd. Someone had to organize them, and Civic Forum was the one to do it. The media were in the hands of the authorities and were not informing the citizens of what was happening in the streets. No one outside of Prague knew what was happening. The Party and the government clearly hoped that the students would lose interest. They exhorted the students to return to their classrooms. They claimed that no one knew about anything in the countryside, and that there the matter would be decided. Meanwhile, students were already traveling out of Prague with video recordings of what had happened on Národní Avenue on November 17.* They wanted to show the video recordings to the workers; after all, these were their children. Many factories would not allow them in. Throughout the countryside, the students stuck up posters, which graphic designers in the Mánes Building† were manufacturing day and night. At night someone would tear down the posters. The students sent videocassettes to Austrian and West German television stations, so that people within the reach of these stations' signals would learn what was happening in Prague.

Svobodné slovo, which was the first to write the truth, shone like a beacon. Then there was the rural edition of *Lidová demokracie*. These newspapers informed citizens of the rise of Civic Forum. *Mladá fronta* soon joined in. The students picked up the next day's edition at night directly from the typesetters and distributed the newspapers themselves, because otherwise, some newspapers never reached the countryside and were mysteriously lost.

On Tuesday, November 21, Kocáb and Horáček of the Bridge were able to arrange a first meeting. Prime Minister Adamec, however,

---

*See note on p. 245.
†Headquarters of the Union of Czechoslovak Creative Artists.

absolutely refused to negotiate with Havel—as if only Saint Nicholas and the angel should come visit and the devil should stay home, because the children had been good and it would be pointless to scare them. Civic Forum decided that they would not allow their delegation to be screened for political purity. They would not attend the meeting unless Havel was their leader. They would refuse to negotiate without him.

Václav therefore got out of the car with the rest of the delegation, but the authorities refused to let him attend the meeting. He decided on the spot that in the nation's interest, the Civic Forum delegation should act without him. This undermined Civic Forum's decision, but later Havel explained his reasons and the Forum approved.

While the meeting took place, he sat in the Presidium lobby and talked with all sorts of people. Acting as porter, he admitted various delegations with petitions from schools and businesses. Upstairs, meanwhile, Adamec was speaking about perestroika. He used incantatory formulas about democratization, removing the shortcomings of the leadership of the Communist Party, etc. It was clear that even at this point he still did not understand what was happening.

Meanwhile they were preparing sound equipment in Wenceslas Square, and Melantrich* loaned Civic Forum its balcony. On the afternoon of Wednesday, November 22, Havel spoke to the crowds for the first time. He spoke about Civic Forum. Jiří Bartoška, an actor from the Balustrade, gave a report of the meeting with the prime minister, which he had taken part in.† Wenceslas Square was so full there was not room for an apple to drop. It was so cold your breath froze. But what happiness it was to hear truth spoken from a balcony and to read it in the newspapers! People were euphoric; they did not need to eat or sleep. Right now, the truth and the incredibility of each moment

---

*The Socialist Party's publishing house.

†Adamec had ruled out further police violence against demonstrators, vowed the regime would not impose martial law, supported the bringing of non-Communists into the government, and backed an "open dialogue" an reforms.

was enough for them. The crowd answered the speakers, talked back to them. Often I wondered where the genius of the crowd was located, who led it, and who thought up its slogans. Was there one person who was the first to shout a slogan, and then the others joined in; or did these words and sentences arise in many minds simultaneously? Perhaps there was some kind of higher direction the crowd was listening to, instructions that were simultaneously whispered into thousands and hundreds of thousands of ears. It was a miracle; I can offer no explanations. Marta Kubišová sang the national anthem.

The television station covered the demonstration from Kontakt studio. Every so often the broadcast was interrupted, and a rock band replaced the live broadcast from Wenceslas Square. Then Wenceslas Square again. It seemed as if they were fighting over the transmitter, and whoever was victorious at the moment broadcast what he wanted to, until his opponent overthrew him.

51 • *Laterna Magika*

Civic Forum was looking for a space where they could take shelter. The visual artists offered the U Řečických Gallery, where Civic Forum was in fact headquartered for the first few days, but it was a small space, and suddenly someone came up with the Laterna Magika (the Magic Lantern theater).* At this point I called Vašek and told him I was at his disposal. That I could perhaps help write statements, communiqués, news reports. Vašek said I should come at once. I was there in twenty minutes.

It was eight-thirty in the morning. Someone in the kitchen told me to make myself some coffee. In a little while, Václav emerged from the bathroom, and then we ran downstairs. From that time forward,

---

*The Prague theater that uses a multiscene format—a combination of film, theater, and ballet. The theater was a great success at the 1958 World's Fair in Brussels and again at Expo 67 in Montreal.

we ran everywhere. He learned not to walk slowly. Aleš Duda drove Vašek's car, and we went to the Laterna Magika. Aleš drove terribly fast. At the Laterna Magika, there were guards at the door, and we went on inside, downstairs. At the door to Václav's dressing room, two men devoted to Václav body and soul were on guard, Stanislav Milota and John Bok. John had also brought some karate students as bodyguards.

I had never been in the dressing rooms at the Laterna Magika. It was a hot labyrinth with no air. There was practically no ventilation, and everyone smoked like chimneys. When we went there nine months later with the president of Brazil, who had asked to see the place that had been the headquarters of the revolution, I could not understand how we had managed to survive there. In the largest dressing room, about three by four yards, the staff—about ten people—held its meetings. Costumes, ballet tutus, and quaint monsters were hanging everywhere. It smelled like make-up, and there were mirrors on all sides. I could not get used to seeing myself everywhere, and I started to feel a little paranoid. The ballet dancers buttered bread, sliced salami, and boiled coffee. The whole Laterna Magika was working for the revolution. Everything was flurried and feverish, but people were unbelievably kind and decent to each other. Today, when I read Civic Forum's first proclamation, I feel goose pimples and once again recall that special atmosphere, when everyone knew we had no other choice. I had already felt it when I saw armed men stationed opposite us on Národní Avenue—I felt that history was buzzing in my ears and that what was happening was what had to happen.

On Friday, November 24, Miloš Jakeš, general secretary of the central committee of the Communist Party, resigned and so did the entire politburo. We danced in Wenceslas Square. Everyone was happy. No one gave any thought to the fact that they still had the army, the militia, and the tanks.

In the Laterna Magika, everyone moved quickly and purposefully. If someone frowned, he saw it instantly in the mirror. During the Civic Forum assemblies, I marveled at the clever and erudite people who had suddenly surfaced after years of stagnant nonhistory and knew exactly what they were supposed to do. They worked long into the night, laughing often. From time to time, it was as if Havel had written an absurdist play that he starred in and directed. I will never forget that he took me with them and I was part of almost everything that happened. Once again I had the exhilarating feeling that I was in the right place at the right time, that this was the best place in the world, and that I did not want to be anywhere else.

Every so often we would hear that there was a bomb in the basement. People only waved their hands and said, "Forget about it; we don't have time." They reacted the same way when people said they should not sleep at home because they would be attacked in the night and either shot or interned, that the army was moving into Prague, that there would be a putsch. Everyone knew that the situation was "either-or," and I do not remember that anyone was afraid.

One of my first tasks was to write Václav's biography for *Svobodné slovo*. This was a major event, because for the first time he was going to be introduced to the nation in *our* press, without distortion. And I was supposed to do it. I was all atremble, but Milan Uhde, who had just that day arrived in Prague, helped me.

On the evening of November 28, Milan came with us to Národní Avenue, where Vašek dragged both of us on the stage that had been set up. All three of us were badly and inappropriately dressed because we had not had time to change clothes. Milan was wearing hiking boots with white shoelaces that shone so brightly that even a spectator in the second gallery could not fail to notice them. Then we went to the German embassy for a party, where Václav accepted the German Booksellers' Peace Prize. The ladies were wearing long dresses, and we arrived in sweaters. We apologized to Ambassador Huber and his wife, and they forgave us.

The brief biography came out in *Svobodné slovo*. History was unrolling at a madcap pace. Time kept overtaking us, and now we were running to catchup. Fortunately, we ran this leg of the course under a lucky star. From time to time I had the feeling that everything was being directed by some higher power. Occasionaly it seemed that we had made a mistake, but then it always turned out later that what at the time had seemed to be absolutely wrong was in fact the best thing we could have done.

52 ▪ *First Dialogue*

It was November 26, 1989. First there was a consultation in the large dressing room, and then we went to a parley with the prime minister. What the Charter had suggested twelve years ago—as well as all the other petitions since—was finally happening.

"You're coming with us," Václav told me. "Adamec also has a woman there."

And so I sat beside him in the Oriental Salon of the Municipal House. The reporters stood behind us, their breath warming the air. They were like a herd of horses trembling, impatient to start the race. In the middle of the table a small Czechoslovak flag was on a stand. It impressed me. I thought to myself that they must be serious if they had put that there themselves. They, after all, had invited us here; not we, them. Prime Minister Adamec offered Václav his hand across the table. Then Václav's bodyguard, Stanislav Milota, threw out the reporters. For the first time in my life, I was at a meeting behind closed doors—at a meeting on whose outcome the fate of this country might depend. The whole world was waiting to hear the result, because, after many years, Czechoslovakia was once again front-page news.

I examined the people on the other side of the table. I had only seen them on television. Adamec, Vasil Mohorita, Marian Čalfa, and Bohuslav Kučera introduced themselves. Mrs. Němcová, the chairwoman of the Women's Union, smiled at me. From then on, I stared almost constantly at the prime minister, watching the expression on his face and how the color of his face changed. Behind him, outside, it was snowing thickly. In February 1948, it had also snowed, I thought. I was surprised that it was possible to talk so normally with these people, that the meeting was businesslike, brief, and quick. But it also surprised me that it could not have taken place sooner. They used the same words as our side of the table; the stock phrases suddenly disappeared; they knew what they were talking about. Both sides were well prepared.

The prime minister was only apprehensive about one thing: the strike should not harm the nation's economy. As if two hours* could do worse damage than forty years of Communist economics, I thought. Václav assured him that the strike was only intended to demonstrate popular support. The prime minister, red (and from time to time purple) in the face, sharply contrasted with the future prime minister, Marian Čalfa, who was terribly pale and sad. At the end of the meeting, I was bold enough to ask the prime minister to let our two friends, Landovský and Gruša, into the country. He made a note to do it. And they actually appeared. Good God, we thought; so it's really happening.

After the parley, Mrs. Němcová came up to me. She asked me what I did. I said that I was a writer and I wanted to be one again. She was astonished that she was not familiar with anything I had written; not even my name rang a bell. I explained why, and it seemed as though she was hearing about it for the first time. Perhaps she had asked me the question because she thought I would want her job. Then, as woman to woman, she confided her concern. I ought to take action in the name of morality, she said. We are, after all, a cultured nation, and the singer Dědeček [Grandfather] had used vulgar words in the song he had sung last night on Letná Plain.† As women, we should be able to see eye to eye and take action, for after all, we know what morality is. I looked at her with panicked eyes. She had signed that

---

*On November 27, A two-hour general strike called by Civic Forum took place in cities and towns all over Czechoslovakia.

†Some three-quarters of a million people had gathered to hear Havel appeal for public pressure on the government to grant opposition demands.

loathsome proclamation against the students, and now she was concerned with morality.

53 ▪ *Letná Plain*

In the afternoon of November 26, there was a second large demonstration on Letná Plain. On the platform, it was terribly cold; the icy wind blew more strongly than it did below. They brought officers from the emergency units of the ministry of the interior who wanted to apologize for how they had behaved on Národní Avenue on November 17. There were three of them. One of them fainted when he saw the million-strong crowd. Civic Forum had their families moved to a secret location and guarded, and the workers of ČKD (the Kolben-Daněk Machinery Works) took the men themselves into their protection. The crowd could boo or hiss even those who had organized the demonstration. We did not know how the crowd would react to this request for forgiveness. The reaction, as it turned out, was splendid. The crowd was friendly and wanted to talk with the speakers. Mr. Adamec did not understand this, and did not listen to the people. Several personal tragedies unfolded on Letná Plain, and one of these dramas was the prime minister's.

Václav introduced him, emphasized that he deserved credit for the process of dialogue, and stood behind him with Dubček,* as their presence gave him protection. The crowd accepted him. Everything was possible for the prime minister. This was his big day. In the morning he had negotiated with the dissidents; in the afternoon he stood with them before the nation. The people accepted the Communist prime minister; he could still form a bridge between his government and the next, between the past and the present. He could be a

---

*It was his first appearance in Prague since his ouster in 1969.

symbol of tolerance—he could show that everyone had a chance to redeem himself, that the Communists would not be hanged from the lampposts, because they were not all bad, nor were they collectively guilty. The crowd chanted, "A-da-mec." I was moved, as he was. He probably had never experienced anything so spontaneous. It must have been the most glorious moment of his life; every politician, after all, longs to be popular.

He started to speak. His first few sentences earned rounds of applause, while he was still sticking to facts and not commenting on them. But the crowd booed his first attempt at commentary, and then the prime minister committed one political mistake after another. He talked about what the crowd no longer had the patience to hear. Several waves of indignation rippled through the crowd. After all, they had not come to stand here in the freezing cold in order to hear the same thing they had heard for years and years. They booed and started to speak, but the man at the microphone was not listening to them. He still could have pulled him together, but he was not accustomed to listening to what other people thought and following their lead. His future career collapsed. Everything, we saw, was being decided here and now, and the people did not accept him. Earlier, during the negotiations, he had emphasized that the street decided nothing, and now he paid dearly for that opinion. The extinguished star briefly shone, and the was extinguished once again. Of course, the light it had given off had only been reflected from another source. To top off his mistake, he mentioned that the central committee of the Communist Party would decide everything at its next session and rectify its shortcomings.

"Too late, too late!" The crowd pronounced its verdict, as it had so many times in the history of humanity, whether for good or evil. And the prime minister still did not listen. He asked them to trust the Party, because he did not understand that now it was no longer enough to offer what would have been accepted as a positive sign and a constructive solution fourteen days ago. It occurred to me that perhaps he was bringing up his comrades because he did not want to betray them.

Maybe he was not foolish but high-principled. Who knows? It no longer mattered. The die was cast.

The reactions to this demonstration on Letná Plain were varied. Students rebelled against Václav Malý, who was the moderator. People in the countryside were angry because everything sounded different on television. Maybe the coffee was too strong.

On Letná Plain, people prayed the Lord's Prayer. If only they could actually forgive each other. If only they could stop lying and stealing, envying and hating.

This is not theater, I told myself; this is the real thing. The crowd sentenced Adamec to silence and thereby concluded an epoch of history. Those who had committed crimes while acting on orders from others they forgave. A national reconciliation. At least for the day.

Vašek had hand-written his speech on a piece of paper. We did not have time to type it over. He wrote with green ink, the color of hope, and there were a lot of insertions. Later I was able to type his speeches over for him. I tried to shorten the sentences, because writing essays had given him the habit of expressing himself in sentences that were too complex. I also tried to pick out anything that resembled the language products of our media. Under the pressure of speed, my efforts were of little use; the empty Communist phrases forced their way in—any other political language had been forgotten long ago. This language will have to be renewed. I resolved that all the proclamations of Civic Forum would address people in a new language, a language that was different from what was usual in the country until then. These words, after all, were forming a new history, one that was altogether different. Of course, it was impossible to live up to my resolution, because we were always racing against the clock, or rather, the clock was always threatening to catch us.

One person who could not bring himself—or perhaps was simply unable—to give up the old phrases was the editor of *Rudé Právo*. One day he announced himself at the Laterna Magika and the volunteer guards let him into the dressing room. I asked if I could be present during the interview. Mr. Lipavský was supposed to write *Rudé Právo*'s first interview with Havel. He sat opposite Václav, and I observed them both. Mr. Lipavský pulled out a tape recorder, but his hands shook so badly he could not turn it on. He was terribly nervous; perhaps he thought his life was at stake. Here in these catacombs, Havel might have him killed. Or maybe he thought the Minotaur lay in wait for him at the end of the labyrinth.

As if he sensed what I was thinking, he said, "I would like to thank you, Mr. Havel, for letting me come see you. After what's been written about you in *Rudé Právo* . . . but you seem quite normal!"

We stipulated that at six o'clock in the evening he would send us the rough proof, and then someone would bring the proof back to make sure that the interview was printed without any further changes. At six o'clock, they brought us something we had to rewrite totally. We only left the questions in their language, in parrotese, into which they had tried to translate Václav as well.

Every day, I cooked a pot of herb tea so that Václav would have something to drink. In the labyrinth it was oppressively hot, and everyone sweated. Talking—and smoking—dried out the throat. The only pot I was able to find was the kind used for collecting urine in a hospital. The pot accompanied us to every press conference, until it stayed behind in the secret apartment,* where we forgot it.

Stanislav Milota was an excellent bouncer. Every day he threw out dozens of people, but he did it with a sense of humor, in a way that made it impossible for them to be insulted. He was always in a good mood and cracking jokes. It was hard for me to believe that not long ago he had been very sick. Now he was full of energy from dawn to dusk. Everyone was euphoric, and the euphoria sustained the workers through an unbelievable number of hours while working with unbelievable intensity. For every radio station in the countryside, they wrote statements calling for people to resist bloodshed and attempts at provocation. The army and militia were still in the hands of the

---

*See Chapter 55, "The Secret Apartment," p. 262.

Communists, and they were threatening that they would defend themselves. Amateurs suddenly developed enormous political sagacity and preparedness. They knew they could not let a bloody confrontation come to pass, that this revolution had to remain unstained by violence and blood. The confusion reached its peak just before the general strike. But at the same time, there was always laughter, joy, love, and song. There was always someone on hand who could bring cheerfulness into an atmosphere of exhaustion and powerlessness. A spark of laughter would be struck amid the ashes of exhaustion. Playwrights also know how to work with laughter. During one of the most difficult negotiations at the Presidium, when there seemed to be no solution to the situation and Prime Minister Adamec was turning purple, Václav declared a minute of silence and a minute of laughter. Since it was a great success, he repeated the technique at other meetings. And they also laughed on the other side of the table.

I remember when a delegation went to Lazarská Street to meet with the Czech František Pitra, premier of the Czech Republic. It was the first time that future Czech Prime Minister Petr Pithart was in the Civic Forum delegation. John Bok and the other bodyguards returned to the Laterna Magika. At Lazarská Street, they had been thrown out. They waited an hour, then two, three, four. Václav had thought the meeting would be an easy one, but apparently this was not the case. At eight in the evening, we started to be afraid. We sent John and "his boys" to Lazarská. They returned empty-handed. They had not been allowed in the building, and no one would speak to them. Then Saša Neuman and I called there. No one answered the telephone. When at last we got through, they told us that the meeting was still in progress. I confess I was afraid they had been taken prisoner and transported somewhere. I was afraid we would never see them again. When they returned, they said they had had the same feeling. The meeting had been interrupted, and their counterparts had left the room for an hour. State Security agents had surrounded them. During the meeting, Petr Pithart sat across from a law school classmate. When Petr was thrown out of the law school faculty this former classmate became dean. Petr, who for twenty years read water gauges and worked in a warehouse, had not seen him since. Until now.

Every day we were flooded with subjects like this for stories, novels, and plays. But we did not even have enough time to make notes so we would not forget them.

Always, this feeling of unreality. I felt I would wake up and everything would be as it was before. I was almost afraid to fall asleep. When I did, it was not sleep, but a kind of fainting spell in which not even dreams appeared. I told Václav how this feeling persecuted me.

"I've got it even worse," he said. "I'm afraid I'll wake up in a cell and tell my fellow prisoners about this strange dream I had."

On Sunday, December 3, Václav went outside for the first time in fourteen days. He and Olga went for a walk in Průhonice park. When he returned to the Laterna Magika underground, he said, "At last, outside under the high and wide heavens, I realized that this is for real and it is definitely not a dream."

For a while, time settled down—it slowed down to a realistic pace, only to run ahead again, still faster. I thought that, to a certain extent, the atmosphere of unreality was the fault of the underground labyrinth of the Laterna Magika where amid artificial light, mirrors, and a limited air supply, everything took on a magic, brand-new form. We only saw the light of day on city squares and Letná Plain. Otherwise we did not crawl out from underground.

At one of the first meetings with the authorities, Václav asked about allocating a building for Civic Forum. In the end, they allotted us the building that had belonged to the Union of Czechoslovak-Soviet Friendship on the corner of Wenceslas and Jungmann Square, the Špalíček building. Here, everything seemed to be more real.

54 • *Špalíček*

Václav acquired a room with a balcony that looked onto the square, where he stood to address the crowd on several occasions. In the room was a writing desk with a telephone on it. What a change from the Laterna Magika, where at the beginning we only had one line! The room also had a long table for meetings and consultations and that's where we all sat. We were always together then. In the adjacent room, there were two writing desks and more telephones. This room was always full of people, whom John Bok and Milota screened, deciding whom to allow inside. Ladislav Kantor, the leader of the musical group C & K Vocal, began to use his great managerial talent to arrange Václav's schedule. The onlaught of requests, suggestions, complaints, advice, and everything else could no longer be left to sort themselves out by themselves. Kantor's skill at organizing demonstrations was also unequaled.

At this point, they asked me to be press spokesperson. They explained that I was the most serious-looking person in the group.

"Look at us," Křižan said to me. "We look like mutineers. You're cut out for it, and you'll be able to handle it. It's what Václav wants."

From then on, I fought with a pack of reporters. They besieged us like an enormous monster with dozens of arms and legs. They knocked into each other, tripped each other up, and stabbed each other in the back. I had known some of the reporters before, but that December, unfortunately, we went our separate ways, perhaps for life. I refused to misuse my influence to further their personal success, and that riled them. Also, they wrote all sorts of nonsense. On one occasion I had to call Křižan in to impress a cheeky reporter with his physical strength and bulk. Once the reporter saw him and heard him, he changed his tune and started to fawn.

"It's the Hydra from Lerna," I said to Václav.

"Be good to them," he said. "We need them. They work for us."

When the bloody events in Romania began, the whole pack flew off in a special airplane to Romania, like some kind of bird of prey. They liked our revolution well enough, but the Romanian one was more dramatic. It made things easier for me. They returned just before the presidential election and with all their earlier strength tried to reach Havel.

55 · The Secret Apartment

Václav said that since he could not concentrate in Špalíček, he would only visit, or actually, commute. Some time in early December, he moved to a secret apartment. It was a penthouse apartment with a large window that framed a large piece of sky and the tips of a crown of old trees. From here, it seemed as though nothing had happened. The room was quiet and cozy. On a table by the window there was a typewriter; here he wrote his first speech for television, which I typed a clean copy of. We drove to the television station together. Václav refused to use a teleprompter. He considered it to be a deception, and he decided to admit he was reading a speech from paper. He was nervous, as he was before all his public appearances. I sat on the podium, and it occurred to me that he would have to get used to it. He was going to have to overcome his shyness. It would cause him a great deal of pain, and he might never get used to it, because although a writer is an exhibitionist, he is a different kind of exhibitionist. He had decided to become a writer because he was not able to show off any other way.

This first television speech, his introduction to the nation, was a great success. On his first attempt, he handled himself excellently. By chance I later spoke with a few young women who complained that Havel mispronounces the letter ř, was a poor speaker, lowered his eyes in embarrassment, scratched behind his ear, and chewed his fingernails.

"And did you hear what he was saying?" I asked.

"Of course," they answered. After the New Year's speech, I spoke with them again, and they said his performance style no longer bothered them. Before, while they were getting used to him, they hadn't really been listening. But once they concentrated on the fantastic things he was saying, none of his habits disturbed them anymore.

To reach the hideout, telephone callers had to ring three times and then hang up. Only on the next call would someone—usually Stanislav Milota—pick it up. The doorbell also had to ring three times, and then someone, usually Stanislav, would go look through the peephole to see who was there.

Václav was calmer in the apartment. Here there was not a crowd of people always chasing him, setting up a nervous vibration around him, their voices roaring in both ears at once. At night, one of the bodyguards who knew karate slept in the hallway on the floor. This man also went to the grocery store. Václav received important visits here. Dubček came, as did Věnek Šilhán, Petr Pithart, and Jiří Bartoška, who was mediating the negotiations with Čalfa.* The top brass of Civic Forum were here daily. Václav commuted to Špalíček for assemblies, and to the Laterna Magika for press conferences and radio programs. Pavel Kohout visited the secret apartment, and Václav later included his comments on emigration in his New Year's address.

---

*Čalfa had replaced Adamec as prime minister; Adamec had resigned on December 7, in an impasse with the opposition on the composition of the cabinet he had named four days earlier.

56 ▪ *Who Will Be President?*

Husák fell, and the question loomed—Who would be president?

I know I was not the first to suggest this to Václav, but he stared at me with a sorrowful look that held a reproach: "Et tu, Brute?"

"You were always one of the people against my becoming president," he said. "And now you come up with something like this."

"I'm still against it," I said, "but when I look around, I don't see anyone else."

"Olga is also against it," he said. "There's a rumor she might divorce me."

Olga came to the evening press conference at the Laterna Magika. Poor thing, her apartment had turned into a second revolutionary council. People were always coming and going, and the telephone rang nonstop. She stood in the corridor of the Laterna Magika and smoked her beloved Petra cigarettes. She gave me one and said, "It's impossible for him to be president. After all, you know it wouldn't suit him. And what am I supposed to do?"

"I don't know, Olga, I never imagined it would happen either."

Nor did I ever imagine it would come so quickly or in this way. I remembered how in the summer Václav had drawn a layout of the political forces and it never occurred to him that the Charter could win. And now everywhere in the streets there were posters that read, "Put Havel in the Castle." The crowd chanted it in the squares.

The candidate for president had to be introduced to the nation. *Disturbing the Peace** was best suited for this.

One evening, three of us were sitting in the secret apartment. The sky was growing dark. The lamps in the park switched on, and the

---

*A book-length interview with Havel conducted by journalist Karel Hvíždala in 1986.

conversation came around to the publication of *Disturbing the Peace*. Václav had promised Melantrich that they could publish it. I objected that he had promised it to the Atlantis publishing house. Tomás Kosta* was preparing to print *Disturbing the Peace* in Germany and to send the whole print run to Czechoslovakia as a gift from the German Atlantis publishing house to the Czech one.

"Call Melantrich," Václav said. "Tell them they have two options. Either they publish it before December 20, or someone else publishes it."

"They'll never make that deadline," I said. "No Czech publishing house has ever published a book in a week."

"Call them," he said.

So I phoned Mr. Kovařík, the editor-in-chief at Melantrich, and told him what Václav had said. For a while there was silence on the other end of the line. I sensed how impossible the demand sounded. Then Mr. Kovařík pulled himself together and said, "But you can't possibly be serious. Nothing like that has ever happened before."

He sounded like Prime Minister Adamec had sounded when, stunned by the cheekiness of the opposition, he had refused to accept their ultimatum.

"Nothing that's happening in this country right now has ever happened before. I'll give you half an hour to think it over. In a half hour, I'll call you, and you can tell me your decision."

I hung up and the three of us grinned at each other. If other people could do the impossible, why couldn't Melantrich?

In the course of a half hour, Melantrich realized they had a chance. The editor-in-chief let me know they would publish the book in eight days. But he needed the manuscript immediately. Could I bring it to him?

Václav said he had a box somewhere with the manuscript for the foreign edition of *Disturbing the Peace*, but it was stowed away in some deep hiding place. There was no time to go look for it. I searched

---

*An editor at Atlantis.

around the apartment for a while, and I found *Disturbing the Peace* on a small shelf above the bed. I stole it from the apartment's owner, ordered a taxi, and rode to Melantrich. There the chief of production was already waiting. He grabbed the manuscript and ran off. The next morning the editor-in-chief, Mr. Kovařík, called me to say that seven of the best typesetters had typeset all night and that they already had two-thirds of it finished. They would need the jacket design the next day. Joska Skalník worked on it all night, and in the morning it was ready. It seemed entirely possible to me that our country would be able to revive its market economy.

On December 20, the book was on sale and people were standing in line for it. As I walked through Wenceslas Square, I smiled as contentedly as a little mouse. A mouse made giddy by the realization that when people want a thing badly enough, everything falls into place. When they want to, they can move the globe, as our future president had written in his acceptance speech for the Erasmus Prize, a prize named for another great fool (cf. *In Praise of Folly*) and great European.

On December 29, after the Te Deum that was part of the celebration for the new president taking office we, Havel's closest friends and supporters, walked through the Castle with Petr Pithart. As we made our way the bell Sigismond rang through the Castle courtyard. The bell was tolling for the old times, just as the keys had rung the same death-knell earlier.* For a while we and Petr stopped, as if the bell prevented us from moving, as if it rooted us to the ground. I burst out crying. I looked at Petr, and he had tears in his eyes. I grabbed his

---

*Sigismond is the largest bell in the tower of St. Vitus Cathedral on the Hradčany, called the Castle. "At the end of the demonstration, . . . the people down in the square make the most extraordinary spontaneous gesture. They all take their keys out of their pockets and shake them, 300,000 key-rings, producing a sound like a massed Chinese bells." Timothy Garton Ash, *The Magic Lantern: The Revolution of '89 Witnessed in Warsaw, Budapest, Berlin, and Prague* (New York: Random House, 1990), p. 96.

hand and said, "This is the most happy moment of our lives." And he nodded.

"Even if nothing else happens," I added.

And only then did everything begin. And it keeps on beginning, over and over again, each time in a different way. As if we will never be through with it.

We entered the State Rooms of Prague Castle. Jiří Křižan was the only person who had been there before us, to see what it looked like. The officers of the fifth department of the ministry of the interior stood on all sides. We were like a handful of invaders in conquered territory.

The secretaries in charge of protocol pounced on me, wanting to know where I had put the biography because they needed it for the Czechoslovak Press Agency. I realized that I only had the one that had been printed in *Svobodné Slovo*, and then the one on the book jacket for *In Different Directions*.

I went to the president and said, "We've hit a snag. We don't have your biography."

And our new president laughed and said: "So tuck yourself into a corner somewhere out of the way and write one."

And it was left in my hands.

▪ Epilogue

A peculiar, extraordinary thing happened, after the Velvet Revolution, and it was—and still is—significant for our world. Czechoslovakia chose as its president an intellectual, a writer, and a dissident who went almost directly from prison to the Prague castle, the traditional seat of the Czech kings and the largest inhabited castle in the world.

It was, in fact, the intellectuals who, in the first phase after the revolution, had to suply democratic politics, a democratic public, democratic laws and all the varieties of power normally found under pluralism. This happened in Czechoslovakia, Hungary, Bulgaria, Poland, and Lithuania. We often ask whether the intellectuals and artists who entered politics lost their spiritual power. I would answer that there was no other choice. The intellectuals who entered politics have enriched not only politics, but also themselves.

In ancient Greece, for example, many politicians were intellectuals and were nonetheless good politicians, perhaps because they were free in their decisions and actions. What liberated them was precisely that they did not want to be politicians; the possibility that they might lose their posts did not enter their calculations. They were not afraid of that. Instead, they considered it immoral to place personal interest above the civic interest. Václav Havel also linked politics to morality. Morality, he felt, ought to be the foundation of every politics.

In the first century before Christ, the wise Pericles governed Greece; in the fourteenth century, Lorenzo Medici governed Florence. Although, historical epochs like these never lasted long, recounting them helps revive in people the romantic dream of wisdom and justice in rulers; qualities that cleansed the rulers, whose robes were so often stained with blood. And these epochs remind those who hold office, at least for a time, of the curses and calluses power causes when unchecked by conscience.

But, in Czechoslovakia, after the revolution, intellectuals governed more or less for the simple reason that there were no politicians left. How could there be after forty years of harsh totalitarianism? Later on, those who for various reasons did not achieve power would accuse the intellectuals of having stolen power for themselves and abused it, but this is untrue. If in 1990, after the first free elections, the intellectuals had wanted power, they could have set four-year terms of office. But they set only two-year terms, headed by President Havel, who in June 1990 was again, for a second time, elected president of the Czechoslovak Federal Republic for two years.

Maybe it was political naïveté. At that time the intellectuals had no idea how long it takes to formulate a program and put it into action. They were intoxicated by easy victory. Where they had expected to find resistance, none had appeared and in the labyrinth of power they had expected to meet the Minotaur, but he did not appear. Meanwhile the forces that had not put up any resistance during the revolution grew like poisonous mushrooms throughout society; they appeared in the soul of almost every citizen, while the old structures quickly adapted to the new situation at hand. How skillfully, for example, they suddenly began to use the Helsinki declaration on human rights. Those who had stifled the rights of others for years suddenly wanted rights for themselves, and they obtained them in the courts. They remained in government departments and bureaus; they continued to govern and govern today in industry. They organized themselves into a smuggling and business mafia.

None of these people is against market economics in principle; they probably do not want to turn back the wheel of history and introduce socialism again, either. They want to make as much money as possible in the temporary confusion, to take as much as possible from a government that is already quite poor, to make themselves rich. They still do not understand that they cannot profitably conduct business in a country that doesn't work, that they cannot be rich in a country that is poor.

As obsesson with material goods, a passion for having—perhaps these are consequences of the collective ownership and social egalitarianism that were implemented unfairly and forced on people under socialism. Perhaps it is a way out of the insecurity and spiritual emptiness that follows every great upheaval. The Communists, after all, had forbidden every spiritual dimension, every attempt at transcendence.

People who are old and retired might want to return to socialism because the prices were lower then, and they no longer have any hope of making money. Either they are already too old, or they don't want to learn anything new; they are afraid to start over, to change their lives, to take risks, to be responsible for themselves. According to polls taken this spring, people in Bohemia, just as in other post-Communist countries, still long for egalitarianism and the further east you go, the more of these people there are. They want everyone to have little, but the same amount. They do not want to have their personal worth appraised and they especially do not want to have to stand up for themselves. They want to hide in the crowd.

Since the time when the Berlin Wall fell and we all celebrated and gave in to euphoria and the feeling that everything was possible, a great deal has changed. We are offering people a market society as the only possible option for development, while in the West, the market has started to stagnate, or to spiral into nothing less than a recession. Even in the United States it has turned out that wealth cannot be perpetual and that we cannot all live in it. Everyone lays claim to human rights, but no one wants to fulfill human responsibilities. Perhaps it might be time to write a charter of the responsibilities and duties of every person and to place it—equal but not separate—beside the charter of rights.

It is harder than we anticipated. Against the truth that the intellectuals were preparing to lay out, the populists put forth a lie, and as it turned out, it is much easier to win with a lie. People do not want to hear the truth. It is unpleasant. The politician who is accustomed to speaking the truth must tell the citizens that they can do everything themselves, that there are no longer any internal enemies to blame, because they themselves are their own deadliest enemy. The politicians who speak the truth must, like Churchill, demand blood and sweat from the people.

The dissident was accustomed to telling the truth to people and he built his whole life on this. But how can a politician who does not lie hold his ground against a politician who does? After all, telling lies, not truths, makes you popular, and many people long to be lied to.

The intellectual politician has a further problem. He is unable to advertise himself, because he's self-critical and sheepish in the presence of government, maintaining a constantly critical position toward power, a distrust of it. The intellectual wants to create ideas, but he doesn't want to repeat them or force them on anyone. Therefore he's not too successful at the practice of politics.

And so, after a two-year period, determined by the intellectuals themselves, it was more or less the pragmatists who won the elections in June 1992. Of course any generalization here is imprecise, the intellectuals' attempt to substitute for nonexistent politicians ended after roughly two years; many intellectuals, however, remained in power. But the majority could no longer fall back on the excuse that they were amateurs and didn't care about power, that they could leave at any time if the people didn't like them. They had to decide to become politicians. Some made this decision; others returned to their original callings, enriched by their encounter with power.

Havel faced the same decision. In his lecture at New York University on October 17, 1991, he described himself as a literary critic who had been suddenly forced to write a novel. For years he criticized the practice of politics as a pragmatic battle for power, whose goal was to gain power by any means; he promoted "apolitical," moral politics, politics based on conscience and truth. Then destiny played him a dirty trick, it invited him to show what *he* could do as a politician. Power dropped into the hands of the man who had written the celebrated essay, "The Power of the Powerless." After almost three years in the presidency, Václav Havel stated that his opinions had not changed, that on the contrary, he believed in them more firmly. It is not necessary to lie in politics, he felt; politics need not be dirty. It is possible, even necessary, to tell the truth, but it is necessary to tell it with tact and taste.

During two years, from June 1990 to July 1992, he made thirty state visits and received twenty-four state visitors. He delivered 107 official speeches and signed, as head of state, seventeen international treaties and agreements. He introduced fifteen proposals for new laws to the federal assembly, among them very significant legislation on the referendum and voting laws, which the parliament rejected. He introduced his own proposal for the constitution of the federal republic. He conducted countless meetings on the composition of the constitutional law of Czechoslovakia, participated in all the important meetings of the Czech and Slovak representatives, visited every region in both parts of the federation, and met with mayors of towns and cities and representatives of national and local administrations. The laws he proposed could have opened up a space for further Czech-Slovak discussions, could have created a system of safety measures to prevent crises. He was always convinced that for the citizens of both republics it was more advantageous to live in a collective state. Unfortunately, this did not work out. The elections in June 1992 showed that the majority of the population of the Slovak Republic had given their vote to the party that was pushing for separation. The separation was the legitimate result of free elections, and in the end it led to the abdication of Václav Havel in July of that year. He did not want to be the liquidator of a federation of whose utility and viability he was convinced; he did not, however, abandon his citizens.

The pragmatists won, as they have so many times before in history. In Slovakia, the populists won, headed by the current prime minister, Vladimír Mečiar. In Bohemia, it was the Civic Democratic Party, headed by the current prime minister, Václav Klaus. Klaus is the father of economic reform, and because the reforms are running remarkably well so far, he's enjoying a good reputation worldwide. Roughly speaking, the prime minister stands for the opinion that the economy must be transformed first, and then, when the state is prosperous, the government can take up cultural and social issues. His opponents accuse him of being uncivilized, of not having enough sense of tradition, of wanting to sell the country out to foreign capital, of being cosmopolitan, of abetting the loss of national identity, and of lacking social compassion.

Klaus and his government assumed the task of dividing the Czechoslovak Republic into two states. It was as bold and unpopular a move as taking up the burden of economic reform.

The victorious party in Slovakia had a policy of slowing and limiting economic reform. Two economies cannot live side by side in one state; it is impossible for them to have the same currency and army, as the Slovaks wanted. They wanted all the advantages of a joint state and none of the disadvantages. And so the division of the state became a necessary operation. The surgery was performed with skill and by the book, but the convalescence will be long and perhaps dramatic. Neither patient is yet out of danger. We still do not yet know whether they will survive, and it is still out of the question to speak of health.

Klaus and his government took up a task that would be impossible to handle well. It is always possible to argue, "If only this had happened," or "This shouldn't have occurred," but at every opportunity— and there are many—at every misunderstanding and mix-up, they can be reproached: "you shouldn't have taken Slovakia at its word then, you should have continued to meet with them, you should have had more patience." These recriminations will continue until both countries—under other circumstances and in another political and economic context, of course—reunited. Václav Havel believes in this, too, and he stands above it all as the independent, nonpartisan, Czech president.

Opinions differ over Havel. Some believe that he should continue as president. He started something and he ought to finish it. People have associated him with a certain hope, and he must not disappoint them. He can leave as soon as it is clear that the ship he launched is afloat and will not founder. Then people will remember him with gratitude. But is this possible? Is it possible to pass the straits between the Balkans and Western Europe with the keel intact and the body not stained with blood? Is it possible for the president to become a playwright again?

Nobody knows.

Some people say that he should not have become president a third time in January 1993. They would have preferred to see him as an independent intellectual, someone who had a free hand and a free mind, who could criticize everything and not have to take responsibility for anything, someone who would be in the opposition against the government's pragmatism. They wanted to see him in a position like Adam Michnik's in Poland, who left the Sejm of his accord and rejected several high government posts and become editor-in-chief of the newspaper *Gazeta Wyborcza*.

Others think Havel ought to have remained the leader of Civic Movement and changed the movement into a political party, into a party of the democratic center, and thus gained greater powers than he has today as an independent president—perhaps he could wield a presidential power like Clinton's or Mitterrand's. Furthermore, in January 1993 Havel became the representative of a divided, diminished state. Admittedly, the divorce was accomplished with politeness and decency; nevertheless, the two nations could not manage to live in what was only a collective home, as civilized nations should be able to do.

In the new political system, parties and their representatives often indulge in party politics, mutually denounce each other, hold grudges—they are more concerned with themselves than with the common good. No democracy can avoid this, but in a democracy as young as the Czech one is, it can be led astray. In these circumstances, an independent president can try to reconcile the divided parties and help them find a compromise. Havel is still the most popular and trustworthy person in the country. He is the one listened to for advice.

Economic reform is in progress; small-scale privatization has taken place; large-scale privatization has gone through two rounds already. A class of businesspeople of every stripe has arisen; people are buying shares; they are founding banks and stock exchanges; since the new year a new tax system is in effect; internal revenue department offices have appeared, as have offices for trade, the economy, customs, etc.— all the tools that Western democracies have used for ages and still use today. At the same time, the Czech Republic's budget is balanced, inflation is under control, and our debt is no larger than absolutely necessary. This process, however, has its unpleasant side effects. We inherited from the old regime a legacy of enormous economic deformation; COMECON collapsed; many businesses lost their markets and cannot hold their own competition. The division into two states left us with further complications involving the links between industrial organizations and markets. Many businesses are in debt; they are unable to pay their bills and are relying on the state to help them, as it has many times before. Production levels have fallen, and therefore the real income of the population has also fallen; prices are rising, and the standard of living has dropped.

The boldness and courage of the reforms, however, meet with respect abroad.

It is remarkable how bravely and matter-of-factly people are coming to terms with the difficulties. The Czechs have one good quality: they are level-headed and matter-of-fact. They adjust quickly; their business sense, a sense for the value of productive work, awakens quickly. But the atmosphere in Bohemia is not healthy, neither ecologically nor morally. Civic conscience, self-confidence, truthfulness, the courage to take risks, sensitivity to one's own and others' freedom— all these values were crushed underfoot for forty years. A new spiritual orientation and the spiritual dimension of life cannot be purchased, nor can they be managed or decreed into existence by any administration. It is a long and complicated process. And so people succumb to insecurity, despair, emptiness. The vacuum of values arouses in them the feeling that everything is possible in a democracy, that they can vent their worst qualities. After every great social upheaval, criminality rises; all the worst human traits surface: envy, hate, looking for enemies, scapegoating, intolerance, radicalism, a primitive cult of consumerism, nationalism, fascism, opportunistic morality . . . Others call upon the government to show a strong hand, to restore order.

All of this is very dangerous, and it is good when the president speaks to the people heart to heart, calls their attention to the rules of decency, restores good traditions and condemns the bad ones. Over and over again, he emphasizes to individuals and to political parties the importance of the spiritual and moral dimension of politics. He is a symbol of the best aspects of every citizen, the best aspects of the whole that all of us form.

Three years full of dramatic changes have passed. Numbered among the good changes: in 1991, the last Soviet soldier left; with the active participation of Czechoslovakia the Warsaw Pact was dissolved; we have become full members of the Council of Europe and associate members of the European Community. The door to the political and economic community of democratic Europe has opened.

Americans remember Václav Havel's triumphant trip during his first visit to the United States in February 1990. They remember his speech in Congress, when he asked the United States to help the Soviet Union, then still in existence, and they remember the celebration of freedom in the Cathedral of St. John the Divine in New York, when the most luminous representatives of American culture paid tribute to Havel. It is not only Americans who connect Havel the person with their hopes for the existence of a better world, but Americans have a special love of hope. That is why almost 20,000 young Americans are currently living in Prague.

The second and third visits of the Czech president to the United States, however, were more sober and practical, and there was no longer so much celebration. The euphoria had vanished; the hard work remained. But in his speech at George Washington University he spoke again of the topic that had concerned him in 1990: the responsibility of each inhabitant of this planet for everything that happens here, and the reluctance to know, help, and share. Again he tried to turn America's attention to the post-Communist East, to convince them that sensible and thoughtful assistance would eventually be to America's own benefit.

In Bohemia and Moravia, according to the constitution, the president is the guarantor of the continuity of governmental power. He cannot be recalled for a period of five years, unless he commits treason or felony, and he is very important, particularly in periods of political crisis, because he is the representative of the identity and integrity of the state. The Czech president is not the chief of the executive branch, nor is he the leader of the parliamentary majority; he has no direct influence on government policy or its implementation. That is the task of the government, which is controlled by parliament. The president names the government and in certain situations can dismiss the lower house. Above all, however, he is the guarantor of the legitimacy of political solutions, the custodian of the political culture and the moral dimensions of politics.

In the winter of 1993 Havel did not wage a presidential campaign. He wrote out his program beforehand in the book *Summer Meditations*. It is an encouraging book, and we are not the only ones who would be happy to live in the nation he imagines. The book offers a vision of hope for our world, a vision that only Havel the writer could articulate.

He can no longer say he does not want to be president and that he did not choose his office. He has accepted it as his lot. Yet in his statement of beliefs, there is still the freedom of an intellectual, of someone who can always return to something he perhaps likes better. Nothing he began is finished yet. None of us know what will come next or what will be demanded of us. It is important, therefore, that the majority of citizens trust him and are willing to listen to what he has to say.

—Eda Kriseová
Prague
June 30, 1993

▪ Glossary of Names

[Note: ČSFR is the Czech and Slovak Federal Republic]

ADAMEC, LADISLAV (1926), Communist prime minister from October 1988 until November 1989.

BARTOŠKA, JIŘÍ (1947), actor; from 1978 to 1991 a member of the Theater on the Balustrade.

BATTĔK, RUDOLF (1924), sociologist and essayist. After the August 1968 invasion, imprisoned for several years; in 1980, again sentenced to seven years in prison as a founding member of VONS and as a Charter spokesperson. Served as deputy chairman of the Federal Assembly from 1990 to 1992, and is member of the Association of Social Democrats.

BEDNÁŘOVÁ, OTTA (1927), an editor for Czechoslovak Television until 1969. Member of VONS.

BENDA, VÁCLAV (1936), philosopher and mathematician. Founding member of VONS and Charter spokesperson. Now heads the Christian Democratic party.

BENEŠ, EDVARD (1884–1948), a significant politician; president of Czechoslovak Republic in 1935–1938 and 1945–1948.

BENEŠ, JAN (1936), writer. Since 1969, he has lived in the U.S.

BĔLÍKOVÁ, JARMILA (1948), psychologist, member of VONS.

BONDY, EGON (pseudonym for Zbynĕk Fišer) (1930), philosopher, translator, left-wing Marxist, poet, prose writer, and ideologue of the Czech underground. The protagonist of several of Bohumil Hrabal's books.

BRATINKA, PAVEL (1946), philosopher and political scientist. Vice-chairman of the Civic Democratic Alliance and Deputy Minister for Foreign Affairs for the Czech Republic.

BROD, MAX (1884–1968), a German Prague writer; author of novels about the Prague milieu. Friend of Franz Kafka; author of his biography and first publisher of his work. After 1938, he lived in Israel.

BRABENEC, VRATISLAV (1946), poet, prose writer, text maker, and rock musician; member of the rock group The Plastic People of the Universe. He emigrated in 1982.

ČALFA, MARIÁN (1946), Communist member of the federal government until 1989. From 1990 to 1992. Prime minister of Czechoslovakia, a member of the Civic Democratic Union, and now an entrepreneur.

ČAPEK, KAREL (1890–1938), prose writer, playwright, essayist, journalist, and translator, who played an important part in forming the spiritual climate of the prewar republic on a deeply humane basis.

ČERNY, ALBERT (1937), actor, member of VONS, imprisoned in 1979; from 1990 to 1992 a representative in the Federal Assembly.

ČERNÝ, VÁCLAV (1905)–1987), literary critic and theorist, historian, editor, and translator. University professor in Brno, Geneva, and Prague. From 1944 to 1945, imprisoned as a member of the resistance; after 1948, persecuted. The author of significant *Memoirs*.

CHALUPECKÝ, JINDŘICH (1910–1990), art theorist and critic, translator. Founder and leading representative of Group 42.

CHRAMOSTOVÁ, VLASTA (1926), actress. After 1968, she was only allowed to appear in public on limited occasions. Later, even this was forbidden once she became an activitist for Charter 77. This led to the founding of so-called "apartment theater," whose advocate she became.

CHYTILOVÁ, VĚRA (1929), screenwriter and director of so-called New Wave films. Best known for *Daisies*.

DEML, JAKUB (1878–1961), Catholic priest, poet, prose writer, political writer, author of prose poetry and collections from daily newspapers; translator.

DIENSTBIER, JIŘÍ (1937), political writer, reporter, playwright, and translator. In the 1960s, a foreign correspondent in the Far East and the U.S. A founding member of VONS and a spokesperson for the Charter. From 1989 to 1992, Minister of Foreign Affairs of the ČSFR, and now heads the Civic Movement.

DOLEŽAL, BOHUMIL (1940), while *Tvář* was in existence, one of the foremost literary critics. Now an adviser to the prime minister of the Czech Republic.

DRTINA, PROKOP (1900–1980), politician, secretary of President Beneš. During the war, an emigré in London; after the war, Minister of Justice; after 1948, removed by the Communists and imprisoned. Author of wide-ranging memoirs.

FABIANOVÁ, VLASTA (1912), actress, member of the National Theater.

FÁRA, LIBOR (1925–1988), painter, graphic designer, typographer, stage designer, and costume designer. Graduate of UMPRUM (the student of Emil

Filla). Worked with the E. F. Burian Theater, the Theater on the Balustrade, the Theater Beyond the Gate, and the Dramatic Club.

FÁROVÁ, ANNA (1928), art theorist, critic, and translator; wife of Libor Fára. Interested above all in trends in modern painting and photography.

FIALKA, LADISLAV (1931–1991), mime, choreographer, dancer, director, and teacher. Founding member of the Theater on the Balustrade since 1958.

FIKAR, LADISLAV (1920–1975), poet, screenwriter, dramaturge, and translator from Russian and German. From 1948 to 1959, editor-in-chief and managing director of Československý Spisovatel publishing house.

FISCHER, JOSEF LUDVÍK (1894–1973), philosopher, sociologist, author of a treatise about culture. He was most influential in Moravia (a professor at Masaryk University in Brno and Palacký University in Olomouc).

FISCHEROVÁ, DANIELA (1948), playwright, prose writer, author of books for children.

FORMAN, MILOŠ (1932), film director, member of the New Wave in Czechoslovak film in the 1960s. Since 1968, he has lived in the U.S. The recipient of several Oscars.

FUČÍK, BEDŘICH (1900–1984), a significant literary critic and historian, editor and translator. In the 1950s, tried on trumped-up charges and imprisoned for many years.

GOLDSTÜCKER, EDUARD (1913), literary historian, critic, German scholar, and comparatist. In 1969, he had to leave Czechoslovakia and he became a university professor in Sussex in England. He has now returned to the ČSFR.

GOTTWALD, KLEMENT (1896–1953), after 1929, the leading figure in the Communist Party of Czechoslovakia; in Moscow during the war; after the takeover, the first Communist president.

GROSSMAN, JAN (1925), literary critic and theorist, theater scholar, stage director. From 1962 to 1968, head of drama and director at the Theater on the Balustrade, where he returned after November 1989.

GRUNTORÁD, JIŘÍ (1952), publisher of the samizdat press Edice Popelnice; in 1980–1984, imprisoned for his activities. Now the manager of a library of samizdat literature,

GRUŠA, JIŘÍ (1938), poet, prose writer, author of literary-critical works, and translator. In 1981, his citizenship was taken away and he was forced to remain in exile. Now the Czech ambassador to Germany.

HÁJEK, JIŘÍ (1913), politician and diplomat; he was Czechoslovakia's ambassador to Great Britain and the United Nations; in the second half of the 1960s, he was in turn Minister of Education, Minister of Culture, and (during the Prague Spring of 1968) Minister of Foreign Affairs. One of the first three spokespeople for Charter 77.

HAŠLER, KAREL (1879–1941), singer, actor, and cabaret performer. Tortured to death by the Nazis.

HEJDÁNEK, LADISLAV (1927), an important philosopher, essayist, and political writer. After 1977, he was twice a spokesperson for Charter 77.

HERRMANN, IGNÁT (1854–1935), writer and journalist who in his works concentrated on the laughable and tragic features of the petite bourgeoisie.

HLAVSA, MILAN (1951), underground musician and rocker. Imprisoned during the campaign against the rock band The Plastic People of the Universe in 1976.

HOLAN, VLADIMÍR (1905–1980), poet and translator, author of lyrical-reflective prose and prose poetry. An important figure in Czech poetry. Since 1949 he has avoided public life.

HORÁČEK, MICHAL (1952), journalist, poet and writer, now an entrepreneur. In 1989, he co-founded the Bridge initiative, which organized the meetings between Civic Forum and the government.

HORNÍČEK, MIROSLAV (1918), actor, prose writer, playwright, and director. In 1955–1960, Jan Werich's partner at the ABC Theater.

HRABAL, BOHUMIL (1914), prose writer, poet, screenplay writer. He has held many occupations, which have had a considerable influence on his work, which held a significant place in the spiritual climate of the 1960s (the Czech New Wave in film drew on a set of his short stories). He was forbidden to publish in the 1950s and once again in the 1970s.

HRUBÍN, FRANTIŠEK (1910–1971), a significant poet, prose writer, playwright, and translator, author of reflective poetry and poetry for children.

HUSÁK, GUSTÁV (1913), a Communist functionary; from May 1969 to December 1987, general secretary of the central committee of the Communist Party of Czechoslovakia; president of the Czechoslovak Socialist Republic in 1975–1989.

HUTKA, JAROSLAV (1947), underground singer. After 1978, he lived in Holland; after the November Revolution, he returned to Czechoslovakia.

HVÍŽĎALA, KAREL (1941), journalist and political writer. In 1978–1989, he lived in the Federal Republic of Germany. In 1986 he conducted a book-length interview with Václav Havel, which was published as *Disturbing the Peace*. He now works for the daily newspaper *Mladá fronta dnes*.

JIROUS, IVAN MARTIN (Magor) (1944), art theorist and critic, poet, political writer, artistic director of the rock group The Plastic People of the Universe. In the 1970s and 1980s, imprisoned many times. Leading personality of the Czech underground.

JIROUSOVÁ, VĚRA (1944), art historian, poet. The former wife of Ivan Jirous (see above), also was very active in the Czech underground.

JUNGMANN, MILAN (1922), literary critic, historian, political writer, and transla-tor. After 1972, employed as a window cleaner. Now acting chairman of the board of the Writers' Council.

JURÁČEK, PAVEL (1935–1989), film director, screenwriter, and dramaturge. Helped create the New Wave of Czech cinema in the 1960s. Since 1979, he has spent part of his time in the Federal Republic of Germany.

KABEŠ, PETR (1941), poet and political writer. In 1966–1968, editor-in-chief of the literary monthly *Sešity*. (Notebooks). In the 1970s and 1980s, he published only abroad and in samizdat.

KANTŮRKOVÁ, EVA (1930), journalist, prose writer, screenwriter. In the 1980s, jailed in connection with her Charter activities.

KAFKA, FRANZ (1883–1924), Prague German writer who came from a Jewish family; author of novels, stories, diaries, and letters in which with a signifi-cant personal artistic form he drew a portrait of the feelings of man in a mechanically functioning, depersonalizing society. His first publisher was Max Brod.

KLÍMA,. IVAN (1931), playwright, prose writer, political writer, essayist, and author of radio plays.

KLÍMA, LADISLAV (1878–1928), philosopher (autodidact), nonconformist thinker, who scorned universal philosophy and called his own position "existencism." Also the author of belletristic works.

KLIMENT, ALEXANDER (1929), dramaturge, poet, and novelist.

KOCÁB, MICHAEL (1954), composer and rock musician.

KOHOUT, PAVEL (1928), playwright, prose writer, political writer, poet, and translator. Since 1978 a resident of Vienna; in 1979, his citizenship was taken away and he was forbidden to return to his country.

KOLÁŘ, JIŘÍ (1914), poet, artist, creator of painterly and photographic poetry, author of collages, "rollages," "crumplages," and other objects. Founding member of Group 42. He has had a number of exhibits in Bohemia, Moravia, and abroad. Since the late 1970s, he has lived in Paris.

KOPTA, PETR (1927), translator, poet, playwright.

KRAUS, KAREL (1920), dramaturge, theater theorist and critic, translator. Worked as a dramaturge at the National Theater and the Theater on the Balustrade; since 1990, dramaturge at the Theater Beyond the Gate II.

KREJČA, OTOMAR (1921), theater director, critic, and theorist. In 1956–1961, head of drama at the National Theater. Until 1968 and after 1990, a director and artistic director at the Theater Beyond the Gate, an important Prague theater.

KRIEGEL, FRANTIŠEK (1908–1979), politician in the era of Dubček's leadership; a signatory of charter 77.

KROUPA, DANIEL (1949), philosopher; from 1990 to 1992 chairman of the Interparliamentary Club for the Democratic Right. Now vice chairman of the Civic Democratic Alliance.

KRUMBACHOVÁ, ESTER (1923), screenwriter and costume designer of New Wave films.

KRYL, KAREL (1944), popular singer, songwriter, and poet. Since 1969, he has lived in Germany.

KŘIŽAN, JIŘÍ (1941), dramaturge, screenwriter, and writer. From 1989 to 1992, he was an adviser to President Havel; now Deputy Minister of Interior of the Czech Republic.

KUBĚNA, JIŘÍ (pseudonym for Jiří Paukert) (1936), poet. Studied art history at the philosophy department at Brno University. In the 1960s, published in *Tvář* and in the anthologies *Similes 1* and *Similes 2*. Now working in monument conservation.

KUBIŠOVÁ, MARTA (1942), singer; in 1970–1989, she was not permitted to perform in public.

KUČERA, BOHUSLAV (1923), until November 1989, the chairman of the loyal Czechoslovak Socialist Party.

KUNDERA, MILAN (1929), prose writer, poet, playwright, screenwriter, essayist, and translator. Taught world literature at FAMU until 1970. In 1975, he became guest lecturer at the University of Rennes in France. In 1979, he was deprived of his citizenship; he remained in France. His prose and essays have been translated into many languages.

Kusý, Miroslav (1931), political writer, philosopher, now professor of political science in Bratislava.

Kvapil, Jaroslav (1868–1950), poet, playwright, translator, and director. In 1912–1921 the head of drama at the National Theater.

Landovský, Pavel (1936), actor and playwright, one of the founders of the Dramatic Club. Since 1978, a member of the acting ensemble of the Burgtheater in Vienna.

Lederer, Jiří (1922–1983), journalist, political writer, literary critic. Until 1969, an editor for *Literární noviny* and *Reportér*. Between 1972 and 1981 he spent six years in prison, after which he emigrated.

Linhartová, Věra (1938), prose writer, poet, art critic, translator. Since 1968, she has lived in Paris.

Lis, Ladislav (1926), one of the activists of the Prague Spring 1968. As one of the Charter 77 spokespeople, he was repeatedly imprisoned.

Lopatka, Jan (1940), literary critic, editor, and theorist of radio creations. He edited worthy samizdat magazines, anthologies, and others. One of the significant actors in the November Revolution.

Machonin, Sergej (1918), theater, literary, and film critic, dramaturge, screenplay writer, and translator. One of the significant actors in the November Revolution.

Macourek, Miloš (1926), Scenarist, dramaturge, poet. With the theater on the Balustrade since 1959.

Malý, Václav (1950), Roman Catholic priest, publisher of samizdats. Charter spokesperson and member of VONS. One of the significant actors in the November Revolution.

Medek, Mikuláš (1926–1974), painter and illustrator. A graduate of UM-PRUM (pupil of František Maika and František Tichý). Author of surrealistic texts.

Menzel, Jiří (1938), screenwriter, theater and film director; he draws above all from Czech literature (Hrabal, Vančura).

Michnik, Adam (1946), Polish political scientist, political writer, and politician; one of the foremost fighters for freedom; an activist in KOR and Solidarity; editor-in-chief of the daily newspaper *Gazeta Wyborcza*.

MILOTA, STANISLAV (1933), photographer. After the August 1968 invasion, which he documented, he was not permitted to work in his field. A participant in the November Revolution.

MLYNÁŘ, ZDENĚK (1930), political writer and political scientist; in 1968, a member of the presidium of the central committee of the Communist Party of Czechoslovakia. After signing Charter 77, he moved to Austria.

MOHORITA, VASIL (1952), chairman of the Communist youth organization until November 1989 and a member of the presidium of the central committee of the Communist Party of Czechoslovakia.

NĚMCOVÁ, DANA (1934), psychologist, Charter 77 spokesperson, and member of VONS.

NĚMEC, JAN (1936), film director from the 1960s' New Wave. From the early 1970s until 1989, he lived in the U.S.

NĚMEC, JIŘÍ (1932), psychologist, essayist, political writer, and translator. Member of VONS, for which he was imprisoned. From 1981 to 1990, he lived in Austria. Now he lectures at the medical school of Charles University in Prague.

NEUBAUER, ZDENĚK (1941), philosopher of phenomenological orientation, originally schooled in microbiology. In the field of microbiology he is known worldwide.

NOVOTNÝ, ANTONÍN (1904–1975), prominent Communist representative; in 1953–1968, first secretary of the central committee of the Communist Party; in 1957–1968, president of the republic.

ORNEST, OTA (1913), stage director. Tried for subversion in 1977 and sentenced to three and a half years in prison.

PACOVSKÝ, LUDĚK (1932), political writer banned after 1968. Since 1978, a member of VONS.

PALACKÝ, FRANTIŠEK (1798–1876), historian, philosopher, politician, and literary theorist. Founder of modern Czech historiography; organizer of Czech cultural, scientific, and social life; leading figure of the national revival. Author of the monumental *History of the Czech People in Bohemia and Moravia*.

PALOUŠ, MARTIN (1950), Catholic philosopher. In 1986, a Charter 77 spokesperson; from 1990 to 1992 Deputy Minister of Foreign Affairs in the ČSFR.

PALOUŠ, RADIM (1924), Catholic philosopher; in 1982, a Charter 77 spokesperson; now chancellor of Prague's Charles University. Father of Martin Palouš.

PÁNEK, FRANTIŠEK (1949), naive poet, author of lyric poetry and song lyrics.

PÁRAL, VLADIMÍR (1932), prose writer, author of stories and novels.

PASSER, IVAN (1933), film director and screenwriter of the so-called New Wave. Since 1968, he has lived and worked in the U.S.

PATOČKA, JAN (1907–1977), important philosopher, student of Husserl and Heidegger; the author of an unusually wide-ranging philosophic work. One of the first three Charter 77 spokespeople.

PAVLÍČEK, FRANTIŠEK (1923), playwright, author of radio and television plays, screenplay writer.

PECKA, KAREL (1928), writer, imprisoned during the 1940s and 1950s. He has written a number of books about the persecution in the fifties.

PETŘIVÝ, TOMÁŠ (1955–1986), poet, political writer, and prose writer. He was imprisoned for his Charter 77 activities.

PETROVÁ, JANA (1966), imprisoned in 1989 for participation in the demonstration for the Jan Palach anniversary. From 1990 to 1992, a member of the Federal Assembly, and now a spokesperson for the Civic Democratic Party.

PIŠTORA, JIŘÍ (1932–1970), poet, writer of feuilletons, literary critic. In the 1960s, a contributor to and editor of *Tvář* and *Sešity*.

PITHART, PETR (1941), political writer, political scientist, historian, author of feuilletons and monographs. One of the primary representatives of the Civic Movement, and from 1990 to 1992, prime minister of the Czech Republic.

PLACÁK, PETR (1964), writer and political writer of the underground; a significant figure in several independent groups.

PROCHÁZKA, JAN (1929–1971), screenwriter and prose writer.

RADOK, ALFRÉD (1914–1976), a significant director and playwright. The creator of Laterna Magika and its artistic director in 1957–1965. In 1968 he went into exile.

RUML, JIŘÍ (1923), journalist and political writer; together with Rudolf Zeman the editor of the samizdat *Lidové noviny*. In 1984, a Charter 77 spokesperson. From 1990 to 1992 a representative to the Federal Assembly.

RUT, PŘEMYSL (1953), playwright, poet, prose writer, literary critic. Now editor of the revived *Literární noviny* and the magazine *O Divadle*.

ŠABATA, JAROSLAV (1927), psychologist, Charter 77 spokesperson. Imprisoned several times. From 1990 to 1992 a minister in the government of the Czech Republic.

ŠABATOVÁ, ANNA (1951), as a student of philosophy, arrested and imprisoned for two years. A Charter 77 spokesperson and founding member of VONS. Daughter of Jaroslav Šabata.

ŠAFAŘÍK, JOSEF (1907), essayist and philosopher; not allowed to publish after 1948 and again after 1968.

ŠALDA, FRANTIŠEK X. (1867–1937), significant literary critic, theorist, prose writer, poet, and playwright. Leading figure in the literary generation of the 1890s.

SALIVAROVÁ, ZDENA (1933), writer, publisher. At the publishing house Sixty-eight Publishers in Toronto, she and her husband, Josef Škvorecký, published books by writers banned in Czechoslovakia, and thus contributed to the preservation of continuity in Czech literature.

ŠAVRDA, JAROMÍR (1933–1988), poet, prose writer, and translator. For his samizdat activity he was imprisoned.

SCHORM, EVALD (1931–1989), a significant film director of the Czech New Wave.

SEIFERT, JAROSLAV (1901–1985), an important poet, political writer, feuilleton writer, and translator. He won the 1984 Nobel Prize in Literature. In addition to his own works, he translated from French the work of modern poets and edited many periodicals and anthologies. After 1971, he was only able to publish part of his writing. His work has had a notable influence on every subsequent generation of Czech poets.

SEKANINOVÁ-ČAKRTOVÁ, GERTRUDA (1908–1986), lawyer. In the 1960s, deputy minister of foreign affairs. In October 1968, as a representative to the Federal Assembly, she came out against approving a treaty for the temporary lodging of Soviet soldiers in Czechoslovakia. A member of VONS.

SIDON, KAROL (1942), film scenarist, journalist, author of radio and television plays. From 1968 to 1969 editor of *Literární listy*.

ŠILHÁN, VĚNEK (1927), economist. One of the creators of economic reform in 1968; a significant politician in the Prague Spring.

ŠIMEČKA, MILAN (1930–1990), philosopher, essayist, critic, and translator. In 1981, he was imprisoned for a year; after the November Revolution he was briefly chairman of the Board of Advisers to the President.

ŠKVORECKÝ, JOSEF (1924), prose writer, poet, screenwriter, literary critic, and translator. Since 1969, he and his wife, Zdena Salivarová, have lived in Toronto, where he is a university professor. Publisher of Czech emigré literature in his publishing house Sixty-eight Publishers.

ŠOTOLA, JIŘÍ (1924), poet, prose writer, and translator.

SOUKUP, KAREL (CHARLIE) (1951), poet and songwriter. He was condemned for his artistic activity and imprisoned. In 1982, he was forced to emigrate.

STANKOVIČ, ANDREJ (1940), poet and critic. In the 1960s, he belonged to the *Tvář* circle; in the 1970s and 1980s, he published only in samizdat (*Kritický sborník*). A member of VONS.

STEIGERWALD, KAREL (1945), playwright and screenwriter. Dramaturge of the Theater on the Balustrade.

ŠTEPAN, MIROSLAV (1945), Communist party chief in Prague until 1989.

ŠTĚPÁNEK, ZDENĚK (1896–1968), a significant theater and film actor.

ŠUSTROVÁ, PETRUŠKA (1947), imprisoned from 1969 to 1971, later a spokesperson for Charter 77 and a member of VONS. From 1990 to 1992, deputy interior minister of the ČFSR; now a journalist.

SVOBODA, JOSEF (1920), stage designer and architect. Artistic director of Laterna Magika since 1973.

TESAŘ, JAN (1933), historian, member of VONS. Since the end of the 1970s, he has lived in Paris.

TIMOFEYEV, LEONID IVANOVICH (1904–1984), a Soviet literary theorist of socialist realism.

TOMIN, JULIUS (1938), philosopher and political writer. In the 1970s, he organized seminars in people's apartments on ancient philosophers. Since 1980, he has lived in Great Britain.

TOPOL, FILIP (1965), underground musician and writer of song lyrics.

TOPOL, JÁCHYM (1962), underground poet, prose writer, and journalist. Editor of *Revolver Revue*.

TOPOL, JOSEF (1935), playwright, poet, essayist, and translator. Dramaturge of Otomar Krejča's Theater Beyond the Gate until it was closed down in 1972.

TŘEŠŇÁK, VLASTIMIL (1950), underground singer, painter, and writer. Since 1982, he has lived in Germany.

TŘÍSKA, JAN (1936), actor, one of the founders of the Theater Beyond the Gate. Since 1977, he has lived in the U.S.

TRNKA, JIŘÍ (1912–1969), an excellent graphic designer, painter, and illustrator, and creator of famous puppet films.

UHDE, MILAN (1936), poet, prose writer, playwright, literary critic, screenwriter, and political writer. From 1990 to 1992 Minister of Culture for the Czech Republic, currently chairman of the Czech National Council.

UHL, PETR (1941), journalist. In the 1960s, a leftist reformer and student leader. Tried with Havel for subversion and sentenced to five years.

URBAN, JAN (1951), journalist and political writer; editor of the samizdat *Lidové noviny*.

URBÁNEK, ZDENĚK (1917), prose writer, theater scholar, essayist, translator. Especially noted for his translations of Shakespeare's plays. Now chancellor of the Academy of Performing Arts.

VACULÍK, LUDVÍK (1926), a significant prose writer, feuilleton writer, cultural and political writer; author of the text "Two Thousand Words," publisher of Padlock Press (Edice Petlice).

VLADISLAV, JAN (1923), prose writer, poet, essayist, translator, author of books for children. Since 1981, he has lived in Paris.

VODŇANSKÁ, JITKA (1944), psychologist. She studied medical anthropology in the UK. She concentrates on psychotherapy and musical therapy.

VONDRA, ALEXANDR (1961), geographer, spokesperson for Charter 77. From 1990 to 1992, he was an adviser to President Havel, and is currently a deputy to the Minister of Foreign Affairs for the Czech Republic.

VOSKOVEC, JIŘÍ (1905–1981), actor, dramatist, songwriter. With Jan Werich, ran the Liberated Theater. After the war became a well-known actor in New York.

VOSTŘEL, DAREK (1929), actor. A graduate of DAMU and law school. He worked in the Rococo Theater.

VYSKOČIL, IVAN (1929), psychologist, prose writer, actor, and playwright. Co-founder of the Theater on the Balustrade and Reduta. Now he heads the Acting Department at DAMU, the drama school of the Academy of Performing Arts.

WEINER, RICHARD (1884–1937), prose writer and poet; Paris correspondent for *Lidové noviny*.

WENIG, JOSEF (1885–1939), stage designer, painter, and illustrator.

WERICH, JAN (1905–1980), an important actor, playwright, author of song lyrics, prose writer, and translator. With Jiří Voskovec and the musical collaborator Jaroslav Ježek, he ran the Liberated Theater. In the 1960s he was artistic director of the ABC Theater.

WERNISCH, IVAN (1942), poet and translator.

WILSON, PAUL (1942), Canadian journalist and student of Czech culture; translator. He has translated a large portion of Václav Havel's prose writing.

Before his expulsion from Czechoslovakia in 1977, he played with the underground rock band, The Plastic People of the Universe.

YENGIBAROV, LEONID GEORGIYEVICH (1935–1971), Soviet clown, actor, mime, and screenplay writer of Armenian origins.

ZÁBRANA, JAN (1931–1984), poet and translator from Russian and English.

ZÁPOTOCKÝ, ANTONÍN (1887–1957), prominent Communist politician; after 1948 prime minister, and from 1953 to 1957 president of the Czech Socialist Republic.

ZEMAN, RUDOLF (1939), journalist and political commentator, radio editor. Editor of the samizdat *Lidové noviny* until 1989, and from 1990 to 1991 its editor-in-chief.

ZUSKA, ZDENĚK (1931–1982), Communist mayor of Prague in the 1970s and 1980s.

▪ Index